Forgotten Books

Madame du Barry

By

Edmond De Goncourt

Published by Forgotten Books 2012

Originally Published 1945

PIBN 1000694836

MADAME DU BARRY

BY

EDMOND AND JULES DE GONCOURT

WITH PHOTOGRAVURE AND
FIFTEEN OTHER PORTRAITS

LONDON
JOHN LONG, LIMITED
NORRIS STREET, HAYMARKET
MCMXIV

CONTENTS

I.

II.

III.

Contents

IV.

V.

VI.

VII.

Contents

VIII.

IX.

X.

XI.

Contents

Contents

LIST OF ILLUSTRATIONS

2

Madame Du Barry

I.

Hardy's Journal dated February 1st, 1769.—Esther du Barry and "Haman" Choiseul.—The struggle between the Encyclopedic Party and the Devotee Party.—The "Republican Multitude."—Choiseul on his defence with regard to his religion.—Certificate of birth of Jeanne Bequs, called "La Du Barry."—Her Childhood.—She takes up her Abode with "La Frederique."—The Community of Sainte-Aure.—The Chateau of Cour-Neuve.—Madame Labille's Millinery Establishment.—The Comte du Barry.—His Past.—His *second-hand Traffic* in Mistresses.—The Supper at Lebel's.

HARDY, a citizen of Paris, who in the eighteenth century had the patience to keep a record of the various events of his time, the rumours and news of the city of Paris, all the things that he saw, heard, and learned, relates in his "Manuscript Journal,"[1] hitherto unpublished, that on the 1st of February, 1769, Candlemas Eve, a priest, who was a friend of his, went to dine at a house the name of which is not mentioned. It was the moment when the gossip of Paris was all about the Comtesse du Barry. At dessert, another priest, who was dining at this house with two of his brethren, invited Hardy's friend, as well as the rest of the company, to drink " to the presentation ;" and as Hardy's friend was not quite sure as to what this meant, and asked whether it referred to the presentation of Our Lord in the

---

[1] Fragments of this Journal have been published by the *Nouvelle Revue Encyclopedique*, but the manuscript has not yet been published in book form.

Madame Du Barry

Temple which was to take place next day, the priest who had proposed the toast, said to him in reply:—" It refers to the presentation which took place yesterday, or is going to take place to-day—the presentation of the new Esther, who is to replace Haman and to rescue the Jewish people from oppression." [1]

Ponder over this scene and those words: they furnish the explanation of Madame du Barry's good-fortune.

In that war of ideas, the great war of the eighteenth century, in that conflict of minds, and of souls, ardent and ruthless, in that civil war of consciences, in which blood no longer flowed, but in which persecution continued, in the time of the excommunication and proscription of public opinion, when a sort of retaliation for the Edict of Nantes was exercised against the militant order of the Jesuits—on that army of old men driven by the hand of Choiseul out of that France where their houses were falling into ruin, in the midst of that rending and clash between the usages of the old French spirit and the new audacities which had for their minister M. de Choiseul—between those two irreconcilable extremes, the Church and Royalty on one side, the Revolution on the other, thinking men no longer saw in Madame du Barry the woman, the courtesan, the lady of the pavement, "the Du Barry": they only saw in her an instrument, a weapon, by means of which a party kills a party. And so it was—strange fact—that in this eighteenth

---

[1] " Journal of Events as they came to my knowledge." By Hardy. National Library MSS. 6680-6682.

century, accustomed to make woman the agent whereby changes of Government could be brought about, Madame du Barry unwittingly rallied around her all the religious sentiments and all the political sentiments which had been thwarted, wounded, humiliated by the minister, Choiseul. All that was left of old France rooted in her beliefs, and terrified by the chain of incredulity in which the links connecting Fontenelle with Voltaire were joined together by the physician La Mettrie, the geologist Demaillet, the physicist Boulanger, the naturalist Buffon, the geometrician d'Alembert,—all the men whose minds were disturbed by the attack which the knowledge of natural things, the exact, positive, material sciences, provoked against the mysteries of the supernatural world,—the men who were opposed to the novelty of governmental theories, to the dream of systems, to the experiment of progress,—those who, after the meeting of the Bishops, believed that the Church and the State were united in life and in death, and saw a political revolution at the end of a religious revolution,—those who so far back as 1765 announced that " the philosophic spirit was destined to give birth to the strangest revolutions and to precipitate France into the horrors of anarchy,"—those again who thought that the human mind was held fast and safeguarded in the future by the education imparted to youth by the Jesuit body[1]—all this

[1] In 1762, President d'Aiguilles declared that, with the destruction of the Jesuits, " Anglicism," otherwise called Republicanism, " would on: day form the spirit of the nation."

great party was condemned to silence its repugnances in order to push forward Madame du Barry into the position in which she might be of service to it. A thousand passions, a thousand devotions, the relations, friendships, memories, interest which a great order leaves behind it, the fright of Louis XV.'s heart in the presence of the " Republican multitude,"[1] over which his successor should reign, the secret resentments of the Dauphin and the Dauphiness against Choiseul, bequeathed in the testament of Louis XVI., the hopes of the Queen embroidering with her hands, which were soon to be chilled by death, an ornament for the first house of the Jesuits after their restoration—all rallied or attached themselves through the party to this State presentation. Hence this understanding, this instinctive complicity around the mistress, those hands and those invisible succours which sustained the Du Barry; hence that breath and that aid of a strong public opinion which carried her to power on the cloud of Psyche.

M. de Choiseul did not deceive himself as to the meaning of Madame du Barry's accession to favour. His reply to every reproach made in detail to his administration was that which he had made in 1765 when the party grouped by Soubise behind Madame d'Esparbes, the same which he again found behind Madame du Barry, had sought to effect his dismissal. " What though people may say," re-

---

[1] An expression used in a letter of Louis XV. to Choiseul dated Fontainebleau, October 15, 1765, and communicated by the Duc de Choiseul to the *Revue de Paris*, 1829, Vol. IV.

marked M. de Choiseul in a sort of justification addressed to the King, "that I have striven to drive out the Jesuits and that I have upheld the claims and pretensions of the Parliaments, on every side, I have taken no step to promote these objects, and have had no other ideas save those which your Majesty has observed when my advice was asked for in the Council Chamber. . . . Finally the great reproach falls on my religion. It is difficult to attack me positively on this serious matter. I never speak about the subject; but, as far as form is concerned, I pay strict attention to decency, and in the conduct of affairs my principle is to sustain religion."[1] And the Duke did not deceive himself. Three years after that time, in a family assembly at the residence of Mesdames, in the presence of the Dauphiness, whom the King's aunts knew to be secretly attached to the person and the policy of Choiseul, the conversation happening to turn on the fall of his ministry, Madame Adelaide exclaimed that the exile of the Duke had saved religion in France, inasmuch as it was manifest that this minister's object had been to destroy it utterly.[2]

What, nevertheless, was this woman to whom the ironies of History assigned and thought fit to entrust such a part as the restoration of the monarchic authority and of the

[1] Memoirs of the Duc de Choiseul, delivered up to the King in 1765, and referred to in the *Revue Française* of July, 1828.

[2] "Secret Correspondence of Mercy-Argenteau." Didot, 1875. Despatch from Mercy to Maria Theresa, May 18, 1773.

religious authority? We are going to tell, as best we can, the story of this woman's life.

"*Jeanne*, natural daughter of Anne Bequs called *Quantiny*, was born on the 19th of August, in the year one thousand seven hundred and forty-three and was baptized the same day. Her godfather was Joseph Demange and her godmother Jeanne Birabin who have attached their signatures along with mine.

"L. Galon,

"Vicar of Vaucouleurs

"Jeanne Birabin.

"Joseph Demange."[1]

Such is the certificate of Madame du Barry's birth, the truth as to her origin,—a truth hitherto ignored or misunderstood by history.

In the midst of contradictory narratives, in view of the evident hostility of the anecdotes and memoirs published the day after Louis XV.'s death, in view of the predisposition towards the paradox of rehabilitations since attempted, and in the face of biographies which seem to take into account only the novel-reading public, it is rather difficult to trace up, to distinguish, and to determine the exact truth with regard to the childhood and early youth of Madame

[1] This certificate of the birth of Madame du Barry, extracted from the records of the civil government of the town of Vaucouleurs, and delivered to Saint-Mihiel, on the 25th of September, 1827, has been confirmed for us by a letter of the Mayor of Vaucouleurs, date the 30th of November, 1859.

Madame Du Barry

du Barry. It is necessary, it seems to us, to be satisfied with probable truth. Besides, that is sufficient for biographies of this kind, and posterity may console itself for not possessing absolute certainty and perfect knowledge as to the precise degree of weakness to which a woman descended who has become a historic personage by chance, and, as it were, by sheer inadvertence.

Out of all the traditions of the eighteenth century which agree in giving Madame du Barry a certain Gomard de Vaubernier as a father, an error to which we shall find the key later on, and a financier named Dumonceau as a god-father, it seems that there is scarcely any authentic fact to be gathered save that the mother and daughter endured great privations in Paris, and perhaps that, before going to Paris, Anne Becu had been the recipient of charity and kindness at the hands of this M. Dumonceau, who was one of the principal persons interested in supplying provisions to the army. It is in this sense that we are going to follow the narratives of the time.

Little Jeanne's mother, left without resources, conceived the idea of setting out for Paris to try her luck there, and her first visit was to the rich financier, whose memory and whose acts of kindness had left an impression on her heart. M. Dumonceau, who had almost forgotten his little *protegee,* was astonished at her pretty face and her arch manner. He gave the mother twelve livres, promising to allow her an equal sum every month to enable little Jeanne to learn to read and write. At the end of some months and some dozens of livres, the worthy Dumonceau became deeply interested in the mother's distress; and, in the ingenuousness of his character, he could think of nothing better than to send the mother and daughter to live with his mistress, Mademoiselle Frederique, a courtesan, who enjoyed almost a reputation at this period.[1]

The pretty child was developing into a charming young girl when Mademoiselle Frederique, who was a lively young woman, thought she was growing very quickly, and began to have some apprehensions as to the future. She persuaded M. Dumonceau, who on another side was preached at by a very pious parent, to make little Jeanne enter the convent of Sainte-Aure.[2]

[1] *La Frederique*, also known by the name of *Souville*, had originally been kept in rather a mean style by M. de Vouvray, Master of Requests. To M. de Vouvray had succeeded one M. de Boisgelin, a follower of the Duc de Berry, who had the beauty removed from the Rue de la Truanderie and installed in a pretty apartment in the Rue de Richelieu and liberally supplied her with everything she needed. This did not prevent *La Frederique* from being a gay woman and frequenting the suppers at the little house of La Brissault and others. *La Frederique* was a tall, beautiful girl, very red-haired, and celebrated for her "accomplished debauchery." *Journal of M. de Sartines's Inspectors.* Dentu, 1863.

"Anecdotes about the Comtesse Du Barry." London, 1775.—This is the book containing the greatest amount of documentary information as the life of Mme. du Barry, and a great portion of it has been made out of the "Secret Memoirs," a book which other books that followed it have only copied and paraphrased. But let us give here a list of the favourite's biographies :—

"Authentic Memoirs of the Comtesse de Barre (*sic*), Mistress of Louis XV., King of France, extracted from a manuscript in the possession of the Duchesse de Villeroy." By the Chevalier Fr. V. . . .,

Madame Du Barry

The daughters of Sainte-Aure were a community whose specialty and aim were quite peculiar. Sainte-Aure did not serve the purpose of a refuge for the frail, a retreat for sinners: this convent was intended to save persons from

London. Printed at the expense of the Publishers, 1772 (one volume, 12mo). This is a little romance which has not the slightest resemblance to the history of Madame du Barry.

"Historic Summary of the Life of the Comtesse du Barry, with her Portrait." Paris, 1774 (one small volume, 12mo or 8vo).

"Cythera's Gazette, or the Secret History of Madame du Barry." London, 1775 (one small volume, 12mo).

"History and Life of the Comtesse du Barry." Pont-aux-Dames, 1775 (one small volume, 12mo).

"Remarks on the Anecdotes of the Comtesse du Barry." By Madame S. G. (oudar). London, 1777 (one small volume, 12mo).

"The Pleasures of the City and of the Court, or Refutation of the Anecdotes and Summary of the Life of the Comtesse du Barry, written by Herself." London, 1778 (one volume, 12mo). A rare little romance which paraphrases the "Anecdotes."

"Letters of the Comtesse du Barry, with those of the Princes, Noblemen, Ministers and others who have written to her, gathered from all Possible Sources." London, 1779. (Apocryphal correspondence.)

"Life of the Comtesse du Barry, followed by her epistolary Correspondence and her Gallant and Political Intrigues." (8vo.) This biography, in which her death is announced, contains a portrait with the words underneath:—"The Messalina whom you see. . . ."

"The Illustrious Victims Avenged." By Montigny. (8vo.) Containing a long notice about Madame du Barry.

"Historic Memoirs of Jeanne Gomart de Vaubernier, Comtesse du Barry. Prepared from Two Authentic Fragments." By M. de Favrolles (Madame Guenard). Paris, Lerouge, 1803 (four volumes, 12mo). This book, written without being subjected to stricture, contains, in three or four volumes, the greater number of fragments seized at Luciennes, and to-day in the National Archives.

"Memoirs of the Comtesse du Barri." By Lamothe-Langon. Abel Ledoux, 1843 (five volumes, 8vo). A romance without the least historical value.

falling. According to the view of the reformers of this institution, it was an asylum open, at a modest cost of two hundred francs, to every young woman who, born of a virtuous family, " found herself in circumstances in which she ran the risk of being ruined."[1] The ten livres were paid for the bed; the little girl was provided with two pairs of sheets and six napkins[2] and the gates of the convent in the Rue Neuve-Sainte-Genevieve were closed upon her.

To a young girl brought up in this fashion, knowing nothing of life except what she had seen at Madamoselle Frederique's, cradled in this luxury of a young girl's existence, with her head and her eyes dazzled by ribbons and fine dresses, to a child spoiled by petting and caresses like this pretty young creature, already coquettish, and already displaying that roguish humour which even Versailles could not restrain, the descent was great and the change severe.

Farewell to the charming little gown, fashionably cut,

[1] " Picture of Humanity and Beneficence, or Historic Summary of the Charities which are practised in Paris."

[2] " State or Picture of the City of Paris." 1760.

" The Comtesse du Barry." By Capefigue. Amyot, 1858.

" Madame du Barry, 1768-1793." By J. R. Le Roy. Versailles, 1858. A pamphlet full of original documents of the greatest interest.

Two fragments are also connected with the history of the Favourite. The first, " Equality Acquired Shadily, or the Little History of Protection," is the most complete narrative of the persecution to which she was subjected in 1793 at Luciennes. The other has no interest save that of its title:—" The Descent of La Barry into Hell, and her reception at Pluto's Court by the Widow Capet, who has become the Favourite Fury of Proserpine."

which she wore at La Frederique's! On this head so full of gaiety behold a double veil of plain black stuff accompanied by a common "guimpe" without starch. Behold on those fair tresses a band of coarse linen which conceals them and falls down so as to cover three-fourths of the forehead. Her gown is of white Aumale serge of an ordinary pattern without any arrangement or superfluous ornament, and her little feet are cased in calfskin shoes yellow and unfashionable, fastened with two similar laces. And no way of avoiding this pitiless discipline as to costume: do not the archives of the community preserve as a model and as a pattern a hieratic statue thus attired?

And everything around little Jeanne is plain, severe, and sad, like her new costume, in this community so curtailed that she has no silver save the plate of the infirmary and no gold save the gilding of the altar. It is the vow of poverty in all its rigour, forbidding to each one personal possession, suppressing the thine and the mine; it is the work of the hands, the work of instruction, while maintaining deep silence. There are prohibited and punished the jests, the dainty airs, the exaggerated or sudden outbursts of laughter, every pleasant phrase, every bantering tone.[1] Vain prohibitions! over which little Jeanne soon jumped, bringing into the austere house the gaiety of her age and her disposition, and causing there the revolution of Vert-

[1] "Constitution of the Nuns of Saint-Aure according to the rule of Saint Augustine." Paris, at Simon's Printing-house, Printer to the Archbishop of Paris, 1786.

Vert. The noise, the bad example of such youthful mirth, vainly chidden and curbed, the contagion of which was to be feared, got the charming little madcap sent home to her mother, that is to say to La Frederique's. La Frederique, considering that the attractions of her *protegee*, now grown up and formed, were more dangerous than ever, and, tired of the mother, whom she suspected of spying on her domestic concerns, conceived the idea of making a great outcry as to the singularly familiar relations of Jeanne's mother with a Capuchin friar named Gomard. Owing to this scandal and the well-simulated indignation of La Frederique, M. Dumonceau had the mother and daughter turned out of doors.

It was about this time that the little girl of fifteen, penniless, and left to face the world, showed herself in the streets like the " Mignonne " of Retif de la Bretonne, carrying in a little open box little " hardware " articles, going from door to door, and offering to everyone who passed her watch-guards, her snuff-boxes, her imitation pearls, her pins with brilliants, her pin-cases, and all the paltry goods which are bought on account of the tradeswoman's bright eyes, and which are paid for as the purchase of her smile; an open-air shop, a rough occupation, such an insignificant business that it seemed a pretext, dubious wanderings up and down the slippery pavement, exposed to the chance of being addressed and having proposals made to her, to the want which leads into temptation, to the servants picking up whatever amuses their masters. Years afterwards, the Comte de Genlis, one of the most fascinating libertines of the age, expressed his astonishment to the Comte d'Allonville when he recognized at Versailles in the woman to whom he was presented a little girl of the streets whom his valet had once brought to him.[1]

During this period a change took place in the family which led to the young girl being rescued from this shady existence. Her uncle, or her pretended uncle, the Capuchin friar, who had got into the priesthood, became, by a pluralism worthy of the period and suited to the man, the almoner of the chapel and at the same time the prompter for the plays performed at the chateau of Cour-Neuve, where the aged wife of Lagarde, the Fermier-general, found amusement for her closing years in society theatricals. The Capuchin aroused in Madame Lagarde's breast such curiosity with regard to Jeanne that the old lady, becoming interested in the pretty young girl, invited her to Cour-Neuve,[2] was soon charmed by her face and by her babble, and retained her services as a lady's companion, a chambermaid, if necessary. Unfortunately it so happened that Madame Lagarde had sons who were young men; ere long

[1] "Secret Memoirs from 1770 to 1830." By the Comte d'Allonville. 1838. Volume I.

[2] An old residence in the neighbourhood of Paris entirely restored in modern fashion, and retaining of its past only a double enclosure of moats always filled with running water. The recreations of Cour-Neuve have been the subject of description in a rare volume :—" New Year's Gifts of Cour-Neuve for the year 1774, dedicated to M. de la Garde, Master of Requests." Cour-Neuve, 1774.

the chateau became the scene of the romance which might naturally be anticipated, the commencement of an intrigue with the seductive young creature; and once more the mother and the daughter fell back from Cour-Neuve to the streets of Paris.

There one must needs eat and live. The little peddleress of haberdashery adopted a calling in which virtue was still a somewhat difficult form of heroism, but in which the temptations had not the same brutality. She entered, under the name of Mademoiselle Lançon, or perhaps Rançon, —the name of the husband whom her mother had just taken—the millinery establishment of M. Labille in the Rue Saint-Honore, a brother of the female painter.

The history of milliners' apprentices in the eighteenth century is neither very long in its course nor very varied for the purposes of narration. Imagine stores, with glass windows all round, where fascinating idlers, handsome noblemen, kept ogling the girls from morning till night; shutters which were used for correspondence, and which allowed the notes folded up fan-fashion to be passed through the peg-holes; little trips out of doors, where the smart milliner's girl, such as Leclerc has sketched her in the series of costumes of d'Esnault and Rapilly, trotted about with a conquering air, her head covered with a big black hat shaped like a calash allowing her fair curls to slip down her rounded, shapely waist squeezed into a polonaise of printed calico garnished with muslin; little shoes with heels and buckles, and a light fan in her hand which she kept moving about as she went along; imagine, at the end of all this, conversations and proposals, and, after the proposals and the responses to the proposals, it was for nearly every one of them, as it was for the little Lançon girl, some Monsieur Lavauvenardiere,[1] or some Monsieur Duval,—or somebody else.

Some have held the view that Madame du Barry carried her irregularity so far that she became the slave of debauchery. They import into this stage of her career the intervention of one of the most notorious procuresses of the age. This is a point of controversy which we must leave to scandal. However, in those first amorous experiments of Madame du Barry may be seen sufficient liberty of choice, sufficient fickleness, a taste and a disgust sufficiently lively and personal to warrant us in assuming that her heart was not quite shattered into fragments.

Soon comes her *liason* with Lamet the hair-dresser, so quickly formed, so quickly broken off, when the milliner's assistant, biting at luxury and acquiring extravagant tastes, had eaten up the last coin of the hair-dresser in the furniture which he bought for her. The hair-dresser fled to England, and the young woman did not know what to do, when her mother, who had become Madame Rançon, brought her into contact with a neighbour, Madame Duquesnoy, who kept a gambling-house in the Rue de Bourbon. A gambling-house! this was always for women of

---

[1] Lavauvenardiere was, according to Soulavie, the first acknowledged or known lover of the Du Barry.

easy virtue the fitting rendezvous, the best place to snatch at fortune; and at the house of the Duquesnoy, in the midst of the circle attracted by her new and strange beauty, the charming Jeanne was not slow in making a conquest of the Comte du Barry, who promised to give her, in the kind of seraglio which he had in Paris, the post of favourite sultana.[1]

The Comte du Barry was a gentleman from the neighbourhood of Toulouse, who made a great boast about his descent from the Barymores of England;[2] but whatever nobility he had came from the municipal office of Toulouse. He had remained in Toulouse up to his twenty-eighth year, occupied in wasting his youth and in diminishing a rather handsome fortune. Then, having exhausted provincial life,[3] he came to Paris with ripened passions, a vague appetite for change and fortune, an ambition which had no object, and ready for anything. Through Madame de Malause, he entered and established himself in good society, and forced his way into acquaintanceships which enabled him subsequently to obtain for his son the position

---

[1] "Anecdotes of the Comtesse du Barry."

[2] The name Barrymore (not Barymore, as given in the text) is well known in Ireland. The Barry family has for centuries resided in the south of Ireland. One of the most distinguished Irish judges bore this name. The title of Lord Barrymore is at present borne by an Irishman, better known by his former name of the Hon. Smith-Barry.—TRANSLATOR.

[3] Jean du Barry left behind in Toulouse his wife, a woman of honorable family, who, it is stated in the "Anecdotes," never wished to owe anything to the favor of the Du Barrys.

of page to the King. Foreign affairs had tempted him at first; but the minister, Rouille, considering that his mind was somewhat green, advised him to take a trip to Germany, and tried his patience for some time by promising to employ him in the assembly of Franconia. After Rouille came Bernis, who still kept him waiting with words; then followed Choiseul, who brutally killed all the Comte's expectations.

Then, Du Barry, whose affairs were beginning to get into an embarrassed condition, abandoned his dreams of diplomacy and directed his attention towards more substantial objects. He obtained from De Berryer an interest in the supplies for the Navy, from Belle-Isle an interest in the military supplies, and then again an interest in the provisions of Corsica.[1] His fortune, set once more afloat by these three sources of income, made him more prodigal than ever in his tastes, in his debaucheries, in gambling and women, in that giddy life, cynical and unrestrained, which gained for him the name of *Roue*. Between this man and La Rançon or rather La Lange—this was the assumed name which the courtesan had adopted—hardly anything else could have happened but what did happen,—a sailing-match in which the parties only looked to what suited the convenience of each of them. La Lange, who appears to have given herself without much relish, remained attached to this *liaison* on account of the money so liberally scat-

[1] Correspondence of the Comte du Barry. *Revue de Paris,* November, 1836.

tered about by Du Barry, on account of that free, irregular, glittering life which becomes a necessity to the woman of pleasure, and perhaps also on account of the education which she derived from that apprenticeship and from that friction which moulded her into the ways of fashionable gallantry, and washed out of her the grisette and the little milliner's apprentice. She associated herself, in this sphere, with some fashionable courtesans, and entered the salon of that species of Ninon, Mademoiselle Legrand, who collected around her the Colles and the Crebillons.[1] To Du Barry, accustomed to overwork his caprices and to use up his passions. when the intrigue was at an end and he had speedily sunk into a state of indifference, the affair became a mere speculation, and the Roue, excited by the ideas and the examples

"Memoirs of General Dumouriez," Paris, Baudouin, 1822. Volume I. The idea was not new with the Comte, for until then, apart from gambling, Jean du Barry seems to have lived chiefly by discovering pretty women, whom at first he found in their lodgings, then made more presentable, and finally brought prominently into relationship with his distinguished acquaintances. A document of the police leaves no doubt as to this kind of traffic at which the Roue felt no shame. The "Journal of M. de Sartines's Police Inspectors" says, at the date of October 2, 1762, with reference to a young lady named Tricot, whom the Comte brought up secretly at the house of a dressing-room keeper in the Rue Montmartre:—"This is one pretty mistress more, whom he will without doubt introduce to some lords after a time, as he has done in the case of previous ones." The same Journal had already said, at the date of September 5, 1761, with regard to one Mademoiselle Beauvoisin, likewise trained by the Comte, who had just caught a rich man interested in the yearly forage-supplies:—"The Sieur Collet has only to stick on well, for, as she always sees Du Barry secretly, his advice will not fail to make things go swimmingly as far as money is concerned."

of the age, calculated the probabilities of the impossible, and measured the scandal without being discouraged by it, seeing that the entire reign and the entire kingdom turned on women ; seeing that so many courtiers, so many ministers, ruled, advanced, and rose and became great only through the mistress.

Nevertheless, this was not the first experiment of the sort made by the Comte du Barry. From the time of Madame de Pompadour, he had sought to make Mademoiselle Dorothee Louis XV.'s mistress. The daughter of the Strasburg water-carrier had even been invited to one of the King's suppers, and her lover " claimed as an introductory favour to be appointed minister at Cologne." It is Madame de Pompadour who gives these details to Madame de Hausset, and she adds :—" I believe the King will not dare to create such a scandal, and luckily Lebel, in order to clear his conscience, has told the King that the fair Dorothée's lover was eaten up with a nasty disease, and he has added :—' Your Majesty does not get cured of that like scrofula.' It was no longer necessary to drive off the lady."

Erecting his batteries, Du Barry was seeking for a Plutus and an opportunity,[1] when Richelieu, in the bad company

---

[1] This idea of *engaging in second-hand traffic* in La Vaubernier had been entertained by the Comte since 1764. We read in the fragments of the " Police Journal," published by Rochefort (" Recollections and Miscellanies," Bossange, 1825, Tome II.), December 14th, 1764 :—" The Marquis du Barry, to whom we are indebted for having brought the beautiful Dorothee to Paris from Strasburg, and

in which he sometimes found himself with the Roue, let it escape from him in the other's presence that, since Madame de Pompadour's death, Louis XV. no longer gave himself up to private debaucheries and that he would be anxious to get an acknowledged mistress. This phrase excited the imagination of Jean du Barry, and he several times brought La Lange to supper in the Marechal's town-house. One day, while crying up the beauties of his mistress, half seriously, half jocosely, he announced to the Duke that he intended her for Louis XV. Richelieu, who had at first found fault with Louis XV.'s fancy for Madame de Pompadour because she was not a person of title, and did not want anyone to be the King's mistress unless she had been presented, smiled with pity, giving him to understand that if he had not other plans for making his fortune, he would not make it very soon. The Roue was not disconcerted; his cynical confidence in his success broke out into a thousand follies, a thousand drolleries, brightening up this supper so that the very recollection of it would amuse Richelieu and that he would refer to it more than twenty times. Du Barry was heard loudly declaring that he would him-

for having introduced the Demoiselle Beauvoisin into society, made his mistress the Demoiselle Veauvarnier (sic) appear in his opera-box last Monday at the Comedie Italienne. She is a lady of nineteen, tall, well-formed, with a noble air and the prettiest face. Certainly he is trying to dispose of her on advantageous terms. When he has begun to get tired of a woman, he has always made use of her in the same way. But, also, it must be admitted that he is a connoisseur, and that his merchandise is always good value."

MADAME DE POMPADOUR

To face page 22

self carry La Lange into the King's bed if nobody else was willing to bring her there. Finally, Richelieu said to him in a jesting tone:—"Well, go and see Lebel; perhaps through his agency your favourite will obtain for one day the honours of the Louvre."[1]

Many pieces of evidence exist as to the first meeting of the King with the Du Barry. In a sort of justification and account of his life addressed in Louis XV.'s reign to M. de Malesherbes, the Comte du Barry, who introduces Madame du Barry as having charge along with her mother of the management of his house, relates that, as he had given up his interests in the Corsican supplies, interests reduced to nothing by the arrangements of M. de Choiseul, Madame du Barry went to Versailles to make an appeal to the minister: it was, according to him, in the course of these solicitations that the King saw her.[2] Another story is more

[1] "Private Life of the Marechal de Richelieu, containing his Amours and his Intrigues." Buisson, 1791, Tome II.

[2] Here is a narrative of the Roue in this letter, which is a sort of autobiography:

"Having no other care at the time save that of watching over the education of my son, a page of the King, and my health being shaky, I confined myself to a narrow circle of acquaintances. And it was then that I begged of Madame Rançon and her daughter, Mademoiselle Vaubernier, to look after the management of my house, and to do the honours of it, which they did for several years with affection and intelligence.

"Excited by gratitude and in order to fortify them against the future, I gave up to them then the interest which I had in the Corsican supplies, which they enjoyed for some months.

"The new arrangements of M. de Choiseul having the result of depriving them of this source of income, they appealed to him to

worthy of credence; it is that of a man who lived in intimate companionship with M. de Choiseul, and who seems to have obtained his knowledge and his information through the confidence of the minister. Dutens wrote to the effect that, after the praises of Madame du Barry poured into the King's ears by Lebel and Richelieu, won by assurance of the Roue, a supper was given at Lebel's, at which Mademoiselle Lange, Sainte Foix—who, it was said, had made her forget Du Barry—and some women were present. It was at this supper that, put at her ease and emboldened by champagne, Du Barry's mistress, with the freedom, the gaiety, and the bewitching follies of a woman who does not think she is observed, charmed the eyes of the King, who, having got notice, gazed at her through an opening made in the wall of Lebel's dining-room. And this first impression was so lively that the King sent for her that very night.

Du Barry's mistress had, perhaps naturally and without any mental reservation, the ingenuity not to affect embarrassment and the good faith not to deceive the King as to her experience. She put aside those skilful grimaces with

let them keep it, and it was during the various journeys he compelled them to make to Versailles that Mademoiselle Vaubernier attracted the attention of the King. M. Lebel was entrusted with his commands, and this last, with whom neither she nor I have had any connection, carried out the execution of them with her alone. Before, however, leading her to Compiegne, he wished that she should only appear there as my brother's wife, a suggestion to which I lent myself then as well as he did, with no other motive certainly save a blind and respectful obedience."

which Louis XV. was surfeited, and the copious display of
confusion which even the cleverest women thought they
owed as a tribute of homage towards the King. She did
not counterfeit ignorance or repugnance or awkwardness.
She was herself; she treated the King as a man, and the
man that was still left in the King came forth amorous
after this first interview. Lebel had not expected such
success; he looked upon it as one of those caprices which
morning dissipates. Terrified at the undignified character
of an attachment in which the King's heart was entangled
as well as his senses, he confessed to the King that he had
deceived him, that the woman whom he had introduced
to him was neither a married woman nor a lady of title,
and he thought it his duty to enlighten him as to the compromising consequences of having this further *liaison* with
her, when the King, stopping him, ordered him to have her
married, and, as soon as the marriage was over, to bring
her to Compiegne.[1]

[1] "Annals of Louis XV." A. Villefranche, at the house of the
Widow Liberty, 1782. Volume II. "Anecdotes about Madame du
Barri." "Historic Memoirs of Jeanne Gomart de Vaubernier, Com-
tesse Dubarry." By M. de Favrolle (Madame Guenard). Paris,
Year XI. Vol. I.

II.

Guillaume du Barry ordered to Paris.—The Forged Vaubernier Certificate of Birth.—The articles of the Contract of Marriage with the Comte Guillaume.—The Bride's Share.—The Celebration of the Marriage and the Husband's Return to Toulouse.—Madame du Barry taking possession of Lebel's Quarters.—The furniture of the Apartments at Versailles.

By order of the King, transmitted through Lebel,[1] the Comte du Barry wrote to his brother Guillaume, a poor officer in the marines, who lived in Toulouse with his mother, and announced to him the good marriage which he had thought of for him.

Guillaume du Barry hastened to prepare in Toulouse the power of attorney[2] by which his mother the Lady Catherine

---

[1] Some days after, Lebel died in such a sudden manner that it was rumored he had been poisoned. Nothing of the kind had happened, but it would seem that, during the representations which he made to the King as to the undignified character of his *liaison*, which he expected to be only a passing fancy, the King, losing his temper, had threatened to strike him with the tongs with which he was going to stir the fire. This threat had brought about such a revolution in "poor Dominique," who was subject to hepatic colics, that a colic seized him and carried him off in two days. ("Private Life of the Maréchal de Richelieu." Buisson, 1791.)

[2] In the presence of the Royal Notary of the City of Toulouse and witnesses named below were present Dame *Catherine Delacaze*, widow of the nobleman, *Antoine Du Barry*, Chevalier of the Military Order of St. Louis, an inhabitant of this city:—

Madame Du Barry

Delacaze, widow of the noble Antoine du Barry, authorized him to contract marriage with such person as he might think fitting; and he rushed up to Paris, and dropped in at his brother's mansion in the Rue Neuve des Petits Champs with an eager and docile zeal in carrying out Jean du Barry's plans.

The contract of marriage was immediately prepared. But there were, in dealing with the future husband and with the King himself, sentiments of pride and shame which were offensive to the lowness of origin of the woman who sought for a husband in order to belong to the King. The real name of the future Madame du Barry, we have said, was, according to the original produced in the suit of the

"Who has made and arranged through her general and special attorney, M. Jean Gruel, merchant, Rue de Roule, Paris, to whom she has given authority on her behalf and in her name, to consent that the noble Guillaume du Barry, her son, ex-officer of infantry, should contract marriage with such lady as he deems fitting, provided in the meantime that she is approved of and accepted by the said attorney so appointed, and that the nuptial benediction should be distributed according to the canonical constitutions by the first priest called upon, without it being, however, understood that the aforesaid lady giving authority is to give anything to her son in his contract of marriage, holding, moreover, that the presents are to have effect notwithstanding superannotation and until express revocation, engaging, obliging, renouncing.

"Made and passed at Toulouse, in our office, the 15th day of the month of July, in the forenoon, in the year 1768, in the presence of the Sieurs Bernard Joseph Fourmont and Bonaventure Calvet, practitioners, residing in this city, undersigned, with the said lady giving authority and our notary.

(Signed) "Delacaze, Du Barry, Fourmont and Sons, Notary."

Madame Du Barry

Du Barry heirs, Jeanne Bequs—according to a communication of the Mayor of Vaucouleurs, Jeanne Becu. On the authority of these two authentic testimonies, which only differ as to the orthography of the name, Jean du Barry's mistress was a natural child. It was thought desirable to disguise a civil condition of which indiscretion and public malignity might make a weapon. These were subterranean, shameful complaisances to which, without doubt, an almoner of the King, Gomard de Vaubernier, connected at the same time with the Rançons, Lebel, and Comte Jean, lent himself. This Gomard would have given a father to the natural child in the person of one of his brothers, Gomard de Vaubernier, whose protests were not to be feared ; he had for some time been dead. And in place of the genuine certificate of birth of Madame du Barry, printed in the commencement of this history, the notaries had, in order to set up their contract, the forged certificate of birth by which hitherto the anecdotists, the romancers, and the historians have been duped. Here is this forged certificate :—

"Extract from the baptismal register of the parish of Vaucouleurs, diocese of Toul, for the year one thousand seven hundred and forty-six.

"Jeanne, daughter of Jean Jacques Gomard de Vaubernier and Anne Becu called *Quantigny,* was born on the 19th of August, one thousand seven hundred and forty-six, was baptized the same day, had for her godfather Joseph de Mange and for her godmother Jeanne de Birabin, who have attached their signatures along with me.—L.

Madame Du Barry

GALON, Vicar of Vaucouleurs; Joseph DE MANGE and Jeanne de BIRABIN."

We see that this forged document[1] certified by L. P. Dubois, the cure of the parish and town of Vaucouleurs, certified also by the Commissary Enquestor, examiner of the town and provostship of Vaucouleurs, gave to the natural daughter a father of noble name.

The witnesses became people of importance, and the peasant, La Birabine, was transformed into the Dame de Birabin. The flattery of the forgers went farther still; it went so far as to make Guillaume du Barry's future wife three years younger by making the date of her birth August 19, 1746, instead of August 19, 1743.

On the 23rd of July, 1768, the contract of this strange stage-marriage was drawn up in the following terms:—

[1] Taking advantage of this forged certificate of birth, in 1814, on the return of Louis XVIII. the Gomard heirs took steps to obtain possession of certain articles which had belonged to Madame du Barry, and which were in public establishments. They presented to the Minister of Finances an Act of Notoriety, averring that the Sieur *Philbert Gomard*, brother of *Gomard de Vaubernier*, father of Madame du Barry, being the nearest relative of the Comtesse at the time of her death, was her heir, an act likewise establishing their filiation as heirs of the Sieur *Philbert Gomard*. They received authority, in order to aid their researches, to take from the Prefecture of the Seine-et-Oise a certain number of papers which were never given back, but of which fortunately a file of documents, THE ACCOUNTS OF MADAME DU BARRY, forms to-day part of the National Library, Manuscript Department, Nos. 8157-8160. The *Gomard* heirs had as yet obtained nothing from their claims except these papers, when on the 17th of April, 1825, the law as to the indemnity of the emigres was re-enacted. At the date of her death Madame du Barry did not

Madame Du Barry

"Before the Councillors of the King, notaries of the Châtelet of Paris, were present:

"The high and mighty Seigneur Messire Guillaume, Comte du Barry, Chevalier Captain of troops taken from the naval forces, residing in Paris in the Rue Neuve-des Petits-Champs, and parish of Saint-Roch, of full age, son of the late Messire Antoine, Comte du Barry, Chevalier of the Royal and Military Order of Saint-Louis and of Dame Catherine Delacaze, his wife, and now his widow, residing in Toulouse, contracting for him and in his name;

"Sieur Andre-Marie Gruel, Merchant, Paris, where he resides in the Rue de Roule, parish of St. Germain l'Auxerrois, in the name and as special proxy for the purpose of the marriage hereinafter referred to of the afore-

possess any real estate, the gift of Luciennes being only for life; but then there came back to the recollection of those heirs the will of the Duc de Brissac and they claimed from the Montemart family, who inherited from the Duke, and who had a considerable share in the liquidation of the thousand million francs, the execution of the legacy made for the benefit of Madame du Barry. Suddenly there came on the scene the *Becu* heirs, who had found out on the registers of Vaucouleurs the genuine certificate of birth, and contested with the *Gomards* their title of heirs to Madame du Barry. Hence a lawsuit between the two branches, and judgment of the Tribunal of First Instance of the Seine of the 19th of January, 1829, confirmed by the decree of the Royal Court of Paris of the 22d of February, 1830, which gave the *Becus* the victory in the suit and recognized them as Madame du Barry's sole heirs.

The *Becu* heirs, in a suit which lasted up to 1833, continued to claim the Brissac legacy. Finally the *Becus* came to a settlement with the Brissacs, but the sum which they received was almost entirely absorbed by the creditors of Madame du Barry and the costs of the lawsuit.

said Dame du Barry Mere, entered into before *Sans,* Royal Notary in Toulouse, in the presence of witnesses, on the 15th of July of the present year, the original of which duly stamped and legalized is, by requisition, left annexed to the minute of the presents previously certified by him to be true, signed and initialed in the presence of the notaries whose names are written hereunder:

" The said Sieur Gruel, by that name, being present and authorizing so far as may be necessary the said Seigneur Comte du Barry on the one part;

" And Sieur *Nicolas Rançon,* interested in the affairs of the King, and the Dame Anne Becu, his wife, whom he authorizes for carrying these presents into effect, residing in Paris in the Rue du Ponceau, parish of St. Laurent, the said Dame before mentioned *widow of the Sieur Jean Jacques Gomard de Vaubernier,* interested in the affairs of *Mademoiselle Jeanne Gomard de Vaubernier,* minor daughter of the said Dame Rançon and of the said late Sieur Gomard de Vaubernier, *her first husband,* residing with them, for this present and as to her consent on her own behalf and in her name;

" Who, in view of the marriage proposed and agreed upon between the said Sieur Comte du Barry and the said Demoiselle Gomard de Vaubernier, which will be celebrated immediately in the face of the Church, have adopted by these presents voluntarily made and reduced to writing the civil clauses and conditions of the said marriage as it will follow in the presence of and with the consent of the high and mighty Seigneur, *Messire Jean du Barry-Cerès,* Governor of Levignac, elder brother of the future husband, the aforesaid nobleman, and of *Claire du Barry,* a lady of full age, sister of the aforesaid future husband.

" FIRST ARTICLE.

" There is to be no community of goods between the said Seigneur and the lady who is to be his future wife, derogating in this respect from the custom of Paris and from every other which admits them to be united; and on the contrary, they are to be and are to remain separated as to goods, and the said lady who is to be the future wife shall have, alone, the enjoyment and administration of the goods, rights, and actions, the movable and immovable property which belong to her and may belong to her as a consequence of *such claim as she may have.*

" ARTICLE II.

" The lady who is to be the future wife marries with the goods and the rights which belong to her, and which will belong to her, in the course of events, *of which she will have the administration,* as is above stated. And her personal effects consist of the amount of 30,000 livres, composed of trinkets, diamonds, clothes, linen, lace, and household articles for her use, the entire proceeding *from her gains and economies,* and of which, in order to avoid confusion with the personal effects of the said nobleman, her future husband, there has been made and drawn up an inventory transcribed on the two first pages of a sheet of notepaper, which is, at their request, left annexed to the minute of the presents, after having been, by the said contracting parties, declared to be true, signed and initialed in the presence of the notaries whose names are here undersigned.

"ARTICLE III.

"All the furniture and effects which are in the houses to be occupied by the future married pair as well in Paris as in the country, other than those enumerated in the inventory annexed as above will be deemed to belong, and will in fact belong, to the said Seigneur, the future husband, and, if in the course of time, the said lady who is to be the future wife makes any purchase of furniture and effects, she will be obliged to get a receipt from the notary to the amount of the goods.

"ARTICLE IV.

"All the property belonging to the lady and the nobleman, the future married pair, and those which they fall in for during their married lives through whatever title, as well movable as immovable, will be deemed to belong to each of them and their successors in their respective lines of descent.

"ARTICLE V.

"The said Seigneur, the future husband, has bestowed upon and bestows upon the lady, his future wife, by way of dowry 1000 livres in yearly income, the capital of which laid out at five per cent interest will belong to the children born of the said marriage.

"ARTICLE VI.

" In the event of the death of one of the future married pair the survivor will have and take out of the effects of the pre-deceased, in the form of right of survivorship, in furniture and goods estimated at their proper value, the amount of 10,000 livres or the like sum in cash, at the option of the said survivor.

"ARTICLE VII.

" It is agreed that the said lady, the future wife, will *remain charged alone with the management and with all the expenses of the household,* as well for food as for the rent of apartments which they will occupy, servants' wages, table-linen, household utensils, keeping up of equipages, feeding of horses, and *all other expenses without exception,* as well with regard to the said Seigneur her future husband as with regard to the children that are to be born of the said marriage, whom she will be bound to rear and educate at her own expense, on the condition that the said Seigneur, her future husband, will be obliged to pay to the said lady his future wife, the sum of six thousand livres as an annuity, so as to provide for his moiety of the said expenses, and maintenance of the household each year from six months to six months, and always in advance, so that the first six months will be payable the day after the celebration of the marriage.

" It is thus that the entire contract has been agreed upon and settled between the parties promising, binding, and renouncing.

" Made and carried out in Paris at the house of the said Seigneur, Comte du Barry, the future husband as below designated in the year 1768 on the 23rd of July, in the afternoon; and have signed hereto: J. GOMARD DE VAUBERNIER, le CHEVALIER DU BARRY, GRUEL, le COMTE DU BARRY-CERES, A. BECU, C. F. DU BARRY, RANÇON." [1]

And let us not forget in this amusing and disgraceful simulacrum of a union before notaries, the personal share of the bride, that trousseau for the purpose of beginning housekeeping estimated at thirty thousand pounds, the result of " the gains and economies " of the lady, of which a reservation is made in the double sheet of notepaper attached to the contract. Jeanne Becu wears a diamond necklace of the finest quality worth eight thousand livres; a tuft for the hair and a pair of earrings shaped like chandeliers valued at eight thousand livres. She wears thirty gowns and petticoats of different materials, silk and gold and silver for every season, estimated at three thousand livres. She wears English, Brussels, Valenciennes, Arras and other laces, as well in the trimming of her dresses as in ruffles, caps, and otherwise, valued at six thousand

---

[1] " Memoirs of the Society of Moral Sciences, Letters and Arts of Seine-Oise," Volume V., 1859.

livres. There are six dozen fine chemises of Holland linen, garnished with embroidered muslin ruffles, one dozen morning gowns all of different stuffs, silk or other material, two dozen corsets, and many other linen and personal articles of attire for the use of this lady, valued at two thousand livres. Nothing is lacking in the wardrobe of this bride, who brings with her, too, the complete bed, with the curtains, head-board, canopy of green damask, hangings of the same kind of damask, eight chairs, four arm-chairs, and two green damask bed-screens, of the estimated value of three thousand livres, and completing the bride's personal outfit to the amount of thirty thousand pounds.

A month after the contract, the marriage was celebrated.[1] The husband set out again for Toulouse. Madame du Barry took possession of Lebel's quarters,[2] then of Madame

[1] "On the 1st of September, 1768, after publication of three banns without any opposition in this parish of St. Laurent and in this of St. Eustache on the 24th, 25th and 31st of last July, in view of the power of attorney given by the mother of the bridegroom to M. Jean Gruel, merchant, of Paris, in the Rue de Roule, to whom she gives power on her behalf and in her name to consent to the present marriage, and in view likewise of the authority given by the step-father and the mother of the bride to Messire *Jean-Baptiste Gomard*, priest, almoner of the King, to whom they give the right to represent them at the celebration of this marriage, the betrothal having been to-day celebrated, Messire Guillaume, Comte du Barry, ex-captain, and Mademoiselle Jeanne Gomard de Vaubernier, aged twenty-two, daughter of Jean-Jacques de Vaubernier interested in the affairs of the King, and of Anne Becu called Cantigny, have been married by us."

[2] All that autumn of the year 1768, Madame du Barry was the mistress in a strictly *incognito* fashion of the King, for his Majesty

Madame Du Barry

Adelaïde's apartment. This apartment was situated in the second story of Versailles, quite close to the King's apartment. And Louis XV. could repair thither every hour without being seen, either by a staircase opening on the balcony of the " Stag's Park "[1] or through the library situated above the great cabinet, one door of which opened on a little landing giving entrance to one of the two cabinets placed at either side of Madame du Barry's bed-room.[2]

[1] The " Parc aux Cerfs," as the student of French history knows, was the seraglio of that most amorous monarch, Louis *le Bien-Aime*. —TRANSLATOR.

[2] Almost immediately (December 22, 1768) the steward of Madame du Barry's house took a lease in his mistress's name of a mansion in the Rue d'Orangerie, intended to afford housing for the equipages and the servants of the favourite. At the end of a few years Madame du Barry's house became so imposing an establishment that her equipages and her servants could no longer remain in the Rue d'Orangerie. The favourite was obliged to rent the Hotel des Luynes, and soon purchased in the Avenue de Paris for the purpose of erecting a large mansion there a pretty summer residence built for Binet, Madame de Pompadour's valet and relative. Ledoux made there considerable enlargements. He even built a chapel there, for which there was a regular chaplain.

In 1770, other quarters were prepared for Madame du Barry at Versailles; but the suite of apartments was given definitely to the Duc de Cosse-Brissac, and Madame du Barry remained in her old suite of apartments, which a plan of Gabriel—" Plan of the Changes and Additions to be made to the suite of apartments of the Comtesse du Barry (July 22d, 1770)"—shows to be completely modified as compared with the former plan. This suite of apartments consisted of a library, which had already existed at the time of Madame Adelaide, a back-library, etc., a drawing-room cabinet, a large drawing-room

being in deep mourning for the Queen, it was not the correct thing, as the " Anecdotes " say, for him to make a public display of his pleasures.

Madame Du Barry

Installed in Versailles, Madame du Barry from the start gave full vent to her tastes for luxury and magnificence. The courtesan who had thought green damask sufficient for her yesterday commenced to surround herself with all the beautiful and agreeable things which she came later on to collect at Luciennes, as if in a boudoir of the furnishing arts. In this dwelling provided for her by her new-found good-fortune, in this succession of small low rooms, which preserve still to-day in the half-light of their shutters with closed wooden bolts the memory of a mysterious voluptuousness, the King's mistress heaped together artistic objects, rarities, bronzes, marbles, chinaware. On the chimney-piece of the salon there was a magnificent pillared clock on which a crowd of china figures disported themselves. In the centre of the salon stood a table garnished with bronzes gilt in dead gold, and the upper portion of which was a marvellous miniature painting after Le Prince. Two chests of drawers faced each other, one of old lacquer-work, of lacquer-work such as cannot now be found, from which came out in full gold relief monkeys gaily dressed; the other was adorned with five plates of Sevres porcelain, five

cabinet, and the room where one could see in the alcove the door of the staircase leading towards the King's apartment. In June, 1772, Gabriel made a large ball-room, which the old suite of apartments lacked, and the cost of which amounted to 14,950 francs, while at the same time he built new kitchens for the favourite. In 1774, Madame du Barry's suite of apartments came into the possession of old Maurepas, as Louis XVI. was anxious to have his minister under his hand in the same way as Louis XV. had his mistress. (National Archives, MSS. Plans of Royal Houses, October, 1773.)

plates which could not be matched in the whole world. The former displayed on its marble surface a bronze group of four figures, the "Abduction of Helen," the latter a Bacchanalian group of boys which had come from the hands of Sarrazin. From the ceiling hung a glittering lustre of rock-crystal, which cost sixteen thousand livres. As the mistress of the place was fond of play, there was in a corner of the salon a chest containing four quadrille-boxes, made of ivory with counters, consolation-fishes, and the other figures encrusted with gold. In another angle slept the harmonies of an English piano-forte, constructed in Paris by the celebrated Clicot, with its flutes, pipes, lute, cymbals, tubes, and blowers imprisoned in a box of rosewood garnished with bronzes gilt in dead gold.

Madame du Barry's chamber was not second to this salon. On the German clock which represented the " Three Graces supporting the Vase of Time," the hour was indicated by a Cupid's arrow. Everywhere porcelain reigned and triumphed. Chests of drawers displayed pictures in porcelain in the style of Watteau and Vanloo. Writing-desks and cupboards framed in their wood plates of porcelain with a green background in which Sevres had loosened its bouquets, while basins for putting in flowers with patterns of blue and gold rockwork traced on them afforded a glimpse of seamen in miniature or grotesque figures by Teniers.

The cabinet had its little writing-table, all plated with porcelain, its ink-horn formed of various portions gilt and chased with consummate art, a timepiece with children's sports painted in Sevres, and a gilt dragon with a dart of marcasite. Passement had put his signature to the thermometer and the barometer so richly mounted in gilt bronze. A thousand objects, a thousand marvels encumbered the shelves: scent-boxes in old lacquer-work, tea-services of Saxe with pictures and miniatures, were still waiting there for the liqueur-case of rock-crystal which Madame du Barry was to buy afterwards at Madame de Lauraguais's sale.

And this luxuriousness and this selectness in the furniture extended into every portion of her apartments.

III.

The Choiseul Monarchy.—The Minister's Brutality towards Madame d'Esparbes.—Influence of the Duchesse de Gramont on her Brother.—The " Bourbonnaise " and the Satirical Prints.—The Roue's Diplomacy aided and sustained by *" La Chon "*—The Marechal de Richelieu in the role of protector.—The Presentation of the Comtesse du Barry at Versailles.—The Perfection and the Childlike Daintiness of the Woman's Beauty.

M. DE CHOISEUL was master of France. He governed through a ministry filled with followers who submitted to the superiority of his talents, to the energy of his will. He dominated through this people of creatures grouped under him even to the lowest class in the State and devoted to what was called " the Choiseul Monarchy." He reigned through the supports which he had created abroad, through the personal obligations of European cabinets towards him, through the *eclat* of a ministry which had restored a semblance of greatness to French politics, and which, taking everything into account, had given peace to Europe, alarm to England, arms to Turkey, and a province to France. He had taken possession of the King, and had got into his good graces by the force of custom, the easiness of his task, the agreeability of his optimistic views, and the charms of his domination; and even Choiseul's enemies, taking into consideration the King's age, and no longer expecting from

41

his sixty years the passions and inconstancies of youth, despaired of a sudden change of masters and of a revolution in the palace deposing *King Choiseul*. In the mean time, the minister, wishing to make sure of the future and to leave nothing to chance, strove to prevail upon the King to marry an Austrian archduchess; in this way he would have his ministry associated with thankfulness in high quarters, the gratitude of a throne, and obtain from the King directly a guarantee of his favour. Thus, having got everything out of his way, what would he have to fear? And did he not already believe himself to be unshakable?

In 1765, a year after Madame de Pompadour's death, an attempt had been made to place Madame d'Esparbes with the King and to get her talked about in connection with him. Madame d'Esparbes had the most beautiful pair of hands at the Court, and the King had let himself be captivated by those pretty fingers which picked cherries so gracefully. Madame d'Esparbes had gone to be proclaimed at Marly, where she had apartments. When M. de Choiseul, in the insolence of his omnipotence, coming over to her, with the consciousness of the insult he was about to fling at her,—it was on the great staircase before everybody—caught hold of her by the chin, and asked her:— "How is your business going on, my girl?" [1] The mistress was killed by these words; the suite of apartments was taken away from her; and the King, to whom Choiseul

[1] Memoir of the Duc de Choiseul, placed in the King's hands in 1765, cited in the *Revue Française*, 1828.

spoke about the way in which he had quizzed her, did not
dare to proceed further with Madame d'Esparbes, who,
some days after, received a letter under royal seal exempt-
ing her from paying her court to the King, and command-
ing her to retire to Montauban to rejoin there her father,
the Marquis de Lussan.[1] Therefore, M. de Choiseul, at
first, regarded the new intrigue with a certain contempt.
He saw there the hand of Richelieu, without deigning to
be annoyed with him. A chilling dignity was his response
to the advances of the mistress, who would very probably
in this opening period of her career, have willingly quitted
her leader in order to find an ally in the Duc de Choiseul
and some friends in his camp. Then the minister came
to realize that he had no longer to deal with a caprice of
the King, with another d'Esparbes. He saw all the passion kindled in the master's heart, all the attractions and all
the solid fascinations of the favourite growing stronger
every day. The vulgarity of the intrigue, and the impossi-
bility, too, of suppressing it, the constraining force of his
thinly-veiled disdain, and the haughty nobility of his character, obliged him to be obstinately resolute and to persevere
in his attitude to the end. Besides, in the position in which
M. de Choiseul now happened to find himself, he lacked
the quality most essential to his *role,* coolness; he was led
into this war with a woman by the passion of a woman, of
his sister, the Duchesse de Gramont.

[1] "Historic Summary of the Life of Madame du Barry." Paris,
1774.

Madame Du Barry

In the little apartments where she lived bereft of all female society since Madame de Pompadour's death, Madame de Gramont had conceived a plan for obtaining the mastery over the King's habits almost by force, and of establishing over his weakness of resolution and his indolence of mind an influence and an interest which would have made him forget the reign of Madame de Pompadour. And she flung herself on this idea with all the fire of her nature, basing her hopes of success on the masculine force of her spirit, associated as she was with half of her brother's political speculations, on the seductive powers of her mind, and above,all on a certain fascination of the dominant order which she was supposed to possess.[1] But the King was tired of the government of political women. Madame de Pompadour's death had set him free, and he did not wish at any cost to go back to this kind of servitude. In spite of his coolness, Madame Gramont persevered; she was putting her trust in obstinacy, in the continuance and the audacity of her efforts, in the effects of obsession and moral violence, when her whole dream was shattered by this little girl of the streets who had been thrown into the Royal bed. It was this disappointment, these resentments of Madame de Gramont, that proved a burden to the minister in his management of public affairs. M. de Choiseul was driven by his sister beyond hostility. Madame de Gramont led him on to outrages; she organized that war of street-ballads, vaudevilles, ribald verses, and satirical publications

[1] "Private Life of Louis XV." London: Peter Lyton, 1785.

which had only the result of plunging the King deeper into his love-affair. She launched forth the " Bourbonnaise," [1] so as to awaken all the echoes of the street-crossings; she got the past of this mistress of the King set to music by all the lamplighters of Paris and of the provinces; and in the zeal of her anger she suggested to Voltaire, whom the minister Choiseul made the vehicle of his wit, the pamphlet of the " King of Bedlam," in which the vengeances of Chanteloup passing over the head of the Du Barry, directed themselves even to her lover. [2]

[1] Air: " La Bourbonnaise "—

> " What a strange thing it is!
> A girl who is dirt!
> A girl who is dirt!
> What a strange thing it is!
> With a King's heart may sport
> And be welcomed at Court."

The past of the mistress was not only described in songs paid for by Choiseul; it also enjoyed the publicity of numerous sheets of paper slipped under cloaks, with words like the following written on them: " September 3, 1768.—There has appeared at Compiegne a Comtesse Dubarri, who had caused a great commotion by her face. It is said that she has made herself agreeable at Court, and that the King has given her a very good reception. Her beauty and this rapid celebrity have led many persons to make inquiries about her. It has been sought to trace up this woman's origin, and, if we are to believe what has been made public about her, she is of very ignoble birth. She has reached her present position by ways that are by no means virtuous, and her entire life is a tissue of infamies. A certain Dubarri, who claims that he is one of the Barymores, and who got her to marry his brother, is the instigator of this new mistress. It is contended that the taste and intelligence of this adventurer in the details of pleasure made him aspire to the King's confidence, with a view to furnishing His Majesty with amusements, and that he will succeed the Sieur Lebel in this function."

[2] See Voltaire's " Roi Pétaut."—TRANSLATOR.

Madame Du Barry

The man who ran Madame du Barry, the Roue, the Comte Jean, was not one of those vulgar debauchees who drown themselves in the wine and the pleasures of life in which they wallow. He had will, imagination, and that fire of swaggering energy which drives the men of his country towards adventures and launches them into the unknown. At the core of him lived and concealed itself, under the waste of low appetites, an activity ready for action, the force to rush at anything big, the torment of desires long wandering and aimless, perhaps the bitterness caused by finding his career broken and by the refusal he had endured at the hands of the Prime Minister. Nature had flung him into life like a good gambler with the audacity to stake his all. The crapulous world in which he had lived, the filthy and ironical society of which he had made the evil acquaintance, had given him that supreme contempt for humanity which makes a man believe that everything happens, and by which he often causes them to happen. Nothing made him astonished at his luck save the astonishment of others; and it was he who was, ere long, to the great amazement of all those who yesterday called him a madman, to pray to God for his brother's death so as to give himself the pleasure of seeing this very stimulating event—the marriage of the King of France to his ex-mistress!

Du Barry was a man of observation; one glance was sufficient for him, in spite of the laughter of Lebel and Richelieu, to divine the future of Madame du Barry. From

Madame Du Barry

that day Du Barry revealed himself, and his genius as a
Mentor made itself seen. On this great theatre of the
Court, where Madame de Pompadour had been found to be
a *gossip*, it was no easy task to maintain the frolicsome girl
of the streets in the style, the proportion, and the propriety
of her new role. It was necessary every moment to protect
her from yielding to the first impulse, to hold her back on
the brink of an awkwardness, of an extravagance, of a
grimace, of a glaring breach of propriety, to drive back into
the recesses of her breast her vivacity and mirthful outbursts,
the hot tears and the petty angers of the grisette. How many
wicked smiles from under fans, and how many laughs at
her expense outside, had that supper procured for fine ladies
at which, in a dispute with the King, the Du Barry, blub-
bering, so far forgot herself as to say loud enough for
everyone to hear her:—" You are a liar, yes, a liar, and the
greatest liar in the world!"[1] And how she amused the
servants with her innocent question about Mercury:—" I
don't know what it is; I wish someone told me."[2] And
what a delight it gave to those who took a hostile attitude
to repeat her comical way of asking—and always with a
childish lisp—for news as to the Marechale de Mirepoix's
sprain:—

' By the way, how is the little *Maressale's* old foot?"[3]

[1] "Complete Correspondence of Madame du Deffand." By M.
de Sainte-Aulaire. Michael Levy, 1866, Volume I.
[2] "The Marquise du Deffand's Letters to Horace Walpole." Treuttel and Wurtz, 1812, Volume II.
[3] "Complete Correspondence of Madame du Deffand." By M. de
Sainte-Aulaire, Volume I.

Madame Du Barry

Those blunders, those stupidities, those faults of education, those treasons of nature Jean du Barry was skilful enough to prevent the recurrence of too often. He had buttressed his ex-mistress with the society, the surveillance of his ugly but intelligent sister " Chon," who was slightly hunchbacked and slightly lame.[1] He himself separated from the favourite, hidden in the gloomy recesses of Paris, far from the Court and from the eyes of the curious, protected her, followed her, guided her, incessantly corresponding with her through a service of boy-messengers, who carried the post on foot between Paris and Versailles, and by means of whom he roughly jotted down to the Du Barry her *role,* her words, and her responses. In short, it was such clever guidance, and there was such an attentive prompter and one of

[1] Jean du Barry had three sisters. One, named Claire, who was familiarly called " Chon," as an abbreviation of Fanchon, did not lack wit and a certain political sense. She had a taste for literature, and had the distinction, the " Anecdotes" inform us, of seeing herself in print in the " Mercure." She was the sister whom the Du Barry preferred, and was the guiding spirit of the house. At one time, the Marquise de Montmorency, to please the favourite, had attempted to marry " La Chon" to the Duc de Boutteville, a gentleman head over ears in debt, but bearing one of the greatest names in France.

A second sister, baptized at one time *Pischy* and at another time *Bitschi* and at a later period called Mademoiselle de la Serre, played beside the " Chon " the part of a helpless creature.

The third sister, called *Catin,* was married to a peasant from Levignac, one Filieuse, who was subsequently astonished at being himself ennobled. Jean du Barry had two brothers, Guillaume, husband of the Du Barry, and Elie, who, as a recognition of the amorous services rendered by the Comte to MM. de Richelieu and De Duras, became a Colonel in the Queen's Regiment and married Mademoiselle de Fumel.

such experience behind the wanton *bombarded* at Versailles, that, during the year which elapsed between the first interview and the presentation, the King's mistress did not give rise, so to speak, to the worst of scandals, to ridicule. The Roue, who had never had any doubt as to success, no longer had any fears. At a whistle from the " Bourbonnaise," he responded secretly with the " Loves of the Duc de Choiseul with his sister the Duchess de Gramont," and openly with a genealogy of the Du Barrys prepared with a great splash in England and connecting the Du Barry with the Barymores. Now that he had got the favourite out of the " Parc-aux-Cerfs," from that common lodging-house erected for the sake of caprice, where she would have disappeared with those who did not even leave the recollection of them in the King's mind, the Comte Jean thought the time had arrived for the presentation, and he urged Madame du Barry to obtain this consecration which gave the mistress so many rights—the right not to be sent away, the right to take part in the journeys of the Court, the right to get into the royal coaches, the right to live publicly with the King, the right to show herself in the Dauphin's apartments, as well as in those of the King's brothers, and those of Mesdames, the right to give orders to the ministers, the right to receive ceremonial visits from the great and from ambassadors, all the rights, in short, without which the mistress was nothing but the mistress,— with which the mistress was the favourite. This was what Du Barry wanted, what he kept pushing Madame du Barry

towards without letting her rest. He did not allow himself
to be satisfied by conspicuous marks of royal favour, or
by the order sent to M. de Marigny to re-establish in the
royal dwellings the communications between the apartments of the late Marquise de Pompadour and the apartments of the King or by the pitiful figure made by the
King at the entertainments of the Comte de Noailles.
He began to find, in spite of all these steps, that
the presentation was put off, and he sought to guess at M.
de Choiseul's game and to defeat it. In anticipation, he had,
for the purpose of the ceremony, which required a woman
of title, discovered in Paris a Comtesse de Bearn, a lady
by no means in comfortable circumstances, the widow of
a gentleman from Perigord, who had died leaving her five
children and a big lawsuit to carry on against the house of
Saluces—a lawsuit which traced its commencement back
as far as Montaigne. Du Barry obtained for the Comtesse
a provision which enabled her to present herself and play
her part of solicitress in a condition suitable to her birth;
finally, he helped her to win her case, and thus secured for
himself a sponsor whose entrance upon the scene seemed to
be heralded by M. de la Vauguyons, attempts to compromise
with the repugnances of Mesdames.

In this big business of the presentation, the Comte Jean
had the support of Richelieu. Undecided at first, having no
great confidence in the duration of the King's caprice, hesitating about publicly compromising himself, in connection
with such a low intrigue, held, moreover, in respect by

Madame Du Barry

Choiseul, whom he feared, flattered, and wished to manage, Richelieu had only joined the party of the mistress in a very subterranean fashion; but when, owing to her daily and familiar relations with the King, he had assured himself that the royal fancy was a serious one, and that it was safe to lay odds on the Du Barry, he took the risk. Jealous of the great place which M. de Choiseul, "that marplot," as he called him, had taken in the daily life of the King, of his dictatorship in the ministry, Richelieu foresaw a means of having his revenge in the elevation of the Comtesse. Devoured by spite, eaten up by a secret envy of a great political position, to which his reputation for levity and for dangling after women and engaging in amorous negotiations had prevented him from having access, he had not abandoned that dream to which the intrigues of Madame de Lauraguais had driven him, on the death of the Marechal de Belle-Isle—the post of Prime Minister; and the least that he hoped for was to enter the Council behind the mistress when she became the Favourite. So it was that the Comte Jean had a devoted ally with the King. And Richelieu said besides that he would not be King if he did not impose his choice on his ministers and his court. It was thus, and as best he could, that Richelieu catechised the King, stimulated his courage, and worked to bring about the presentation.

But it was on one side of Richelieu, in the younger branch of his family that Madame du Barry found her great fulcrum, her boldest and most serious supporter. She found him in that representative of religious authority and of monarchic authority, the protector of the Jesuits, the man whose entire life had been a duel with M. de Choiseul, a duel which at that moment threatened to have the scaffold for its closing scene—M. d'Aiguillon.

M. de Choiseul belonged to the Jansenists, to the Parliamentarians, to the philosophers, to the party of reform of Church and State, to the first harvest of liberty, to the conspiracy of the future. M. d'Aiguillon belonged to the traditions of his family, to the school of his grand-uncle, Cardinal de Richelieu, to the wisdom of the past, to the theory of the absolute rights of power, to the party of social discipline, to the doctrine which makes of monarchic government a pleasant state of things tempered by a theocracy. In those two men everything was antagonistic, the interior administration of the country as well as the plan of her alliances on the map of Europe. They were the two champions and the two extremities of their age. The conflict between their personalities was a conflict of principles, and the ideas of the time circulate around their quarrels. The Duc d'Aiguillon, the lover of Madame de Chateauroux[1] banished in 1745 from his little suite of apartments through the jealousy of Louis XV., and in disgrace for many years, did not obtain admission to his old quarters till 1762, his re-entrance, so to speak on the stage of Versailles, where he became the

[1] Madame de Chateauroux was as yet only Madame de la Tournelle, and the Duc d'Aiguillon only the Duc d'Agenois. The Du Barry's future minister did not become Duc d'Aiguillon till January 31, 1750.

To face page 52

intimate friend of the Dauphin. Alarmed at the influence of D'Aiguillon over the mind of the religious prince, and knowing that from that moment he had been assigned the post of Minister of Marine by the devotees of the Court, Saint Sulpice, and perhaps the remorse of Louis XV., Choiseul had raised up La Chatolais as the conqueror of Saint-Cast. There, in that province of Brittany, where the Jesuits, authorized by the Governor, D'Aiguillon, were taking steps to effect a restoration, Choiseul had launched that cruel portrayer of the Jesuits, in his celebrated report. So then, above D'Aiguillon, whom the Choiseul party accused of extortions; above Choiseul, whom the D'Aiguillon party accused of having poisoned the Dauphin and the Dauphiness, it was Jesuitism and Philosophism, which were wrestling for the mastery; and this great trial with eighteen centuries as witnesses became the arena where the two spirits which still divided France and contended for the world struggled, advanced, recoiled, triumphed, and succumbed in turn, according to the vicissitudes and the rebounds of human affairs. One day, the disappearance of Madame de Pompadour gave Choiseul entire domination over the King. Another day, a murmur from Broglie on Choiseul's Austrian policy withdrew D'Aiguillon from his position of obscurity and set him afloat once more. But at last the successive deaths of the Dauphin, of the Dauphiness, and of the Queen had left the adversary of the Minister-King very feeble and quite ready to collapse in his duel, in his long and interminable trial. And in the helpless condition in which

Madame Du Barry

D'Aiguillon found himself and the ideas whose fate he held in his hands, Choiseul's enemy turned towards Madame du Barry as a suppliant. In order to deal out strong blows, an acknowledged mistress was needed to promote the interests of the devotee party. In spite of these supports, the presentation was slow in coming. Already the month of January was far off when Paris every day awaited the event with feverish curiosity. It had been almost positively announced that it would take place on Sunday, the 29th of January. But M. de la Vauguyon, despatched by the Marechal de Richelieu to Mesdames to inform them that, according to the protocol, Madame du Barry had gone to visit their ladies-in-waiting, had seen Madame Adelaïde abruptly turn her back to him and to the little discourse in which he preached submission to the wishes of the King. It was only a drawn game; the presentation would have certainly taken place the following Wednesday, a day for which the King in leading out the Duchesse de Choiseul, de Gramont, and de Mirepoix, had only invited the last. No. And some days after this, the King, while hunting, had a fall from his horse, which once more put off the presentation.[1] In the midst of all these delays the Comtesse got afraid of the consequences which this presentation might have for her in the future, and, pretending that she had sustained a sprain,

[1] "The Marquise du Deffand's Letters to Walpole." Treuttel and Wurtz, 1812. A missive emanating from the King's palace (Archives Nationales O'411) announces that the accident which had happened to the King would not have any troublesome consequences, that there was no fracture, but only a bad contusion.

remained obstinately fixed in her lounging-chair. In February, Madame du Deffand, who boasted of having won all her bets, laid a wager that the mistress would not be presented, that the King would not do such an indecent act needlessly.

The months of February and March passed without anything being done. Evidently the King was hesitating. He was eager to overcome his last hesitations, to play a game of bluff with regard to any feelings of shame he had left on behalf of his daughters. The triumvirate of Du Barry, Richelieu, and D'Aiguillon called upon their creature for a supreme effort, a scene of tears in which, casting herself at the King's feet, she implored of him to put a stop to the insulting remarks as to her presentation which, though it had been announced in the foreign newspapers, each day seemed to defer. . . . The King gave way. On the 21st of April, 1769, on his return from the chase, Louis XV. declared that the presentation would take place on the following day, that it would be unique, that it would be the event that had been in question for a long time—the presentation of the Comtesse du Barry.[1]

The great day arrived. Paris rushed to Versailles. The curiosity of an entire people beat at the gate of the park. The presentation was to take place the night after the function. The hour was approaching. Richelieu, in his capacity of First Gentleman, was at the King's side. Choiseul was on the other side. Both were waiting, counting the minutes,

[1] "Anecdotes about the Comtesse du Barry," London, 1775.

glancing at each other, watching the uproar around them, and keeping a keen eye all the time on the King. The King, ill at ease, restless, agitated, was looking every moment at his watch, and was astonished at the delay. He walked up and down, mumbled words which he did not finish, grew impatient at the noise which reached him from the gates and the avenues, and the cause of which he wanted to know from Choiseul. " Sire," replied Choiseul, with his sarcastic finesse, " the people, having been informed that it is to-day Madame du Barry is to have the honour of being presented to Your Majesty, have rushed from every quarter to witness her entry, not being able to be at the reception which Your Majesty will give her."

The hour had long passed. Madame du Barry did not make her appearance. Choiseul and his friends were radiant with joy. Richelieu, at a window-corner, felt his assurance giving way. The King went across to the window, and glanced out into the night: nothing. At last, he made up his mind, and opened his mouth to countermand the presentation. " Sire, here is Madame du Barry," exclaimed Richelieu who came to recognize the Favourite's carriage and livery; " she will come in if you give the order." And at these words, Madame du Barry appeared behind the Comtesse de Bearn.[1] She entered adorned with diamonds worth a hundred thousand francs, which the King had sent her, adorned with that superb headdress, the arrange-

---

[1] " Memoirs of the Marechal Duc de Richelieu" (by Soulavie), 1793. Volume IX. " Private Life of the Marechal de Richelieu."

ment of which had made her miss the hour for the presentation, attired in one of those triumphal costumes which the women of the eighteenth century called "a fighting costume," armed with that toilette in which the eyes of a blind woman, the intuition of Madame du Deffand, saw the destiny of Europe and the fate of ministers.[1] And it was an apparition so radiant, so dazzling, that at the first moment of surprise the greatest enemies of the Favourite could not escape the fascination of the woman and gave up slandering her beauty.[2]

All the representations, all the portraits, all the pictures which Madame du Barry has left of herself, all those mirrors which seek to immortalize immortal beauty—marble, canvas, engraving—display and reflect in our eyes the most charming seductions of form, the most delicate attractions, the most dainty perfection of a body and a face which seem to realize the ideal of the pretty Frenchwoman of the eighteenth century.[3]

[1] "Letters of the Marquise du Deffand." 1812. Volume II.

[2] "The Gazette of France" announces the presentation in these terms: "At *Versailles, April 26, 1769.* On the 22d of this month, the Comtesse du Barri had the honour of being presented to the King and to the Royal Family by the Comtesse de Bearn."

[3] We trace this picture of Madame du Barry especially in the two portraits of her by Drouais in the Devere sale (March 17, 1755), portraits which seem to us the originals exhibited in the Salon of 1769.

To the amorous correspondence of Madame du Barry with Lord Seymour, possessed by M. Barriere, was attached a lock of the Favourite's hair. I have been able to touch this hair, and I have never met with any human being's hair so completely resembling silk.

Madame Du Barry

Her hair was the most beautiful, the longest, the most silky, the most blonde in the world, blonde of an auburn tint, and curling like the hair of a child,—hair which preserves on the forehead of a woman, as it were, an adorable survival of the little girl. She had (charming contrast!) dark eyebrows, and curved dark lashes, almost curling around her blue eyes, which one scarcely ever saw quite open,[1] and from which stole coquettish sidelong glances out of those half-shot orbs—the genuine look of passion. Then came a little nose finely cut and the delicate curve of a dainty mouth. Hers was a skin, a complexion, which the age compared to "a rose-leaf steeped in milk." Her neck resembled the neck of an antique statue, lengthened by Parmian sculpture so as to sway delicately on the round low shoulders. And then an arm, a foot, a hand. . . . and a thousand beauties of detail. There were in her the victorious youth, the life, and, as it were, the divinity of a Hebe. Around her floated that atmosphere of intoxication, that flame of an amorous goddess which made Voltaire write this line on beholding one of her portraits:

"Such beauty for the gods alone was made."[2]

[1] "Recollections of Madame Vigee Lebrun." Fournier, 1835, Volume I. Here we have the simpering look, the theatrical look of the two portraits exhibited by Drouais in 1769, criticized by the Salon haunter of the "Secret Memoirs" without having seen. Madame du Barry.

[2] Literally: "The original was made for the gods."—TRANSLATOR.

IV.

Repugnances of titled women towards the Favourite.—Purchase of the Marechale de Mirepoix's "Chaperonnage."—The Duchesse de Valentinois, the Marquise de l'Hopital, the Princesse de Montmorency.—Skilful effacement of the Favourite.—The Bellevue Supper. The Gift of Luciennes.—The Courtiers' Meannesses and the Chevalier de la Marliere's Dedication.—Portrait of Chancellor Maupeou.

So the Comtesse du Barry had been presented by Madame de Bearn to the King, to Mesdames, to the Dauphin, and to the children of France. The day after the presentation, which was a Sunday, she was present at the King's mass, in the chapel of the Chateau, the place which had been occupied by the late Marquise de Pompadour. That day, there were very few lords and ladies of the Court in the train of the King; but it was noticed that he was accompanied by a numerous train of bishops, at the head of whom was the Archbishop-Duke of Reims to whom His Majesty spoke several times during the service. After mass, Madame du Barry appeared at Mesdames' concert, and also at the Dauphin's.[1]

All the wishes of Madame du Barry were crowned by this presentation. She slept in the enjoyment of a great victory; but her triumph was not absolute. It remained for

[1] "Journal of Events that Came to my Knowledge." By Hardy. National Library MSS.

her to wipe away and to conquer the last sentiments of decency of the Court, the repugnances of women of title, the protestations and hesitations of the great names of Versailles, in the presence of an accession to power so abrupt, a good-fortune so new. In the month of May, in the journey to Marly following the presentation, where the King stayed until the Whitsuntide holidays, the women invited displayed so much coldness that nearly everybody felt ill at ease. The rumour even circulated that the Princesse de Guemenee had failed to meet Madame du Barry, and that she had received orders from the King to retire to the society of the young ladies to whom she had been the governness in succession to Madame de Marsan. In the midst of the sulkiness of the ladies who were present, play was carried on in an icy fashion. Some noblemen refused to deal the cards under the pretext of being short of money. The Favourite, however, played, and (unhappy creature!) when she punted at faro, had she not the ill-luck to exclaim: " *Ah! my goose is cooked* " *?* [1] " We must needs take your word for it, Madame," one sharp-tongued player said in reply, while picking up the money she had lost, " you ought to be a good judge," [2] an insolent allusion to her mother's position as cook to Mlle. Frederique. Madame du Barry, made the subject of puns, shunned, and isolated, was forced to beat a retreat towards her own set, and to confine herself to a very limited circle, in other words, to Madame d'Alogny and that old lady-litigant, the Comtesse de Bearn.

[1] Literally: " Ah! I am fried " (i.e., done for).—TRANSLATOR.
[2] " Anecdotes about Madame du Barry." London, 1775.

Madame Du Barry

The mistress's faction was secretly working to secure for the Favourite some social props, to purchase for her the "chaperonnage" of a great name under the monarchy. For this *role,* the most strong-minded of her counsellors had cast eyes on the Marechale de Mirepoix, that needy personage always plunged in debt, and always hunting for a little ready money" which she spent in buying trifles." Since the month of January, the King had been holding conferences with "the little Marechale," which seemed to have had no result. At last, the weak woman, who was so much crushed by debts, though her brother was the Marechal de Beauvau, and she was the friend and ally of Choiseul, consented to become the Du Barry's *travelling* and *supper companion* for the yearly sum of a hundred thousand francs, for which she got neither a contract nor a warrant, but merely a bond by means of which she was kept at will, and might be subjected to every kind of humiliation.[1] The Marechale had been promised the " Nantes Lodges " by the Du Barry, but eventually the King made a gift of the place to the Favourite herself.[2] In spite of this heart-breaking expe-

---

[1] "Letters of the Marquise du Deffand to Horace Walpole." Volume II.

[2] The " Nantes Lodges " were the present made by the King to the Du Barry as a New Year's gift in 1770. The memoirs of the time estimate the income at 40,000 livres a year. In the inventory of the papers of the Comtesse du Barry, removed from Luciennes to the Archives of the Seine-et-Oise on the occasion of the sequestration of 1793, delivered up to the Gomard heirs in 1825 and since lost, we find :—" *New File of Papers.*—Documents relating to the letting of booths, shops, sheds, erected on the counterscarp at Nantes, granted

rience of an influence utterly of no account at Court, the offensive indifference of the Du Barry to her person and to her health, the unfortunate old woman was destined to descend to such abasement as to write to the Favourite on the overthrow of Choiseul: " Madame, I present my compliments to you on your triumph, which is as brilliant as your conquest "—a letter which drew from the indignant pen of the Duchesse de Choiseul this terrible paragraph intended for the benefit of the lady paying the compliment : " Never imagine, I implore of you, my dear child, no matter under what pretext, whatever turn you may take, for whatever purpose in the world it may be, that you could render us the least service through the Marechale. There are no evils that I should not prefer to the opprobrium of being indebted to anyone whom I despise."[1]

But the " Fairy Urgele," as the old Marechale was called, was not sufficient; an entire train was needed to accompany the mistress. It was easy to get the Duchesse de Valentinois, who was already a little mad, already more or less in a dying condition, but who had still some good days here and there ; and a conquest was made of Soubise's mistress, the Marquise de l'Hopital, whose reputation, torn by all the

[1] " Complete Correspondence of Madame du Deffand." By M. de Sainte-Aulaire. Levy, 1866. Volume I.

to Madame du Barry as only a usufruct during her life, by the King's warrant dated December 23, 1769. Account of the Sieur Dardel, manager, and of the Sieur Couilland de la Pironniere, receiver of the produce of the said shops, etc. Documents and plans relating to them. Leases of the said property drawn up in 1771."

silly babblers of the time, had nothing that could be lost. Finally, the Princesse de Montmorency was won by working on her husband's desire to become the manager of the Dauphin.[1]

Madame du Barry, at bottom, filled her role very decently, and it was impossible even for her enemies not to render justice to the propriety of her demeanour. Raised from such a low to such a high position, flung suddenly towards such a height of greatness and into the dazzling splendour of a world to which she had been an entire stranger, she escaped dizziness, vertigo. She preserved, in this perfectly superb adventure, coolness and an unruffled ease of manner. She had, in everything and in the spectacle which she furnished, an equilibrium which might not have been expected from a life like hers, and which astonished her enemies. Foreigners passing through Versailles praised her manners, in which there was no boldness, arrogance, or affectation.[2] Modesty was her style and her habitual practice. She avoided opportunities of exhibiting herself, outlets for the display of vanity. She dealt skilfully with the jealousies of women, and she cleverly made it a matter of prudence to be beautiful. At Court she did not lay great store on her position, disposing of her favour in such a way as to annoy nobody; and the madcap who was so extravagant in the years that were to follow was satisfied at

[1] "Letters of the Marquise du Deffand to Horace Walpole," Volume I.

[2] "Letters of Horace Walpole." Didier, 1872.

this period with an interest which the King had given her in the office of the Fermier-General Virly, and in the money with which a very generous lender assisted her,—her able brother-in-law, the Comte Jean. The Roue knew how to be the King's banker by lending to his mistress.[1]

Gradually, around this favourite so easy-going, so pardonable, better fixed, better established each day, more stable, the quarantine became less severe. Individualities extricated themselves from the bonds of an order, a faction, a coterie. The conspiracy of coldnesses was dissipated; the fine airs became less dry; human respect, the fear of the public and of neighbours became less great. People began in corners of Versailles to gather in groups of two or three in order to have the courage of a little levity; and the end of it was that scarcely anyone was scandalized at hearing at Bellevue Madame Flavacour declaring herself ready to join in a game with Madame du Barry, or the Duc de Richelieu saying in a loud tone, while taking his place beside her, that " he was entirely Madame du Barry's." And the Marechal, having presently got up a little game of lansquenet in order to teach it to the mistress, gallantly lost 250 louis, and, when the King laughed at him and asked him why it was that he had lost so much money at such a quiet game, the Marechal answered him with this snatch from an opera:

[1] "Unpublished Correspondence of the Comte du Barry." *Revue de Paris*, November, 1836. The Roue says in his letter addressed to M. de Malesherbes: "In order to sustain her new position during the first fifteen months, in which she received no pecuniary favour, I drained my pocketbook and pledged the rest of my resources."

Madame Du Barry

"The best of us all
Into debt may fall
Without knowing the reason why."[1]

The King burst out laughing, and with the King every other person in the salon of Belleville.[2]

This supper at Bellevue in the month of June was much commented on by the politicians of the Court. It became, according to the expression of a manuscript sheet of the day, the thermometer which was to advise the courtiers as to "the degree of heat or cold" they were to import into their respective assiduities with one or the other hostile party. The amiably amorous words of the King were repeated, as well as his open acknowledgment of the happiness he felt at possessing her for the first time in this beautiful site. Madame du Barry was exhibited, placed by the King at a

[1] "Le plus sage
S'enflamme et s'engage
Sans savoir comment."

[2] "Letters of the Marquise du Deffand to Horace Walpole." Treuttel, 1812, Vol. I. The King set out from Marly on June 21, 1769, in order to go and sleep at Bellevue, and to repair to the Chateau of Saint Hubert. The King came to Saint Hubert to observe, in company with Madame du Barry, the passage of the planet Venus across the sun, and the explanations of the royal lover to his ignorant mistress and his caressing efforts to make her see the star through a telescope, gave occasion to some verses of a courtier:

"What shall we be told by this telescope,
This Venus and this sun?"
("Que nous diront ce telescope,
Cette Venus et ce soleil?")

table between him and the Comte de la Marche, on account
of the friendship of this Prince for the lady, as Louis XV.
put it, and he allowed the other guests to seat themselves
at table just as they liked. The remark was made that the
Comtesse's nephew, young Du Barry, who had quite recently come from the King's apartment, had been admitted
to the conspicuous honour of this supper. To these shining
marks of favour shown towards the Du Barry faction were
pointed out by way of contrast some symptoms of Choiseul's
failing influence. He was represented as arriving at the
head of a group which, in the course of the guests' walk
around the park while waiting for supper, almost dissolved
in order to join the hostile group of the Marechale de Mirepoix and of Madame de Flavacourt, so that in the end the
minister walked all alone. Allusions were made to the concentration of mind displayed by the minister at the supper,
which was very gay, and to the lines of care on his forehead while the King was playing whist.[1]

As against the influence acquired by the mistress, the
Duc de Choiseul had recourse to the manœuvre which
Fleury had made use of with such success when he wanted
to bring force to bear on the will of Louis XV.: he left the
Court and went to Chanteloup. But, on his return, if he
found his credit again complete and the good graces of the
King at the same point, he also found Madame du Barry's
favour remarkably advanced with the King, who made her

---

[1] "Anecdotes about the Comtesse du Barri." London, 1775.

LOUIS XV

To face page 66

Madame Du Barry

a gift of Luciennes,[1] and the circle of her acquaintances strangely extended. The Favourite had made so many recruits and in every grade at Court, she was already so well propped up by those around her that she had been able to show her gratitude to Madame de Bearn.[2] The emulation

[1] This chateau had been given up to the King by the Duc de Penthievre, who, having had the misfortune to see his son, the Prince de Lamballe, die, had taken a disgust to it. Here is the deed of donation:

"*Warrant of Gift of the Mansion of Louvetiennes in Favour of the Comtesse du Barry.*

"To-day, July 24th, one thousand seven hundred and sixty-nine, the King, being at Compiegne, and wishing to give to the Comtesse du Barry a mark of the benevolence with which His Majesty honors her, has granted to her and made her the gift of the mansion of Louvetiennes, its gardens and appurtenances, of which the enjoyment had been already granted by His Majesty to the Comtesse de Toulouse, and after her to the Duc de Penthievre, who has resigned them so as to enable them to be enjoyed by the said Comtesse du Barry during her life in so far as the said mansion and appurtenances extend and allow, comformably to the plan laid down in the His Majesty's General Direction of Buildings, which commands and orders M. de Marigny, Lieutenant-General of the Province of Orleans to put his hand to the execution of the present warrant and have it countersigned by me, Under-Secretary of State, and by his commands. Signed LOUIS, and lower down, signed PHELYPEAUX (National Archives, Register of Warrants).

"It will be noticed that the donation is for life only, thus differing from the donation made to Madame de Pompadour in the Champs Elysees, which is made to her in such a way that she can dispose of it as her own property without restriction."

[2] The "Anecdotes" speak of a sum of 100,000 livres paid to the Comtesse de Bearn for the presentation of Madame du Barry. Is the statement made in the "Anecdotes" exact? However that may be, the Comtesse de Bearn seems to have continued to find herself in a rather wretched condition so far as her resources were con-

in meannesses began to find an outlet, and a story was told
about the note of the humorous hunchback, the Duc de
Tresmes, to the Favourite: "*The Comtesse du Barry's
marmoset has come to return her visit.*" So then there was
no longer lacking to Madame du Barry anything that a Favourite can command at Court: she had friends, courtiers,
valets, and buffoons. She had not long to wait for men of
letters. Since the beginning of 1769, one of them had the
courage to send her his book with this dedication:

"Madame:—Nature has lavished on you her rarest
gifts; the happiest destiny seems to preside over your career,
and the affability, the beneficence, luckiness of character
still much more essential, will, without doubt, gain applause
with profitable competition. You will surrender yourself,
Madame, to everything most favourable which those esti-
mable qualities inspire in you. You will honour the sciences,
the arts, and all that appears to you worthy of marked distinction, and you will thereby show that discernment and
that real merit always independent of circumstances, and

---

cerned. In a letter sent on the 4th of July, 1771, it is said of the
King's house: "You ought to be persuaded, Madame, with all the
desire I have to be able to render you a service, and although the
circumstances may not be quite favourable for obtaining pecuniary
favours, that I shall not fail to speak to the King as well as to the
Comtesse du Barry about the situation in which you find yourself and
the need you have that H. M. should come to your succour." In
another letter sent on July 25th, 1772, advice is given to her to have a
request made by an advocate to the Council containing the reasons
which put her in the condition to ask for the favour which she so-
licits. (National Archives, "Letters Missive O' 413, 414.)

much superior to those frivolous surfaces under which false grandeur too often thinks it can hide its pettiness from our gaze.   I am with respect,

" Madame,

"Your very humble and very obedient servant,

" The Chevalier de la Morliere." [1]

[1] The book had for its title: "Fatalism, or Collection of Anecdotes to prove the influence of Fate on the History of the Human Heart." By the Chevalier de la Morliere, 1769. The dedication procured for the Chevalier the sale of his volume, and an invitation to supper from the Favourite, who gave him "a distinguished reception."

Other men of letters imitated the Chevalier de la Morliere, and amongst the volumes which the library of Versailles possesses, while some books bear the arms and the device of the Du Barry, four works have in their first page a dedication to the Favourite.

The first bears the title of "Royalism, or Memoirs of Du Barry of Saint-Aunet and of Constance de Cezelli, his Wife, Heroic Anecdotes under Henry IV." By M. de Limairac. The author, in his dedicatory epistle, announces to the Favourite that the traits of heroism which he develops are taken from her family.

The second work, of which the words are by Douin, Captain of Infantry, while the flowers are designed and engraved by Chevalier, Lieutenant of Infantry, and the text is printed by Drouet, an ex-soldier of Infantry, is a small almanac published by Blaisot in Versailles, containing 50 plates and 48 mottoes, and as many horoscopes for every state and age. This "Almanach of Flora" for 1774 has at its head printed in red, with a portrait of Madame du Barry, a sunflower looking towards the sun.

"The star is constant,
And faithful the flower."

The third work is entitled "Moral Tales and New Idyls of D—," and Solomon Gesner, Meister, Translator of the Idyls, addresses the mistress of Louis XV. in these poetic terms:

Madame Du Barry

While the social circle of the Favourite began to be formed, her faction made an important recruit; it definitely got hold of the man who had in 1768 been created by Choiseul Chancellor of France under the promise of ruining D'Aiguillon in his suit brought up that year before the parliament of Paris. A strange figure of the time was this Maupeou. A greenish countenance, like a mottled face, as the Duc de Brissac expressed it, a countenance whose extravasated gall he sought to hide under a layer of white and

---

> " May Beauty, Art and Genius win the praise
>   Of all who owe allegiance to their sway:
>   May my poor Eclogue, simple, harmless, gay,
>   Arrest for one brief moment your sweet gaze!
>   Like you, its beauty needs no gaudy dress—
>   To Nature's hand it owes its loveliness;
>   Like you, a subtle charm around it clings,
>   So that, when robed as a poor shepherdess,
>   It wins the hearts of heroes and of kings."

(This is nearly a literal rendering into English verse of the French original.—TRANSLATOR.)

Finally, the last work is a poetic collection containing two comic operas, "Love's New Year's Gifts" and "The Newly-Married Man," of which the author, Cailhava, has written on the first page these verses:—

> "Borne in a vision high into the air,
>   Methought I saw the Cytherea fair,
>   The tender Hebe to whom lovers pray,
>   Since she loves all things beautiful and gay;
>   Her bright eyes scanned my book, and by her smile
>   I guessed its pages did her soul beguile."

(This version, too, is as nearly literal as possible for an English version of French verses.—TRANSLATOR.

red,[1] eyes which seemed at the same time mistrustful of snares and seeking for prey,[2] while they were veiled by a look of kindness, a physiognomy slily villainous, disguised under the sprightly mask of the comic actor. With this, the tongue which loves gilded phrases, which is insinuating, caressing, and fond of addressing others familiarly on the slightest occasion, and which bores all who possess the least influence with its politeness and exaggerated deference. While he never read a book on legislation, philosophy, or politics, Maupeou read men through and through, penetrating into their hidden recesses, and into the secret basenesses of their mercenary souls. He had put aside the magisterial get-up, that robe under which France was accustomed to see its Chancellor, and he could be seen playing the *agreeable* at clubs, theatres, pleasure-resorts, suppers, and balls. Surrounded with the delicate luxury of a courtesan, the magistrate lived in a mansion, which was a boudoir, sober by temperament, chaste through the feebleness that accompanies a valetudinarian complexion. Under those appearances and those lies of frivolity, Maupeou concealed the windings of an enormous ambition combined with the perpetration of slow and premeditated vengeances. With such a man gratitude necessarily has little weight; he was one of those who belong always to the

[1] " The English Spy, or Correspondence between my lord All-Eye and my lord All-Ear." John Adamson, 1774, Tome I.

[2] Extract from the " Memoirs of Horace Walpole." Year 1771. " Letters of Horace Walpole." By the Comte Baillon. Didier, 1872.

strongest, or rather the strongest belonged only to him. And at that moment, when the struggle between the two parties had been seriously entered upon—it was D'Aiguillon's papers which made the assertion[1]—he was dreaming of *hitting two at once,*—he dreamed of destroying at the same time Choiseul and D'Aiguillon, according only a brief respite to the last. Besides, his political views—let us say it by way of justification on his behalf—made ingratitude a duty with him. A creature of Choiseul, he kept buried in his breast sentiments and a political plan entirely opposed to Choiseul. He secretly cherished a profound hatred against the Parliament, from which he had received marks of insulting distrust,—which wished to *mercurialize him.* A partisan of authority like D'Aiguillon, but with other forms of development, other methods of action, new methods, he had the ambition to bring about a revolution against the Parliament which, by putting into the hands of Royalty a complete authority and an initiative without control, would have permitted the King to give satisfaction to the rights and to the interests which the Revolution of 1789 was destined to arm against Royalty.[2]

Since the presentation of Madame du Barry, the Chancellor had laid claim to a relationship of which till now he had kept the secret. He no longer called her anything but " my

[1] " Memoirs of the Ministry of the Duc d'Aiguillon." Buisson, 1792.

[2] " Maupeou's Memoirs," yet unpublished, indicate the tendency till then unknown of his plans and ideas.

cousin." [1] By his assiduities, by his indefatigable complaisances, by an abasement of character which nothing offended, by all those courtier's buffooneries which drag the Chancellor's robe into the farcicality of a masquerade, Pantalon-Maupeou imparted to the Favourite, bored with the seriousness of the Court, the habit and the need of his person as an amusing butt. And it so happened that the man who had promised Choiseul the ruin of D'Aiguillon promised Madame du Barry the overthrow of Choiseul, binding himself to obtain from the King the destruction of that great force of M. de Choiseul—the Parliaments.

[1] "Private Life of Louis XV." London: Peter Lyton, 1785. Vol. IV.

V.

The Review in the Royal-Lieu at Compiegne.—The Honours of Chantilly paid by the Prince of Conde to the Comtesse du Barry.—The Two Portraits by Drouais in the Salon of 1769.—Choiseul's Act of Submission.—Louis XV.'s Letter with reference to his Mistress.—Chignons *à la Du Barry*.—Flung from a Stag to the King's Pavilion.—Bouret's Design.

ON the 10th of July, the King quitted Versailles to go to the camp at Compiegne. Madame du Barry accompanied him on the journey. Putting aside this time the modesty of her external equipage, of her *incognito,* the Favourite travelled in three carriages with horses, with relays ordered at the different stages as if for the King. In the arrangements made for the journey, Louis XV., in order to avoid bickerings and manifestations of contempt towards his mistress, had erased from the list of women drawn up in the preceding year the Duchesse de Gramont, the Comtesse de Brionne, the Comtesse d'Egmont, the three ladies of the Court who had pretensions to beauty and the most incensed at the Du Barry's triumph.[1] On the 22nd of July, the King

[1] The exclusion gave occasion to a blackguard caricature referred to in the "Secret Memoirs" and with the title of "The Battle of the Anagrams." It represented the three beauties of the court in the character of the Three Graces, flying in tears before a beauty of the street, with a shameless countenance and lascivious attitudes which were indicated by the anagram of the word "grace." Let us

74

brought Madame du Barry to witness the spectacle of the review of the Swiss regiments of Boccard, Lochman, Sonneberg and of the German infantry of Royal Bavaria, Deux-Ponts, Nassau, the Esterhazy hussars, a detachment of the corps of Royal Artillery escorted by forty cannons, &c.[1] The Du Barry in her brilliant phaeton[2] was the queen of the camp. She treated magnificently the officers of the regiment of Beauce, in which her brother-in-law, Elie du Barry was serving, and the Colonel, M. de la Tour du Pin, after the King had passed, had the same honors paid to the carriage of Madame du Barry as are rendered to the carriage of the Royal Family. Choiseul, raging at those high marks of distinction accorded to the mistress, reprimanded M. de la Tour du Pin, and forbade him to waste military honours in this way in the future. What happened? Louis XV. wrote rather sharply to his Minister of War :—

" It is said that you have scolded the Chevalier de la Tour du Pin about Madame du Barry, because she dined in the

---

[1] The National Library possesses a little volume printed without place or date, entitled : " Condition of the Troops which are to pass in review before the King at Compiegne in the year 1769, and which will form the camp in the plain of Verberie, which camp will begin to be formed on the 1st July and will be complete on the 15th of the said month."

[2] " The Life and the Memoirs of General Dumouriez." By Berville and Barriere, Baudouin Brothers, 1822. Vol. I.

---

here mention the rarity, at the present time, of caricatures of the reign of Louis XV., and let us complain of not finding a single one of the caricatures relating to Madame du Barry in the Cabinet of Engravings or in any other collection.

camp, and because the greatest number of officers dined at her house on the day of the review.

"You have promised me that I should no more hear her talked about by you."[1]

The journey to Compiegne had been preceded by a sojourn of Louis XV. at Chantilly; but the presence of Mesdames had not allowed apartments to be given to Madame du Barry, who had done nothing, it was said, but come there secretly to sleep one night. On the return from Compiegne towards the end of August, the Comtesse was officially invited to accompany the King to Chantilly. And of this princely dwelling, of which a Conde had paid the honours to Louis XIV. and his court, another Conde now paid the honours to little Lange, driving her out in a calash at hunts, showing her to the place of honour at public suppers, and seeming finally to dedicate to her the flowers, the fireworks, the flourishes of his entertainments.

The presentation at the Court was, for a mistress, like emerging out of utter obscurity and being crowned with an existence of glory at Versailles; the exhibition of paintings at the Salon of the Louvre was the presentation of the mistress to Paris. All of a sudden came celebrity for her beauty, her grace, for that face until now unknown, to-day

---

[1] Letters of Louis XV. to the Duc de Choiseul, communicated by his nephew, the Duc de Choiseul. *Revue de Paris*, 1829, Tome IV. It is an autograph letter. In answer to this letter the Duke wrote to the King giving a long explanation, in which he said he had only given notice to M. de la Tour du Pin that honors ought not to be paid to her when the King was in the camp.

brought into the light, and of which the charming and brilliant engraving of the period was about to make a popular
portrait, a portrait which all Europe bought. The friends
of Madame du Barry selected, then, to paint her this year,
when the exhibition took place, the artist who painted the
portraits of beautiful and pretty women of great reputation,
the painter of Madame de Pompadour's last portrait—
Drouais. And this artist, captivated by the double character of frankness and archness which constituted the origi-
nality of Madame du Barry's beauty, had conceived the
idea of representing the favourite in two portraits in which
she would be seen in one case under the veil of woman, in
another under the disguise of a man.[1]

---

[1] Diderot rather severely criticizes these two portraits, which, it
must be confessed, like all the portraits by Drouais, are rather me-
diocre pictures. Here is the appreciation of the critic: "If I am to
make any remark to you on these two *portraits*, it is that the original
was, for the time being, the talk of Paris. It was said, and by people
in good society, that they did not resemble each other, and that
Madame du Barry was better. The artist added that there were the
materials for producing a portrait more agreeable, that in her *portrait as a man* there was a constraint which it was painful to see, no
harmony, a head which did not belong to the body, and under this
disguise of costume a body thin, limp, shrunk. The artist did not
doubt that these *two portraits* would be the most stared at of all the
portraits in the Salon. He, therefore, put into them all his skill, and,
if they are bad, this proves that it is not always in an artist's power
to succeed. The efforts which he makes, then, the task which he
imposes beforehand on himself, are very capable of puzzling his brain
and of making his brush unreliable; this is certainly what happened
to Drouais, and what would have happened to a greater master than
he was."

Madame Du Barry

In the first portrait[1] attired in a robe with a white tunic all puffed out, over which ran a garland of roses round the shoulders, the Du Barry appeared, with a string of pearls on her neck, fresh and laughing with the innocence of a young Flora, in a mythological costume, which she wore habitually in her little suite of apartments and arrayed in which the courtesan knew how to please the King. In the second portrait, she is in a riding habit.[2] The co-

[1] Here is the list of portraits of Madame du Barry engraved as Flora:

The COMTESSE DU BARRY. *Painted by Drouais, engraved by Gaucher.*

The place of this small portrait is at *the artist's*, with the privilege of the King, and dated 1/70; the second place is at Bigny's, the King's Lancer, Riding Court of the Tuileries.

An engraved portrait, larger than that of Gaucher, shows her to us in the costume of Flora in a frame of flowers, to which is attached a quiver, a bow, and a lighted torch. On the tablet can be read:

"MADAME LA COMTESSE DU BARRY."

Finally, a copy from these different portraits has been made in aquatint in England on a larger scale, and has been published with the inscription underneath:

"THE COMTESS OF BARRE."

[2] Here is the list of portraits engraved of Madame du Barry in her riding-habit:

THE COMTESSE DU BARRY. Painted by Drouais, engraved by Bauvarlet. The proofs before the letters are worth from 200 to 300 francs.

Another: THE COMTESSE DU BARRY. Marilly del. Lebeau sculp. Frame ornamented at the base with doves pecking at each other, and the verses:

"The Graces and Love her with worship surround;
By the Arts in their turn she is graciously crowned!"
(Les Graces et l'Amour sans cesse l'environnent
Et les Arts avec eux tour a tour eux couronnent.)

Madame Du Barry

quettish print by Beauvarlet, which may be described as the official portrait of the Favourite, shows us the waist caught in a vest with military facings, while around her bare neck and between her breasts plays, like a man's frill gaping

---

Another: THE COMTESSE DU BARRY. Paris: Duchaine, Rue Saint-Jacques and Bligny, Riding school at the Tuileries. There is a list before No. 213.

Another: Legrand, sculp., and at the end of the verse:

"To please is not her only care in life."

(Plaire n'est pas l'unique soin pour elle.)

Four other detestable portraits, the first fabricated for a book bearing above the words: Tome IV., page 159; the second, *Printed and sold by* Henri van Dussen, London, 1775; the third, J. G. Jaenniske, sculp.; the fourth, E. Bonneville, sculp., and below, *M. Jne. Gomart de Vaubernier.*

There is still a sheet in which the portrait of the Du Barry figures in the midst of portraits of Charlotte Corday, of Bailly, of Barnave, of Luckner.

Finally a couple of aquatints of the portrait of Beauvarlet have been made in England. The words inscribed on it are: "Drouais pinxit; J. Watson fecit Madame de Barre. Engraved from a drawing after the original picture painted by Drouais in possession of Louis XV., published 25th Th., 1771."

Lastly, Bonnet has made of this portrait two reproductions in colour:

The first, a pendant of the little portrait of Marie Antoinette, but without any of her qualities, has in the frame beribboned and surrounded with flowers the following inscription: "MADAME LA COMTESSE DU BARRY." England, by Bonnet, 1769. The second reproduction, drawn in red or in blue, and sometimes made to imitate a pastel, is the head of Madame du Barry, represented at her natural size in her riding-habit. The inscription is: "Drouais pinx. Bonnet, sculp. MADAME LA COMTESSE DU BARRY, Paris, Bonnet, Rue Galande, between a candle-stick-maker and a packing-case-maker."

Let us complete the list of portraits engraved at the time by the portraits which represent other paintings besides the two portraits of Drouais.

slightly open, a large piece of English lace. She has a smooth head-dress, and two or three patches stuck here and there set off the rebellious expression of that charming, saucy little face.[1] Therefore, what a crowd, what a crush there

[1] Independently of the two portraits of the Salon of 1769 (sold at the Devere Sale, March 17, 1855) Madame du Barry has been the theme for portraiture many times by the painters of her time. Drouais, the favourite painter of the Comtesse, has again on exhibition in the Salon for 1771 a picture of her as one of the Muses veiled in transparent drapery, which accentuates the nudity of her entire form and allows the legs to be seen as far as the knees. A critic has said of this portrait: "Drouais has once more failed to give a true portrait of the Comtesse du Barry, when he to-day presents her to us with the attributes of a tarnished and almost faded Flora." Whether it was owing to this criticism, or that there were quite enough of nasty jokes as to the nudity of her charms, or whether it was due to the clamour of the devotees, the portrait was withdrawn almost as soon as it was exhibited.

The same year the "Secret Memoirs" announced that Greuze was

There is, first of all, a coarse portrait engraved by some anonymous person of Madame du Barry as a Bacchante.

Another portrait in which Madame du Barry is represented in Court dress and with a large headdress of feathers, bears at the foot of it these words: "Jeanne Gomard de Vaubernier, Comtesse du Barry. Decapitated in Paris on the 18th Brumaire, the year 11 (9th of December, 1793), at the age of 42. Bonivet, sculp. a la pointe. This is the portrait which Favrolle put at the head of his "Historic Memoirs."

Finally, a last portrait of Madame du Barry, the rarest of all her portraits, without doubt done in London in one of her journeys in search of her diamonds, the watch with a handkerchief tied with a loose knot, a short tippet with big folds, a white robe, the waist of which is under the breast, in fact, a toilet which already heralds the fashion of the Directoire. Underneath, "R. Cosway, pinxit. J. Conde, sculp. M. la Comtesse du Barry, London. Published by J. Conde, February, 1794, and sold by I. Tompkins, No. 49 New Bond Street."

was around these two canvases! It was even so big a crowd that, one day, Walpole, who had come to the exhibition to see the two portraits, had to abandon the attempt.[1]

On the day when Madame du Barry, accompanied by a train of painters and sculptors, repaired to the Salon, every one was ordered to go out,[2] according to the orders of M.

[1] Letter of the 30th of August, 1769. "Horace Walpole's Letters." Didier, 1872.
[2] "Letters of Madame du Deffand to Walpole." Treuttel, 1872, Tome I.

striving for a portrait of the favourite. It is the portrait figuring under No. 46 amongst the objects chosen by the Committee of Arts at Luciennes after the execution of the Comtesse; a portrait also catalogued: "An Unfinished Picture representing the Dubarry as a Bacchante."

Madame Lebrun relates in her "Memoirs" that she made three portraits of Madame du Barry. The first, painted in 1786, represented the mistress of Luciennes in a three-quarters' bust, in a white dressing gown, with a straw hat surmounted by a feather. A second portrait, painted, like the first for the Duc de Brissac, showed the Comtesse du Barry dressed in white satin, and holding a crown in one hand. Subsequently, Madame Lebrun found at a sale the face all daubed with rouge. A third portrait, commenced by Madame Lebrun in 1789, and which she had left with only the arms and waist outlined, and found again by the *emigre* at the house of the Comte Louis of Narbonne, on his return to France, was resumed and finished.

In a love letter of Rohan-Rochefort, there is a reference to a portrait begun under the Revolution by Letellier.

Finally, the Museum of Versailles preserves under the number 4537, a portrait of Madame du Barry by an unknown painter (is it a copy of Drouais?) in which she is represented in a dressing-gown, with her hair uncombed, leaning on a dressing-table, and stirring a cup of coffee with a little spoon, with Zamor in front of her carrying a tray.

And let us not forget also that she has been painted, in one of her latest trips to England, by Cosway.

Madame Du Barry

de Saint-Florentin, who prescribed for the new Favourite's reception the same ceremonial as in the case of Madame de Pompadour.

In view of all the conspicuous testimonies of favour shown this year to Madame du Barry by the King. who was becoming more infatuated about her from day to day, in view of the increasing influence she employed from association with Richelieu, D'Aiguillon, Maupeou, Maillebois, and Broglie, feeling the secret disloyalty to himself of men of high rank whom he thought to be on his side and of illustrious ladies who were only longing for the moment to imitate the example of the Duchesse de Mirepoix, perceiving in short in the atmosphere of the Court the symptoms of the serious and lasting domination of a woman establishing her position by the love which she had won, Choiseul thought it expedient to give way. The minister came to declare to the King his respect for the wishes of his master and for the desires of the woman who enjoyed his favour.

The graceful face of Madame du Barry was almost as frequently made the subject of treatment by sculptors as by painters. Pajou did a bust of her, that bust which had such a great success at the Salon of 1771, that official bust reproduced in plaster. And this bust he redeemed and modified in the attitude, the adjustment, and the arrangement of the hair, even five times, as we may see in his memorandum given in the Appendix. Caffieri in 1770 made that delightful bust entirely in plaster which is in the Library at Versailles, a piece of sculpture much superior to that of Pajou, who makes the mistress a Bourbonian and unintelligent, while Caffieri has reproduced the archness, the complaisances, the effrontery of that face so nymph-like, even to the saucy outlines of the quivering nostrils.

Madame Du Barry

He begged of the King not to hold him responsible for the tone of hauteur adopted by his sister and his wife towards Madame du Barry, as he had done everything in his power to bring them to exhibit a very different attitude. But Richelieu, the *friend to suspend and to depend on,* said to Du Barry that she should be distrustful, as the Duc de Choiseul was only keeping up a brave heart against ill-fortune. And Madame Du Barry, who, in the beginning of her favour, had told the Duc that, if he wanted to make advances to her, she would meet him half-way, found that he was too slow in making these advances.

This act of submission on the part of M. de Choiseul had not restored him to Louis XV.'s good graces. He found himself very rarely summoned or invited to the cabinet suppers. The favourite, when he was her partner at whist, did not spare him the grimaces, the mockeries, the shrugs, all the little revenges of the *pensionnaire,* which if they did not lower his credit in his own department, "caused a fall in his estimation amongst fools." At this time, the minister, who, a year before, had been all-powerful, asked, for the Vicomte de Choiseul, the post of captain-lieutenant of Light-Horse: Madame du Barry prevented him from getting the appointment.

Thus menaced, M. de Choiseul remained still confident in the extent of his plans. He was reassured by the difficulties of the political crisis with which Europe was threatened, by the support of the magistrates, the men of letters, and all the persons who were scandalized by the King's new love-affair either on moral or social grounds. Besides, the King stuck to his minister. He lived in the belief that M. de Choiseul was the only man capable of carrying on public affairs, the only one who possessed the art of keeping the enemies of France divided and deprived of the opportunity of disturbing her. He regarded him as the man who was necessary, indispensable, the keystone of European peace. He dreaded a new figure on the scene, the bustle of a change, the interference for even a moment with the customary programme of the monarchy. Did he not see, at the first rumour of Choiseul's disgrace, the Lieutenant of Police coming to announce to him the lowering of the Royal credits, the Prince of Starhemberg asking for explanations on the part of the Prince de Kaunitz in the name of Austria, and all the ministers of the Bourbons in Europe, attached to M. de Choiseul by the " Pacte de Famille "[1] following Prince Starhemberg? In order to get rid of his embarrassment, Louis XV. broke through his ordinary habits, and, without seeking to effect a reconciliation between his minister and his mistress, as he had already tried to do in the case of the Bellevue supper, he entered into an explanation with M. de Choiseul, revealed to him how matters really stood, and defended Madame du Barry against his hostility and his suspicions.

The King wrote to his minister this letter, the authenticity of which is incontestable :—

[1] Students of French history may remember the importance of the " Pacte de Famille " in pre-Revolution days. — TRANSLATOR.

Madame Du Barry

" I begin with M. d'Aiguillon. How can you believe that he is able to replace you? I like him well enough, it is true, on account of the trick I played on him a long time ago.[1] Hated as he is, what good could he do?

" You carry on my affairs well; I am perfectly satisfied with you; but take care of followers and persons offering you advice. You know Madame du Barry; it certainly was not M. de Richelieu who made me acquainted with her,[2] though he may know her, and does not venture to see her, and the only time he has seen her for a moment was by my express orders. I thought of making her acquaintance before her marriage. She is pretty; I am satisfied with her, and I am every day enjoining her to be careful about those who gather about her and offer her advice; for you may well imagine she has no lack of them. She has no hatred of you. She knows your talent, and has no ill-will against you. The exasperation against her has been frightful, and wrongly so, for the most part. They would be at her feet if—so goes the world.

"She is very pretty; she pleases me; this ought to be enough. Do people want me to take a girl of rank? If the Archduchess were a lady such as I might desire, I would

[1] The King is here alluding to the Duchesse de Chateauroux, carried off by him from the Duc d'Aiguillon.

[2] Sara Goudar, in her " Remarks on the Anecdotes of Madame la Comtesse Dubarri," says she had it on good authority "that the King had by accident cast a glance at her in a crowd, and had then lost sight of her; but this first glance having made an impression on him, he imposed on Lebel the task of finding her again.

take her as a wife with great pleasure; but I would like to see her and know her beforehand. Her brother has been looking out for one, and he has not succeeded. I believe that I would be better able to judge than he is, for it is necessary to bring things to an end; and the fair sex otherwise would always be giving me trouble; for most certainly you will not see a Madame de Maintenon in my case. Here is, I think, enough about it for this time."[1]

An interview, a three hours' *conversation* between M. de Choiseul and Madame du Barry during the sojourn of the Court at Fontainebleau, was the result of this letter, but each of them brought to the conference their respective distrusts, prejudices, and requirements. They remained on a hostile footing with a little more display of hypocritical forms. And M. de Choiseul was angry at the step he had taken, which his friends looked upon as a fault, "since it had not produced any good result."[2]

Madame du Barry was beginning to occupy the attention of Europe. What was told about her past, what was known of her sway over the King's senses, what transpired of her secret triumphs over the Prime Minister, what her engraved portraits said of her beauty and her grace, made the Favourite an enigmatic personage, a historic figure full of unexpectedness and novelty, towards whom the curiosity of

[1] Letter of Louis XV. to the Duc de Choiseul, communicated by his nephew, M. le Duc de Choiseul. *Revue de Paris*, 1829. Tome IV. It is an autograph letter.

[2] "Letters of the Marquise du Deffand to Walpole." Treuttel, 1812. Tome I.

Madame Du Barry

foreigners was attracted. And Walpole, having come across from England, almost immediately after his arrival, hurried to Versailles to have a look at the woman who was loved by the King of France. He saw Madame du Barry in the chapel. Accompanied by her inseparable sister-in-law, the Favourite came and sat down at the foot of the altar in the lower part of the church, without powder, without rouge, *without having made her toilet.*[1] The English lord, who compares himself somewhere in his carriage painted and gilt to the grandfather of the Loves, strongly expresses his astonishment at this small show of state, at this absence of ceremony, on the part of the mistress in the palace of Louis XIV. It was because Madame du Barry brought to the Court the indolent and soft habits of body of her former life, a gay woman's taste for free and easy ways, a repugnance towards the exigencies and the sacrifices of official full dress. She thought her hair too beautiful to spoil it with powder, and always refused, Madame Lebrun declares, to put on rouge. She loved to have around her person the sense of being unrestrained by external things, the floating of soft garments, the fluidity of tissues, a toilet which retained a little of that deshabille of the bedroom, of the boudoir. Even at the cabinet suppers, which had hitherto seen women only in full dress, Madame du Barry accustomed Louis XV. to see her come to table in her ordinary costume. And, in this voluptuous fashion, she wore those

[1] Letter of September 17, 1769. "Horace Walpole's Letters to George Montagu." Janet, 1818.

87

loose chignons, invented, designed by her for her former lover, the hairdresser Lamet, those *chignons à la Du Barry*,[1] which, stuck to the head, though not appearing to stick there, resemble a woman's hair ready to fall off with her head thrown back.

The remainder of the autumn, in that nomadic life of the Court, in those continual changes of place, by means of which Louis XV. sought to beguile the solemn ennui of Versailles; in those sojourns at Choisy, at Saint-Hubert, at Fontainebleau, the King had the satisfaction of seeing Madame du Barry with a train of fine ladies who had been conquered and won. Madame du Barry most frequently accompanied her Royal lover in that pretty masculine costume which Drouais' picture has popularised. It was in this dress of a huntress that, during the journey of the Court to Fontainebleau, she posed for the flinging of a stag to the King's Pavilion with Bouret, the great inventor of adulations towards courtesans. He led Madame du Barry towards the Venus sculptured by Coustou for the King of Prussia, a statue for which the gallant Fermier-General, divining the love of the King, had got the Favourite's figure substituted.

---

[1] Madame du Barry could not merely be credited with inventing the chignons which bear her name. The "Anecdotes" also attribute to the taste and the coquetry of Madame du Barry the invention of the "greluchon," a long pin, the top of which was drawn into her chignon, putting it in at the left. The name had made virtuous women disapprove of it, and the *greluchon* ("fancy man") had only been adopted by *fashionable ladies*.

MADAME DU BARRY

To face page 88

VI.

Nomination of the Abbe Terrai to the post of Controller-General.—Choiseul alarms the Favourite with the announcement of the Dauphiness's Arrival.—The Continuation of the Case of D'Aiguillon Accused of Acts which *stained his Honor*.—The Chancellor's "Jobbery."—Madame du Barry becoming D'Aiguillon's Mistress and the Instrument of Choiseul's Dismissal.—Removal from the Records of the Palais de Justice of the Minutes of the D'Aiguillon case.—Coolness of the King towards Choiseul.—Denunciation of the Abbe de la Ville.—The Rising of the Council of September 21, 1770.

THE year 1769 ended badly for M. de Choiseul. On December 21st, at a council held in Versailles and composed of members of the Councils of State, of Finances, of Mails, the Controller-General, Maynon d'Invau, a creature of Choiseul, whose financial plans had been criticized by the Chancellor, laid them down on the desk changed, corrected, modified, declaring that he had nothing better to present. Maupeou addressed the Council, and gave a highly-coloured picture of the distress of France, and demonstrated the insufficiency of the plans presented by the Controller-General. Thereupon, Choiseul defended his protege and his operations. The Chancellor replied with much vehemence, and triumphantly refuted the remarks of the Duc de Choiseul. The King, not hiding his ill-temper, broke up the council, and withdrew into his cabinet, the door of which he shut violently.[1] Then the Chancellor was sent for, and remained for half an hour in conference with the King. There was determined upon the nomination of the Abbe Terrai, whom the Chancellor had beforehand buoyed up with the hope of passing one day from the Controller-General's office to some less dangerous department in the gap which would be made by the approaching retirement of Choiseul. It was one enemy the more and in possession to impede and thwart all the projects of the minister, an enemy whose hostility Choiseul was sure to exasperate, owing to his levity of disposition, by uttering satires and mockeries with regard to his economical ideas. On the evening of the Council, when the Duke foresaw what would be the result next day of the conference between the King and the Chancellor, he displayed a gaiety which made him write to one of the women who supped at his house : " It will be like Charles VII., to whom people said, ' You cannot lose a kingdom more gaily.' "[2]

M. de Choiseul, in spite of his gaiety and his affected carelessness, was beginning to find, as he bluntly expressed it, " that the jade caused him much embarrassment." [3] He could not keep from feeling restless ; he moved about on the high roads, rushing from Versailles to Chanteloup, and

" Memoirs concerning the Administration of Finances under the Ministry of the Abbe Terrai, Controller-General." London: Adamson, 1776.

[2] "Letters of the Marquise de Deffand to Horace Walpole." Treuttel, 1812. Tome I.

[3] "The Life and Memoirs of General Dumouriez." By Berville and Barriere. Baudouin, 1822, Tome I.

Madame Du Barry

from Chanteloup to Metz, giving charge to those around him and perhaps diverting his own thoughts with a kingly train, a table with forty covers. He went even so far as to make some concessions to circumstances. He confined himself within the limits of his three ministerial offices which he held through the Duc de Praslin. He no longer affected supremacy over the ministers of state.[1] The last hope he had left rested on the Dauphiness's arrival, on the influence which she would exercise, according to all anticipations, over the King, on the tone of decency which she would bring back to the Court. Beforehand, he finessed round Madame du Barry, who used to say that at times *the Court stank in her nostrils.* He exercised a secret terror over her, had advice given to her by M. de Noailles to go away, to yield up her place for a moment, to take the waters at Barege.[2] Without Richelieu, Madame du Barry would have gone; but Richelieu opened her eyes, and she stayed, sustained in this resolution by D'Aiguillon. The Archduchess once installed in Versailles, the umbrage with which the Favourite inspired the King, the reports by means of which she prejudiced his mind against the young Dauphiness, soon changed the original sentiments of Louis XV. into coldness, and ruined, with Marie Antoinette's credit, the last chances of the minister.

In the month of March of this year, 1770, Madame du

[1] "History of France during the Eighteenth Century." By Lacre telle Delaunay, 1812, Tome IV.

[2] "Anecdotes about the Comtesse du Barri." London, 1775.

Deffand, thanks to her apartment, which she compares to a theatre with changes of scenery, in which the Mirepoix, the D'Aiguillons, the Chabrillants, the Bedas, succeed to the Beauvaus, the Stainvilles, the Praslins, who met without fighting and without flying on this neutral ground—thanks to everything that was said, avowed, confessed around her— in the unconstraint of conversation, Madame du Deffand predicted that the year would not pass without a great revolution,[1] announced, nine months beforehand, the overthrow of Choiseul and the accesion of D'Aiguillon to power.

The everlasting case of D'Aiguillon went on with animosities on each side carried to an absolute pitch of frenzy. The Duc de Choiseul understood that, in his contest with Madame du Barry, the Duc d'Aiguillon was the soul of the " clique," as the society of Chanteloup called the opposite faction: he wanted to bar against his rival the road to the ministry by an infamous condemnation. D'Aiguillon, as we have pointed out, finding himself at the same time the butt of the hatred of the Chancellor and of Choiseul, was glad to find a prop in the Du Barry. In the memoirs written by Soulavie, on the authority of his papers, the Duc d'Aiguillon declares that he had not taken any step to secure the protection of the Favourite, whom he did not know, and whom he had never seen. Madame du Barry must have taken the initiative in the matter. In her hatred of Choiseul, and with the knowledge she possessed of the opposition

---

[1] " Letters of the Marquise de Deffand to Horace Walpole." Treuttel, 1812, Tome II.

which he exercised over D'Aiguillon, she proposed to him
this alliance. However, the support given in the beginning
by Madame du Barry to the Duc d'Aiguillon had little effect. On the retirement of Marechal d'Estrees, she could
get nothing for him.[1] And for a long time the action of
D'Aiguillon, who had no official access to Versailles, was,
contrary to the assertions of the memoirs of the period, only
a subterranean action exercised through messages, intro-
ductions by private staircases, mysterious interviews, and
even this action was countermined by the tortuous machinations of the Chancellor, who only backed up his new ally
in a half-hearted and very treacherous fashion. It was
he who, in spite of the rage of D'Aiguillon, had got the idea
of the judgment of the former governor of Brittany adopted
by that erratic Court of Peers which sat in the Queen's antechamber. It was he, too, who, at the close of three sittings,
and on the matter taking a favourable turn, had the Peers'
judgment replaced by a Bed of Justice on the 27th of June,
where a declaration was registered annulling all the procedure—a Bed of Justice which did not end the conflict, and
the clearest advantage of which to D'Aiguillon was to be
nominated for the journey to Marly and to be invited to sup
with the King.[2] From all this political perfidy of the Chancellor resulted the famous decree of the 2nd of July, which
dishonoured the Duc d'Aiguillon, declared him " accused
of acts which stained his honour," and suspended him from

[1] " Anecdotes about the Comtesse du Barri." London, 1775.
[2] " Private Life of Louis XV." London: Peter Lyton. Tome IV.

his functions as a peer until judgment had been given in his case.

The brutality of the affair, of the act of the Parliament, opened the eyes of the Favourite, who, very ignorant of political affairs, had perhaps to reproach herself with not having rendered to D'Aiguillon all the services demanded by his position—and that not through lack of good will but solely through a failure to see through all the Chancellor's *jobbery*.[1] To-day, she felt herself personally touched and, as it were, conjointly responsible for this infamous note striking at the man whom she protected. Next, in order to keep herself in the Favourite's mind, he had access to her at all hours; his role of canvasser, concealed and almost secret, had now ceased. Through his post of commander of Light Horse in the King's Guard, which she had got refused to the Comte de Choiseul and had obtained for D'Aiguillon, Choiseul's antagonist had the right to work with the King, to belong to the Council, and finally to be on visiting terms at Versailles. And so well did the politician understand the importance of establishing himself and becoming a personality at Court that for this command of Light Horse, for which there had never before been paid more than from five to six hundred thousand livres, he had decided to give twelve hundred and fifty thousand livres.[2]

[1] "Memoirs of the Ministry of the Duc d'Aiguillon." Buisson, 1792.

[2] "Letters of the Marquise du Deffand to Horace Walpole." Treuttel, 1812. Tome II.

Madame Du Barry

It was then that D'Aiguillon, in conjunction with the Chancellor, took hold of Madame du Barry, gave her a daily lesson, and took care that her hatred of his rival should be permanent. He forced her to use her influence with the King to bring about the exile of the Comtesse de Gramont.[1] He excited, he inflamed this nature without affection, without resentment, without passion, without interest for the people of Versailles, to whom at bottom the new Favourite showed no more of her real nature than a woman shows to actors with whom chance leads her to act in a society theatre. He disturbed her self-satisfaction in the midst of her triumphs. He filled her indolent mind with alarm. He lost sight of nothing that could drag her lazy and indifferent character into the struggle. He represented to her untiringly that there would be no security for her so long as the Duc de Choiseul would remain at his post. He

[1] In the month of July, 1770, at the performances which took place at the theatre of Choisy, whose dimensions were too contracted to contain the Royal Family with all their retinue, it happened that the ladies of the Palace, having taken possession of the front seats, refused to make room for the Comtesse du Barry, the Duchesse de Mirepoix, and the Comtesse de Valentinois. Some sharp words were exchanged, and the most malicious escaped from the lips of the Comtesse de Gramont, lady in waiting to the Queen. The ladies who had been subjected to this affront made a complaint, and the King sent the Comtesse de Gramont into exile fifteen leagues away from the Court. Let us point out once more that it was the Comtesse de Gramont, mother of the Duc de Gramont, and not the Duchesse, sister of the Duc de Choiseul, as we have it printed by mistake. Madame du Deffand said when speaking of the exiled lady: " I only met her two or three times. She appears to me silly, bold and gossiping."

repeated to her that her position made it necessary for her to get the Prime Minister dismissed from office. He drove into her light brain the idea that the best means of ruining him was to confound his cause with the cause of the Parliaments and to describe him to the King as the soul and master of that ambitious body which was always ready for opposition and for encroachment, and which was striving to usurp the privileges of the throne. To show the King that those two steps, simultaneous and working in harmony, the dismissal of Choiseul and the subjection of the Parliaments, would make obstacles disappear, would facilitate the progress of the Government and the recovery of taxes, would remove, in short, all risk of war,—such was the subject in which D'Aiguillon, fostering his ambitions along with his revenges, strove to make Madame du Barry take an interest. He took advantage of her frolicsome disposition to train her for the comedy, and to make her influence the King's mind by taking part in a number of farcical scenes. He put into her hands those oranges, with which she blew up the ministry: "Away with Choiseul! away with Praslin!" The gaiety of the Favourite, the element of the street arab in her disposition, her young and riotous folly, her warbling laughter, her childlike arguments, her bird-like talk, that lisp so pretty in her mouth, all were turned and bent by Choiseul's adversary towards that great object—the overthrow of the Ministry and the destruction of Parliament.[1] In this

---

[1] "Secret Memoirs to Serve for the History of the Republic of Letters." Vols. V. and VI. "Annals of Louis XV." A. Villefranche

role which he made the Favourite play, D'Aiguillon was one day touched by a tender sentiment, which gave the actress persistence, heat, devotion, almost intelligence. As a man of his time, he understood that, in order to make a woman entirely his, he should become her lover. Perhaps, indeed, he mingled with this diplomatic love a little desire for revenge for the nasty trick to which Louis XV. referred in his letter. Nevertheless, whatever alloy of interest, of vengeance, of real passion there was in the court which he paid to Madame du Barry, he knew how to touch this facile heart. And when Madame du Deffand wrote, " The D'Aiguillon is on good terms with the Du Barry," good in the full meaning of the word—the *best possible,* as it was then said—she only gave utterance to a fact of which all Paris was aware. He was now the official " cavaliere servente " of the mistress. During the illumination of the Park at Versailles, when fetes were given at night in celebration of Marie-Antoinette's marriage, Choiseul might be seen giving his arm to the Princess de Beauvau while D'Aiguillon gave his arm —a lover's arm—to Madame du Barry.[1] On the journey to Compiegne, it was the same eagerness, the same attention, the same arm given everywhere. Then, in the midst of amorous words, the lover recalled his case, demonstrated the

[1] " Historic and Political Memoirs of the Reign of Louis XVI." By Soulavie. Treuttel and Wurtz. —— X. Tome I.

at the house of the Widow Liberty. 1782. " Private Life of Louis XV." London, 1785. " History of France during the Eighteenth Century." By Lacretelle Delaunay, 1812. Tome IV.

inanity of the reversal of the decree of the 2nd of July, appealed for an act of good pleasure and royal favour, which he at length succeeded in snatching through his mistress from the vanquished King.

On the 3rd of September, the King arrived at full speed early in the morning at the Palace in his hunting equipage, preceded by Du Vol and the four bodies of huntsmen. There, he fixed himself on the stool of the Duke of Noailles, his captain of the guards, and gave orders to carry off from the record-office the minutes of the D'Aiguillon case, of which the Chancellor accordingly took possession. The Duc de Choiseul had refused to appear at the Palace, and had set out on the previous night for Ferte Vidame.[1] The Minister-King tottered under the blow.

The thanks of the Duc d'Aiguillon to Madame du Barry took the form of a princely present. The Duke gave her a vis-a-vis, in which the entirely new arms of the Favourite and her device, " Boutez en avant," were surrounded with a bed of roses, in which doves were pecking in the midst of pierced hearts, torches, and all the accessories of love, surmounted by a splendid wreath—an equipage much superior in taste and in costliness to the carriages which the Dauphin had gone to seek at Strasburg.[2] Everybody would see in this present, which cost 52,000 livres, the public announcement of a *liaison*, the suspicion of which did not seem to displease M. d'Aiguillon.

[1] " Memoirs of the Ministry of the Duc d'Aigullon." Buisson, 1792.
[2] " Secret Memoirs of the Republic of Letters." Vol. V.

Madame Du Barry

Whilst this hostile influence was being exercised over the King's mind by D'Aiguillon and the Chancellor against Choiseul, against the Parliament, against the other Guise,[1] against that other League, to which a revolutionary spirit was ever being imparted, the Duchesse de Gramont was an exile from the Court and was carrying with her through France her anger and her resentment. Under the pretext of travelling, of taking the waters, she saw on her way the members of the Parliaments had conferences with the leaders, told them that the Parliaments depended for their existence on her brother, bound them to the fortunes of a ministry which would carry in its fall the liberties of Parliamentary power, and thus organized over the Court and over the King himself a sort of pressure on and intimidation of public opinion.[2] The King, kept informed of the proceedings and the violent remarks of his minister's sister, became colder towards Choiseul. He continued working with him and inviting him to his suppers, but without honouring him with a word of civility or confidence. The cabal redoubled its efforts, and instigated Madame du Barry to use all her caresses to wrest from the King the *lettre de cachet* which would bring the struggle to an end. The letter was

[1] According to Soulavie, a note sent to Madame du Barry and placed under the King's eyes, must have had something to do with Louis XV.'s last determination. This note declared that M. de Choiseul had Maria Theresa's promise in writing of a little province in full sovereignty with a guarantee to his descendants, if he succeeded in indemnifying the House of Austria to the prejudice of the Prussian monarchy for the losses it had caused.

[2] "Private Life of Louis XV." Peter Lyton, 1785. Tome IV.

perhaps written one evening in a moment of intoxication, of weakness, and of amorousness; but next morning nothing could persuade the King to send it off.

An incident, at last, precipitated Louis XV.'s resolutions, and compelled him to make up his mind definitely. One of the forces on which Choiseul relied, as we have said, was the impression made by him on the King that he alone preserved peace and was able to maintain it. This was the impression towards which D'Aiguillon and Maupeou directed their attack. They undermined it at first secretly and with words of hidden meaning. They spread the story that the Duc de Choiseul, seeing his credit declining, was anxious to excite war so as to make himself necessary, and they murmured that he alone was able to rouse the Spaniards to attack Falkland Island and to take the garrison prisoners, that he alone had protracted the negotiations about this affair. Louis XV., reading all Choiseul's despatches, was not ignorant of the fact that his Minister considered the army, the navy, and the finances in no condition at this moment to support a war against England; but the persistence of the accusations plunged him into greater doubts each day, and prevented him from taking up Choiseul's defence.[1]

[1] The Duke's spirit, at the same time light and audacious, seemed, it must nevertheless be admitted, at this critical moment, tempted by the chances of a war, a descent on England. Do we not in the month of November, a month before his fall, see the Minister display on the Council-table the celebrated plan of a descent prepared by La Rosiere and Beville by the orders of M. de Broglie, during the years 1764, 1765 and 1766. Did he not send for the Du Barrys exiled by him to attend this Council to declare to the King the possibility of success?

Madame Du Barry

When D'Aiguillon had led Louis XV. to the point of irresolution and uncertainty that he wanted, he made Madame du Barry come forward. Taking the King unawares, the Favourite told him that, since she could not persuade him, it was for the interest of the State and the interest of his own peace to enlighten himself, that nothing was easier, that he had only to send for and question the Abbe de la Ville, M. de Choiseul's clerk, who was entrusted with the task in question. Now the party knew that this Abbe, ex-Secretary to the Embassy,[1] who had been highly

[1] "The Abbe de la Ville," says Besenval, "started in the world by becoming a Jesuit. He then left this order to become a secular priest. Engaged as preceptor to M. de Fenelon's children, he followed him in that capacity in his embassy to Holland where soon his talent and his intrigues easily had the advantage over the limited ability and shallow intellect of M. de Fenélon. The Abbe became a confidential person, and was made Secretary to the Embassy. He remained for a long time in Holland with success in that post, and was only recalled to take the position of Chief Clerk in the office of Foreign Affairs."

And on Terrai's refusal to supply the funds, he obtained a guarantee for the purpose from Foulon. It was at this very Council that Choiseul got for himself an order for three millions to pay his debts. The King signed the order, but forgot to write "good for three millions." Foulon, to whom the Duke showed it on coming back from the King's presence, drew his attention to the matter, which had been forgotten. M. de Choiseul said he would have it set right at the earliest opportunity. And this first opportunity was only indicated by the date of the 22nd of December, the day when the King had decided to dismiss him, so that this cash-order was not paid, and the tail-end of the adventure necessitated the demolition of Choiseul's mansion. ("Memoirs of the Ministry of the Duc d'Aiguillon." Buisson, 1792.)

regarded and treated with the utmost confidence in the office of Foreign Affairs, had ceased to be a clerk owing to M. de Choiseul's habit of writing with his own hand despatches of even the smallest moment. He was sure to give his support to everything that would be done against a minister who despised his counsels, his experience, and his person. On the 21st of December, 1770, the King, in the presence of Madame du Barry, asked the Abbe de la Ville, whom he had secretly ordered to come to his cabinet, where were the negotiations for the maintenance of peace, and what were M. de Choiseul's intentions. The Abbe replied that he could not give an account of the matter to His Majesty, because the despatches of the Duc de Choiseul had not been communicated to him, but that if the King wished to know the main portion of their provisions, he had only to order that minister to have a letter sent to the King of Spain declaring to that Prince that His Majesty absolutely wanted peace, and that no consideration would make him take part in the war if it were declared. " If M. de Choiseul obeys without any rejoinder," said the Abbe de la Ville, " this is a proof that his designs are directed towards peace; if he raises objections, it is because he wants war." The King entered the Council-chamber, and with that slight quivering of the chin which was with him the sign of internal disturbance, he ordered M. de Choiseul to write a letter to the King of Spain. M. de Choiseul, who had just sent a courier into Spain with conciliatory proposals,—and the D'Aiguillon party was not ignorant of the fact,—replied to the King that, before writing, it was necessary to await the answer to the plan for an arrangement, and that it would be time enough to write when that was refused. The King broke up the Council without saying a word.[1]

[1] "Memoirs of Baron de Besenval." Paris: Buisson, Year XIII. Vol. II.

VII.

On Sunday, December 23rd, 1770, Louis XV., after
signing a contract, flung the pen angrily on the table in
place of giving it back to the Secretary of State. This
touch of irritation which the King displayed against the
Duc de Choiseul was noticed. In the evening, the King
said to the Prince of Conde :—" Prince of Condé, will you
be here to-morrow?" "Yes, sire." And the Prince, contrary to his custom, slept at Versailles in order to be ready
for any emergency.

Now the Prince of Condé was not one of those who
waited with the least impatience the fall of Choiseul. He
had made arrangements with the Du Barry which would
place in his hands the direction of political affairs. Here
is what happened :—Cromot, First Clerk of Finances, who

had been informed by Lebel in 1768, during the journey to Compiegne, of the frantic love which the King had conceived for his new mistress, and who had urged Laverdy to tease Choiseul and entangle him in his plans, had been discharged in the month of September of that year. Brought back by the Abbe Terrai,[1] he resumed his post in December, 1769, animated by the desire to avenge himself and openly declaring that he would find a means of ruining the Duke. · Almost immediately, in the month of January, he asked the Duc de Choiseul, through the Abbe Terray[1] the way in which sixty-four millions given for war purposes had been applied. The Duke, accustomed to account to nobody save the King, refused to answer. After this there was a suspension of payment of rescriptions and great debates in the Council, from which the Duc de Choiseul issued exulting over his somewhat ostentatious offer of *Madame de Choiseul's diamonds* to secure subsidies for Holland. Thereupon, Cromot, enraged at finding himself beaten, fell back on Madame de Monaco, the Prince of Conde's mistress, whom he induced to win over the Prince by the bait of the successorship to the Duc de Choiseul. Nocturnal meetings were held during Shrovetide at M. de Fontenelle's house, and the Prince pledged himself to cooperate with the Chancellor and the Abbe, and to be their advocate with the King, on condition that Madame du Barry should grant him: (1) the command of the armies, (2) the choice of suc-

---

[1] This personage's name is spelled by MM. de Goncourt in both ways—" Terrai " and " Terray."—TRANSLATOR.

cessor to the post of Minister of War, and (3) the post of Grand Master of the Artillery.

The articles had been agreed to by the mistress.[1]

The King, by way of keeping his word to the Prince of Conde, went up to his own apartments, and before going to bed directed the news of his minister's dismissal to be despatched to the King of Spain, in accordance with a formal pledge which he had given to inform him first of this event. Choiseul, who enjoyed a still greater preponderance at the Court of Madrid than at the Court of Versailles,[2] had asked and obtained a promise that, on this pledge, the King of Spain should have the word of honour of the King of France. The all-powerful minister controlled the postal arrangements; he flattered himself that he knew the courier well enough to ward off his disgrace by some stratagem similar to that to which he had resorted in February, 1765. But the courier was despatched by side-roads that night; and, when the King was going out to hunt next morning, he sent the *lettres de cachet* to M. de la Vrilliere. The King's letter to M. de la Vrilliere contained these words :—" The Duc de la Vrilliere will convey the following orders to MM. de Choiseul, and will bring back to me their resignations."

The *lettre de cachet* in the King's handwriting and not

---

[1] "Memoirs of the Ministry of the Duc d'Aiguillon." Buisson, 1792.

[2] "Memoirs of Baron de Besenval." Paris, Bandouin, 1821, Vol. I.

countersigned, which the Duc de Choiseul received from
De la Vrilliere was thus worded:

" I order my cousin the Duc de Choiseul to place his
resignation of the post of Secretary of State and of Post-
master General in the hands of the Duc de la Vrilliere,
and to withdraw to Chanteloup till there is a fresh order
from me.

" LOUIS. (¹)

" At Versailles, this 24th of December, 1770."

Louis XV. when sending the *lettres de cachet* to M. de
la Vrilliere, said to him:—" You will inform M. de Muy
that I give him the post of War Minister." M. de la Vrilliere, after his interview with Choiseul, returned to Paris,
and communicated the orders of the King to the new Minister of War, who accepted the office. But, as soon as
he had accepted the post, the honest man, he who was
called the " Montausier of Louis XVI.'s reign," spoke to

---

[1] We give here the historic text of this letter communicated by the
Duc de Choiseul to the *Revue de Paris* in 1829. To the letter for the
Duc de Choiseul was annexed this letter of Louis XV. to the Duc de
la Vrilliere: " The Duc de la Vrilliere will convey the orders herewith to MM. de Choiseul, and will bring back to me their resignations.
Were it not for Madame de Choiseul, I would have sent her husband
to another place, because his estate is in his management; he will
be as if he were not there, and will only see his family and those
whom I may permit to go there." The letter addressed to the Duc
de Praslin, according to the " Annals of Louis XV.," expressed in
the several terms, contained only these two lines: " I have no longer
any need of your services, and I exile you to Praslin, where you will
go in twenty-four hours."

Madame Du Barry

La Vrilliere about his embarrassment. "What!" said M.
de la Vrilliere. "But—Madame du Barry!" replied De
Muy—"how is that to be managed? I cannot, all the
same, carry my portfolio there. I will never submit to it.
What am I to do?"

La Vrilliere, according to the terms of which he was
aware, had believed he saw at the first moment a suitable
man for the office of War Minister in the Prince of Conde.
He thought on the rage of the Prince, who was sure to
assume that he had been deceived. There came back, at
the same time, to his mind a vague remark of the King
which made him cherish the hope of the office for his
nephew D'Aiguillon. And in a Machiavellian fashion he
persuaded De Muy to write a line explaining his position
to the King. Thereupon De Muy wrote the clumsy letter
in which he spoke of "the inflexibility of his character."

The King, immediately on his return after hunting, saw
only one letter with reference to the post of War Minister.
He was not satisfied. He communicated the terms of the
letter to Madame du Barry, who uttered "peacock's
screams," and said that De Muy had insulted her. The
King got into an unmanageable temper, would listen to
nothing more, and went to bed. That night, all parties
went scouring the country. "Chon" sent a courier to De
Broglie. Cromot started for Chantilly. On the 26th, Versailles became the scene of pugnacious contests, "a Hell
and a bear-garden." The Chancellor, who had his usual
attack of catarrh, was confined to his bed since the 24th:

he had himself conveyed in the very crisis of his illness to the Du Barry's residence. He declared that all was lost if De Broglie appeared in the Ministry, and devoted himself to gratifying the desires and ambitions of Conde, who would bring to these combinations the authority of a Prince of the Blood.

Next morning, the Prince of Conde, brought back by Cromot, arrived at Chantilly in time for the mistress's little levee. She listened politely to his complaints, and said:— "I have not been able to get the better of the King. He has failed me—don't be angry with me for it. But I warn you that since yesterday nobody can approach him. He is coming here, and you will have a chat with him. Wait there!" The King came in, said a few words, but did not answer when addressed. Conde kept going round the subject:—"But it is said De Muy refuses. . . . But if your Majesty had not fixed on any choice. . . . But there are some subjects. . . . If Your Majesty permitted, a person might be named. . . . I will take good care not to designate,—much less to indicate" . . . . Not a word from the King. The Prince of Conde snatched up the Royal Almanac, stopped at Monteynard's name, spoke well of him as one whom he had seen working under his own orders, ended with the assurance that he doubted whether a better man could be found. He offered to send an express messenger for him. It was impossible to get from the King a "Yes" or a "No." The Prince of Conde left, despatched three couriers by three different routes into

Dauphine. The sire was found supping in a melancholy fashion with M. de Marcheval. He was brought up to Paris. He was presented by the Prince of Conde, and here was a Minister of War without the King having opened his mouth.[1]

But the news as to the influence and weight of the Prince of Conde with regard to the new ministry spread over Paris, and three carriages were at the gate of the Palais Bourbon on New Year's Day, 1771. The Chancellor, making a turn-about-face, gave the Du Barry to understand that it was useless to overthrow a despotic minister if one was to be re-created in a Prince of the Blood. And, some time afterwards, when ordered to go to Chantilly by Monteynard, who had to endure the affront of seeing his nomination of Maillebois brutally reversed by Louis XV., the Prince of Conde found himself amongst the persons who had come to have an audience with Madame du Barry. At first, there was an embarrassing silence. The King, seated in front of the fire, with his feet close to the mantelpiece, kept gazing at Madame du Barry as she walked in the diagonal, laughing to herself at the annoyance of the prince, who, having obtained nothing, and being no longer able to keep his temper, ended by saying :—" After all, this is very cruel! for you promised me the post of Grand Master of the Artillery." " It is true, I did promise it to you: well, I take back my promise!" the airy mistress hurled at his back while she put out her tongue at him in the glass.

[1] " Memoirs of the Ministry of the Duc d'Aiguillon." Buisson, 1792.

Madame Du Barry

Never perhaps did a Favourite work with less personal animosity for the fall of a minister than Madame du Barry did for the exile of Choiseul. She ended by exhibiting some conscience in the role which the enemies of Choiseul assigned to her; she never exhibited any zeal in it. Were it not for those around her who drove her on, excited her, and were every moment dragging her away from the dainty task of arranging her toilet and from the light thoughts of a pretty woman; were it not for "the givers of advice," who forced her to have opinions about matters which bored her, to excite herself about the affairs of the ministry and to have political views; were it not for the lessons and the obsessions which would fain absolutely mould her levity and her giddiness to a strong and constant will; were it not for D'Aiguillon, who kept teasing her, managing her, occupying her day and night with his ambition and his hates, and trying to drive into her heart a little of his vindictiveness; were it not for this director to whom Madame du Barry gave and was destined to give with her changes and her caprices, "more trouble to rule than all the foreign negotiations," there is no doubt that the Favourite, yielding to her soft instincts, to her conciliatory disposition, would have very speedily adopted an accommodating course of action which would have spared her weak brain the anxiety of an extreme conflict.[1] Since the beginning she had sought for his good graces; and some of

[1] It was she, the Du Barry, who said to the Marechale de Mirepoix: "Just imagine one hating M. de Choiseul without knowing him!"

her letters show us the amiable and almost humble tone of
her thanks to the minister.[1] Vainly did she, a little later,
make overtures of peace to him, while declaring herself
" ready to meet him half-way," to let him be master of every
favour if he would only let her be free for all her whims.
Without bearing any spite for the contemptuous way in
which her advances were received, she got the reversion of
the governorship of Strasburg for Choiseul's brother, the
Comte de Stainville, or allowed him to get it. Even when
the war of insults was started and carried on by the
Duchesse de Gramont with all the violence of her character, Madame du Barry did not still lose patience or hope.
She did not give up the idea of bringing back M. de Choiseul by the aid of third parties. For a long time, she tried
to make him understand that he was persisting in a struggle
against an enemy more powerful than himself; and, when
driven to extremes, she only yielded without any zest to the
necessity of the situation. On his departure, though dismissed by the Favourite, M. de Choiseul did justice to the
woman. As he was quitting Versailles in obedience to the
King's *lettre de cachet,* seeing from the end of the court
a woman at the window of Madame du Barry's apartment,
and thinking that he recognized her, he bowed, and kissed
his hand to her.[2] It was a pretty gesture and a final act

[1] "Letters of Madame du Barry addressed to the Duc de Choiseul,
communicated by his nephew." *Revue de Paris,* 1829, Tome IV. See
appendix.
[2] "Memoirs of a Traveller who is taking a Rest." By M. Dutens.
Bossange, 1806. Tome II.

of courtesy, with which we feel glad to see M. de Choiseul's ministry closing.

The victory only softened Madame du Barry's sentiments with regard to the exile of Chanteloup. When D'Aiguillon, the jaundiced and implacable man, who, longing to carry out to its last extremity the ruin of Choiseul, wanted to deprive him of his post of Colonel-General of the Swiss Guards and the Grisons without any indemnity, it was Madame du Barry who selected M. du Chatelet, the common friend of M. de Choiseul and M. d'Aiguillon, to move the King and obtain some compensation for M. du Choiseul. It was to her that M. du Chatelet thought it right to carry his complaints as to M. d'Aiguillon's harshness and injustice. Madame du Barry immediately replied that, in spite of the reproaches she had to make against M. de Choiseul and the excessiveness of his demands, she would try to procure for him the best treatment possible;[1] and, when M. du Chatelet seemed to be doubtful about the matter, she gave her promise to hold a bond chargeable on M. d'Aiguillon. On foot of this charge amounting to two millions D'Aiguillon only consented to allow M. de Choiseul a pension of 50,000 livres to the account of the charge and 200,000 livres in ready money. Finally, when all the hopes of Choiseul and of his friends seemed about to be dashed by the obstinacy of D'Aiguillon and the ill-will of the King,[2] M. du Chatelet

[1] "Memoirs of the Duc de Choiseul, written by Himself and Printed under his eye at Chanteloup in 1778." Paris, 1790. Second Part.

[2] According to Madame du Deffand, who is well informed, in a

was astonished, touched, when he saw in the salon of Choisy Madame du Barry talking in an almost angry fashion to M. d'Aiguillon and exclaiming as she left him, " It is a nice thing that this should be so!" then going over to the King who was leaning on the mantelpiece, speaking to him, beckoning towards M. d'Aiguillon to come and back up what she said, and never letting the King slip away from her till he uttered these words, as he sat down to play: " Sixty thousand livres pension and one hundred thousand crowns in cash."[1]

Now that Choiseul was exiled, the Chancellor and D'Aiguillon, this time united by a common resentment, worked together to give the final blows to the Parliament [2] which, a

[1] " Memoirs of the Duc de Choiseul, written by himself." Paris, 1790. " Memoirs of Besenval." By Berville and Barriere. Baudouin, 1821.

[2] The fall of Choiseul and the future dismissal of the Parliament gave birth to a caricature, which, like all the caricatures of the eighteenth century anterior to the Revolution, cannot be found. It is described in the " Secret Memoirs," in which the Chancellor, the Controller-General and the Comtesse du Barry are seated round the King. The first President is depicted as carrying towards them a little hamper containing heads, purses, and other things. Some of the contents of the hamper suggest ideas contrary to decency, and the point of the caricatures appears to be that while the Chancellor makes a rush for the heads and the Controller-General for the purses, Madame Du Barry's instincts lead her to rush for the unmentionable articles in the hamper. (Note slightly modified from the original for obvious reasons.—TRANSLATOR.)

letter of which M. du Chatelet was the bearer, the Duc de Choiseul asked (1) for his liberty, (2) the payment of his debts, three or four millions which he had spent of his wife's estate and two others from

few days before the fall of the Minister, had suspended the examination of the affairs of private individuals, giving as a pretext for this revolutionary measure that its members in their profound grief had not their minds sufficiently free to decide as to the goods, the life, and the honour of the King's subjects. On the night of the 19th or 20th of February, 1771, each member of Parliament was awakened by two musketeers, who presented him with an order of the King to resume his functions, to which he had to attach a "yes" or "no" without making any remarks. Some of them, influenced by the terror of their wives and children, had the weakness to recant.

But, next day, when they were collected in a body, the timid went back upon their feeble acquiescence of the previous night. On the following day, they were awakened a second time by a prisoners' usher, who gave them notice of a decree of the Council declaring their places confiscated, forbidding them thenceforth to fulfil their functions, or even assume the title of member of Parliament. And after this usher came two musketeers bringing them *lettres de cachet* which exiled them into distant provinces.[1]

[1] "Private Life of Louis XV." London: Peter Lyton, 1785. Tome IV.

---

different creditors, and on this point he recalled the favour granted in November by the King rendering null the omission of the words, "Good for three millions." "Is this the resignation?" asked the King of M. du Chatelet. "No, Sire, but the proposals which the Duc of Choiseul makes to Your Majesty." "I do not want the letter; I want the resignation." And the unconditional resignation having

Madame Du Barry

These violent measures were wrested from the will of
the King by the cackling of Madame du Barry, who, at
the promptings of her advisers, kept repeating after each
remonstrance of the provincial Parliaments: " Sire, one
more representation for the purpose of taking away from
you gradually the Royal authority, and coming a long distance to dethrone you! In the month of March, while
Maupeou was looking out for the elements and the men
of his new Parliament, intriguing, jobbing, corrupting, the
Favourite was induced to buy for 24,000 livres the portrait
by Vandyke of Charles I., King of England, from the collection of Baron de Thiers.[1] This picture, hung so as to be
seen on entering Madame du Barry's apartment, suggested
to her a dramatic appeal to the imagination of the King,
who every day heard his mistress saying: " France, do you
see this picture? If you let your Parliament do it, it will
have your head cut off, as the Parliament of England had
Charles I.'s." [2] By these threats of dispossession of authority, by these threats of violent death in the presence of
the portrait of the decapitated English King, issuing from
a beloved mouth at every possible opportunity, Madame du

[1] " Secret Memoirs of the Republic of Letters." Tome V. London John Adamson.

[2] "Annals of Louis XV." A. Villefranche, at the Widow Liberty's,
1782. " Private Life of Louis XV." London, 1785. Tome IV.

been sent from Chanteloup, the King put it into his pocket without
reading it.

Madame Du Barry

Barry brought about that celebrated Bed of Justice of the 15th day of April, 1771, at which were read the three edicts, the first dissolving the Parliament of Paris, the second dissolving the Court of Aids, and the third transforming the Great Council in the new Parliament. The King terminated the sitting with these imperious words: "I forbid every deliberation contrary to my will and all representations in favour of my former Parliament, for I will never change." And the phrase, "I will never change," was uttered by the King, Madame Necker declares, while turning round towards Madame du Barry, concealed behind a gauze curtain.[1]

The complete victory gained at the same time by the Duc d'Aiguillon over Choiseul and over the Parliament did not, however, permit Madame du Barry to introduce the ex-Governor of Brittany into the ministry at the first moment. At one time, the Duc d'Aiguillon had been mentioned for the Ministry of Marine, but the Favourite was persuaded that the hour had not arrived for giving the post to her *protege*, that this hasty appointment might put people's minds into a greater ferment,—that it was much better to wait till "they were accustomed to look at the Duke in a state of innocence."

The main result, it must be admitted, was that the private animosities which divided the members of the Coalition

---

[1] "Miscellanies extracted from the Manuscripts of Madame Necker." Pougens, Year CI. Vol. III.

only ended in the exclusion of both sections, and prevented any serious and definite appointment.[1]

The Prince of Conde, who, in the opening months of the year 1771, had considerable influence, was hostile to the Duc d'Aiguillon, and Monteynard, the Minister of War manufactured by his Highness, was the servile instrument of his antipathy.

Maupeou, when the business of the Parliament had been disposed of, became again an ally from whom the Duke had everything to fear. D'Aiguillon could not, and would not, when he came at last to be minister, have the evidence produced at the hearing of his case given up: " The evidence is there," said the Chancellor to everybody; " they follow me everywhere iike the seals, to Compiegne, to Versailles, to Paris, and to Fontainebleau. I can begin the proceedings over again when I wish." [2]

Terrai, who had obtained the temporary occupation of the Ministry of Marine, and meant to keep it, belonged still entirely to the Chancellor.

The Comte de Broglie, " the little intriguer " eternally blinded by ambition, interest, and anger—" three passions," says Dumouriez, " which have always dominated him "—the Comte de Broglie, the *protege* of the Duchess de Mirepoix, the cherished pet of the Du Barry's two sisters-in-law, the

---

[1] " Private Life of Louis XV." Peter Lyton, 1785. Tome IV. " Letters of the Marquise du Deffand to Horace Walpole." Treuttel, 1812. Tome II.

[2] " Memoirs of the Ministry of the Duc d'Aiguillon " Paris, Buisson, 1792.

MADAME NECKER

To face page 118

Madame Du Barry

" Chon " and the " Bischi," with the object of supplanting D'Aiguillon, strove to give the Favourite as a lover one of his intimate friends, the Chevalier de Jaucourt[1] the gentleman who was called " Moonshine " owing to his talent for telling ghost-stories. Lastly, Maillebois, the third member of the triumvirate composed of D'Aiguillon, De Broglie, and Maillebois, who had the promise of the command of the army under the orders of Conde, if France entered on a campaign, and whose appointment to the post of one of the four directors of the war had been so brutally annulled by the King, no longer brought D'Aiguillon any warm co-operation.

But D'Aiguillon had too great a hold over Madame du Barry to allow all these smothered resentments and all these secret intrigues to have any other result save to retard by a few months the accession of the Duke to the ministry. Since the month of April, he had got De Boynes, pushed on by him, to obtain possession of the Ministry of Marine, taken away from the Abbe Terrai. De Boynes was recognized as the foremost man amongst the contending faction, and Maupeou felt that he had been placed there by D'Aiguillon as a substitute for him if he relaxed his efforts for the destruction of the magistracy.[2] Behind the scenes, the Duc d'Aiguillon was already the master; it was he who made the great administrative and diplomatic changes of the

[1] " Memoirs of the Ministry of the Duc d'Aiguillon." Buisson,1792.

[2] " Historical and Political Memoirs of the Reign of Louis XVI." By Soulavie. Treuttel, 1801. Tome I.

month of March—and that during his sojourn for a week
at his chateau of Veret—his object being that the big blows
should be struck during his absence.[1] Strong in the amorous protection of the Favourite, he had also had, during his
journey to Paris, the support of the Prince Royal of Sweden,[2] to whom the first house that was open was the house
of the Dowager Duchesse d'Aiguillon, who had closely cultivated the acquaintance of Count Schaeffer when he was
in the Swedish Embassy. The Duc d'Aiguillon was nominated to the office of Minister of Foreign Affairs in the
month of June, 1771.[3]

[1] "Letters of the Marquise du Deffand to Horace Walpole."
Treuttel, 1812. Tome II.

[2] The Prince of Sweden, while paying court to the Choiseul party,
presented a gold collar to Madame du Barry's dog. On his accession
to the throne, Gustavus III. wrote to her : " The part which you took
in my successes renders them still more agreeable to me. The Baron
de Lieven has made me a faithful report of the kindnesses which
you have shown him, and I thank you for them sincerely. I count
with confidence on the sentiments which you have always manifested
towards me, and I do not doubt that I may often have occasion for
speaking to you of the gratitude with which I pursue very sincerely
the Comtesse du Barry."

[3] The " Copy of a Letter written from Paris on June 10th, 1771,"
describes in those terms the notification of the appointment of the
Duc d'Aiguillon: "Last Thursday all the foreign ministers, having
been invited to sup at the house of Duc de la Vrilliere, went there
without being informed of the reasons for that supper, of which they
were for a long time ignorant. The King, having been told that
they were all assembled, appeared with a laughing face, accompanied
by the Duc d'Aiguillon, whom he introduced to them himself with the
announcement that he had appointed him Minister of Foreign Affairs, and that they should in the future deal *directly* with him *for*

Madame Du Barry

The appointment of D'Aiguillon was celebrated by Madame du Barry by a grand dinner at Luciennes where sat at the Favourite's table with the minister's wife, his mother, that patroness of the Encyclopedists, that harbourer of the Abbe de Prades during his persecution, that gross atheist with a crooked nose, a wild look, and a disordered mind,[1] whom the society of Chanteloup never believed likely to meet the Favourite on terms of social equality. There were present at this dinner all the Ministers of State, the entire diplomatic corps[2] with the exception of the ambassadors to Spain and Naples, the only ambassadors who were not on visiting terms with the Favourite.

The bilious nature of the man, the grudges he had accumulated for so many years, the experience of eating out his own heart in disgrace and separation from the Court, which had already planted in his diseased mind the irritating germs of a malady of which he would die, the liquified

[1] "Unpublished Correspondence of Madame du Deffand." Colin, 1809. Tome II.

[2] The ambassador for England was very favorable to the Duc de Choiseul's adversary, and Paris commented strongly on a dinner given by him exclusively to the d'Aiguillon faction, in the month of February, 1772. The Ambassador of Spain, that Power all devoted to Choiseul, refused on the contrary to go to the dinners given by d'Aiguillon and by Madame de Valentinois, at which the Sultana was a guest.

all that would belong to this department. The assembly was so speechless with the *pleasure* which this news *gave* it, that the Duke was not in any way complimented, and the entire supper passed in the most majestic silence."

bones, the bones like *wax in the dog-days*,[1] drove the Duc
d'Aiguillon, in his hour of triumph, to personal vengeances.
Jarente, the Bishop of Orleans, was exiled;[2] M. d'Usson was
replaced in Sweden by M. de Vergennes. Breteuil, who
had already ordered his carriages, saw himself refused by
Madame du Barry the audience which had been promised
to him, and was recalled from the Ambassadorship of
Vienna. Rulhiere lost the post and the pension which he had
at the office of Foreign Affairs.[3] D'Aiguillon struck high
and low, right and left. *Lettres de cachet* were suspended
over the heads of the Archbishop of Toulouse, the Marechal de Duras, Governor of Brittany, the Duc de Goutant,
M. de Malesherbes, President of the Aides, M. de Tru-
daine, and even the Lieutenant of Police, M. de Sartine.
Madame du Barry, whose lover had for a moment aroused
anger by piquant anecdotes, and satirical verses and songs,
said openly that all Choiseul's friends were to be removed,
and his creatures deprived of posts and employments. There
were some months of terror; everybody was in a state of
mortal apprehension,[4] women as well as men. All the Court

[1] "Historical and Political Memoirs of the Reign of Louis XVI."
By Soulavie. Treuttel, 1801. Vol. I.

[2] The Bishop of Orleans had induced Madame Adelaide to go and
cast herself at the King's feet to ask for Choiseul's recall.

[3] "Secret Memoirs of the Republic of Letters." Tome IV.

[4] "Letters of the Marquise du Deffand to Horace Walpole,"
Treuttel, 1812. Tome II. In a letter of the 11th of September, 1771,
published by the Comte de Sainte-Aulaire, the fear of the Duchesse
de Choiseul for her own friends and those of M. de Choiseul clothed
itself in a pretty simile: "I have a dreadful fear of M. d'Aiguillon.

Madame Du Barry

ladies who had been the leaders in the wars of the Salons, and who had inflicted such cruel wounds on D'Aiguillon and the Favourite with their jests and their pretty sarcasms, such as Madame de Brionne whose contempt for the *clique* had been so intense, Madame d'Egmont, who did not want to have even her portrait in the same room with Madame du Barry,[1] Madame de Noailles, whom a literary sketch of Gustavus III. presents to us storming against the Chancellor, against D'Aiguillon, against Du Barry, in short, against all those patriotic and philosophic fine ladies who were at the same time excited to almost revolutionary pitch in a sentiment of independence against the King's good pleasure and of evecration against his mistress,—those women felt themselves menaced by D'Aiguillon through their husbands, their lovers, their allies. It was thus that she whose action had on the attitude of the Duc de Choiseul towards Madame

---

[1] Madame d'Egmont had promised her portrait to Gustavus III. She wrote to him: "Put it in my power to send you my portrait. I cannot do so without a positive assurance that you neither have nor will have that of Madame du Barry." She returns to the charge in another letter: "Sire, it is said that you have asked for Madame du Barry's portrait; people even go so far as to say that you have written to her. I have denied it at every risk, but it has been maintained to me in such a positive manner that I beg of you to authorize me to deny it on your behalf also. No; it cannot be." Finally, in a last letter she says: "I still ask you for an answer as to Madame du Barry's portrait. Pray be kind enough to let me have your word of honour that you neither have it nor will have it." "Gustavus III. and the Court of France." By Geoffroy. Didier, 1867. Tome I.

He takes every kind of form. He is like the wicked genii of the 'Thousand and One Nights.'"

du Barry an influence perhaps as great as that of the
Duchesse de Gramont, she who wished that the minister
should be " at daggers drawn " with her own sister-in-law,
the Marechale de Mirepoix, she whose insolence of speech
had never known any restraint, she who wrested from the
King almost with violence the permission to go to Chanteloup[1] saw her husband, the Marechal de Beauvau, deprived
of his post of commander at Languedoc. Destitution, persecution, exile, the illustrious lady bore in the assurance that it
was only a trifling thing to suffer compared with the honour
of securing liberty and preserving themselves against despotic power. Unhappily for the maintainance of such beautiful doctrines, the people at Court were then all head over
ears in debt, and could only keep themselves up through the
favours of the King. The Marechal de Beauvau had 700,-
ooo livres of debts on which he paid interest and more than
450,000 francs demanding immediate payment. He was
obliged to petition the King in order to obtain a little money,
obliged to make an appeal to be allowed to remain employed
as Lieutenant General—a position which gave him a salary

---

[1] With regard to Chanteloup, let us give this letter addressed by
Vrilliere to Maynon d'Invau, asking permission to call on the Duc
de Choiseul. It refers to the displeasure felt by the King at these
visits without any attempt by him, however, to forbid them. " I have
submitted to the King the letter in which you express a desire to
go to Chanteloup, and His Majesty has done me the honour to say
in reply that he had never granted anyone permission to go there, but
that he had not refused, and that he had left those who asked him
for liberty to do it to decide for themselves as to what course they
would take in the matter."

of 37,000 francs. And the superb household, which had commenced by braving the King, ended by asking him for alms.[1]

So with the Beauvau household ; so with other households of the Court, reduced, subdued, enslaved by the question of money.

The intimidation of society, of the Salons, of women, having thus been obtained, seduction was employed with Princes of the Blood, who had been vainly invited by *lettres de cachet* to the Comte de Provence's marriage in order to bring about their desertion in the business of the Parliament and to lead them back to the Court. In this negotiation, Maupeou showed a knowledge of human nature in its most secret depths, a discernment in the choice of agents entrusted by him to work upon human weaknesses, a really extraordinary skill in managing souls and corrupting men.

Before the Prince of Conde, who had been abandoned by the Comte de Clermont's death to his floating, irresolute character, so that he no longer remained obstinate in his oppositions, he held out the dazzling perspective of the marriage of " Mademoiselle " with the Comte d'Artois. Some councillors, won over by Maupeou, insinuated to the Prince de Conde that he should draw closer to the Court, and inflame, before it would become a question of a foreign princess, the budding attachment of the Prince for his daughter. The Prince of Bourbon was dragged by the

[1] "Letters of the Marquise du Deffand to Horace Walpole." Treuttel 1812. Tome II.

Chancellor in his father's train by the paltry bait of the Knighthood of the Holy Ghost, which the young Prince had been disappointed in not getting at an age when the Princes of the Blood are habitually decorated,—which led some jokers to say at the occasion of the first journey of the two princes to Versailles " that the Father and the Son were going to look for the Holy Ghost."

After the letters of submission of the House of Conde, the Chancellor was not slow in obtaining letters of submission from the House of Orleans. With the Duc d'Orleans Maupeou made use of Madame de Montesson's ambitious desire to become Duchesse d'Orleans, to raise herself to the dignity of first Princess of the Blood. Addressing himself directly to the woman, he persuaded her, with his irresistible powers of speech that to induce the Prince of Orleans to come back to the Court was the best way to win over to the success of her project Madame du Barry, whose will constituted the will of the King.[1]

As for the Duc de Chartres the Chancellor pandered to his desire to be something by the possibility of succeeding the Duc de Penthievre in the post of Grand Admiral.

All the Princes of the Blood except old Conde, who remained inexorable, became from that day forth devoted friends of the Du Barry, courtiers of the antechamber, who

[1] When the Prince subsequently urged Madame du Barry to obtain from the King publicly permission for his marriage with Madame de Montesson, the Favourite replied to his importunities: " Big father, go and marry her; we'll see how to satisfy you better afterwards."

implored of the Favourite to tell them the day and the hour when they might have the honour of offering her their " respectful " homage.[1]

[1] "The Annals of Louis XV." A. Villefranche. At the Widow Liberty's, 1782. Second Part. "Private Life of Louis XV." Peter Lyton, 1785. Tome IV.

VIII.

THE life, the entire life of Madame de Pompadour belongs to history. It is a life of business, of intrigues, of negotiations, a sustained political *role*, a public exercise of power, hourly communications with ministers, ambassadors, secretaries of state, military men, bankers, lawyers, management of the interests of the nation and of the will of the King,—a life which had a weighty influence on the destinies of France and of Europe. The life of Madame du Barry can neither justify nor satisfy a similar curiosity on the part of posterity. It has neither the same share in the business of the state nor the same claims on history. Take away from it the one incident—the conflict with Choiseul—it is nothing but the existence of the best-kept wanton in the kingdom. It is the senseless dream of a woman of pleasure, a frenzy of expenditure, a luxurious extravagance; it means millions flung away on caprices of fashion; millions flung away on rare jewellery, point-lace, silk, velvet; millions on things the cost of which is *immensely high*—

Madame Du Barry

a river of money, the royal treasure scattered over a mob of tailors, of milliners, of seamstresses, of embroiderers, of lace-makers, of ornament-makers. . . . Every morning—and this was, indeed, the little levee of this woman, who set such slight store on honours and dignities—the Favourite, half-nude, gave audience in bed to workmen and workwomen of well-known reputation who brought for her first awakening the prettiest objects invented by the imagination of the maker of gewgaws, the most perfect articles produced by the handiwork of the time, not letting a day pass without buying something, without ordering something.

Orders, supplies, invoices,—this made up her whole life: it is contained in those four volumes of accounts purchased, some years ago, by the National Library,[1] precious accounts which are really the only memoir to which the Du Barry regime has any just claim.

Open them, these accounts; they will not fail to repay you. They will tell you about the watch adorned with diamonds bought from Lepaute for 5,400 francs by the Comtesse, and the necklace " for a slave," and the " respectful assortment of costumes " worn by her in such a year and such a month. They will give you the name of the book which she sent out to be bound at the Libraire Vente, with her armorial device, " Put forward! "[2] They give

[1] " Madame du Barry's Accounts." National Library. Manuscripts. French Supplement, 8157, 8158.

[2] The Library of Versailles possesses 349 volumes with the arms of Madame du Barry. Some of them, bound during her regime as

you details of the theatre-dress of which she made a present to Raucourt[1] or to Lekain,[2] and her coffee-napkins, which she would have only of Indian dimity, and even the last dressing-gown which she presented to the King with the cushion and the slippers. Here it is her ordinary livery of chamois-cloth and her full-dress livery of crimson velvet. Even Zamore—the "nigger," the trades-people quite shortly and disrespectfully called him,—you will find with his green dress-coat of Saxony trimmed with gold-lace, behind the Comtesse's pretty running-footman, who, squeezed into his polonaise of sky-blue cloth and his legs covered with chamois-colored knitted silk breeches, brandished as he ran that superb cane-knob chased by Roettiers, of which the inexorable accounts will tell you the price almost down to a farthing.[3] If it pleases you to see Madame du Barry's wardrobe, you may go over the review of *full-dress suits,* robes with *hoop-petticoats, robes of respecta-*

[1] The "Secret Memoirs" relate, under the date of January 10, 1773, that Madame du Barry having given the choice to Raucourt of three robes for his use or a theatre-dress, Raucourt chose a theatre-dress.

[2] Madame du Barry gave Lekain a costume in the Greek style and a costume in the Roman style. The two costumes cost 4,808*l.* 45*s.*

[3] The entry dated the 4th April, 1774, gives the price of this cane-knob as "546*l.* 9*s*"—TRANSLATOR.

Favourite, are in red morocco with the arms on the covers; the others, more modestly bound, are covered with calf and sheepskin. These last have on their backs, in the midst of myrtle-wreaths, the arms and the device of the Favourite. I have found, in this style of binding, the "Grecourt" of Madame du Barry. See the work of M. Paul Lacroix on the Favourite s library.

Madame Du Barry

bility and a robe de toilette, robes at 1,000, at 2,000, at 3,000, at 5,000, and 10,000 livres, supplied by the ordinary dealers in silk-goods—Buffand, Lenormand, Assorty, Barbier, Bourjot. Here we have coming from the establishment of her dressmaker, Madame Sigly, robes with a silver ground adorned with bouquets of feathers; robes with a white ground and wreaths of roses; robes striped with big gold plates running into the flowers and the eyelet-holes; robes with a mosaic ground worked in gold and framed with myrtle; and Amazon's robes of white Indian silk, which cost 6,000 livres!

But the gold and the silver are not enough: embroidery comes to shed over the silk the flowering rain of its patterns. Davaux, the Comtesse's embroiderer, embroiders for her completely, after the patterns of Michel de Saint-Aubin, white silk robes in silk-cloud and spangles of colour.

Then there are the ruinous trimmings, all the ornaments which a robe in those days could bear, the thousand fancies of that great artist in gewgaws, Pagelle, the man-milliner of " Traits Galants " in the Rue Saint-Honore—the silver blond-laces, the chiccory head-bands set off and picked out with jasmine, the little bouquets fastened with little knots in the hollows of festoons, and the wreaths, and the bracelets, and the fur-tippets, and the top-knots, and the court-tassels, which brought up the price of a robe to 10,500 livres. Then, when the robes were finished, began the lace,—the lace, that luxury of woman; and reckon the trimmings of a dressing-gown at 2,500 livres, the

Madame Du Barry

English morning-wrapper at 4,000 livres, the ruffles at 600, the needle-stitched head-dresses at 1,400, and the toilettes of Point-d'Argentan at 9,000![1]

From the toilet, from this big business and this big wastefulness of Madame du Barry, the inventory of her follies will lead you to her other caprices, to her temptations, to her taste for bawbles, to her love of pretty nothings. You will follow her in her purchase of porcelain at the King's manufactory. The vases with ears and goats' heads, the lozenged baskets, the chestnut trays, the tea-pots with green ribbons and gilt hatching, the biscuit-groups, the basins of royal blue for putting in flowers with trellises and birds. dozens of which were destroyed by fire before being successfully finished, the breakfast services with figures of grotesque Chinese pattern, which were set apart for the days when the King supped at Luciennes and necessitated two months and a half of work from the first painter of the manufactory, and the service with little roses and wreaths of three hundred and twenty pieces, the ordinary supper-service,—all the Sevres of Madame du Barry is summed up and exhibited for your benefit.

Soon, in this prodigious inventory of so many prodigalities, in the list of expenditure in which seem to be set out by the steward of a Cleopatra the cost and the particulars of pearls melted through a woman's whim, you shall find

[1] See in the Appendix some fragments of these accounts. The estimated cost of cloth, lace, &c., after Madame du Barry's death, reached more than 200,000 livres.

the precious metals—silver, gold—with which her table
shone proudly, with which her toilet decked itself.[1] Read
the memorandum[2] of that great carver in silver, Roettiers,
whose association with Germain procured for the eighteenth
century the marvels of his plate utensils, those models,
those chasings, of which now only a wreck, a sample, is left
here and there. The memorandum describes in full detail,
it sketches so to speak with technical words, all this service
of Madame du Barry, of the most finished shape and carried to the highest pitch of polish, on which the most skilful of Roettiers's journeymen silversmiths spent half his
nights for whole months. An interweaving of myrtle and
laurel is the mark and, so to speak, the device of all the
pieces. The chandeliers with their rams' heads and their
laurel wreaths represent the four Elements; infants' sports,
with trophies of arrows and quivers, may be seen above the
doorways.

Ere long silver is not sufficiently rich and magnificent
for Madame du Barry. She aims at possessing the envy
and the insolence of a service entirely of gold, of which the
helvings will be blood-red jasper, spoons of gold in which
Cupids hold up garlands of roses, a gold coffee-pot adorned

[1] M. Paul Lacroix has informed me that there is in the possession
of the successor of Lepot of Auteuil, Madame du Barry's notary,
a detailed inventory of all the household goods belonging to Madame
du Barry. I direct the attention of students of archæological details
to this document, considering that the numerous descriptions of
artistic objects given here and in the Appendix are sufficient for a
general history of Madame du Barry.

[2] See this Memorandum in the Appendix.

with feet and antique foliage, a gold milk-pot with a spout hollowed by channels in which myrtle-leaves are displayed, while the lid has projecting leaves crowned with a group of roses.

There is, in fact, an entire toilet-service of gold with which her desire is gratified and for which Roettiers gets the order. All Paris talks about it. It is said that the Government made an advance to Roettiers of the fifteen hundred gold marks, which he asked for setting about the work.[1] The inquisitive gathered round the silversmith's establishment, and those who are lucky enough to get in front feel glad at having seen the mirror surmounted by two Cupids holding a wreath. But scandal, or rather the excessive expense, brought the work to a stop; and we find in Madame du Barry's accounts an indemnity to Roettiers for a gold toilet-service which he had commenced. All those beautiful things, so much wealth, this furniture worth millions, those rare objects, those trifles and those marvels, required a temple suitable for them, a nest, a fairy pavilion, which should be, in its grace, in the charm of its details, in the miniature perfection of its proportions, in the delicacy of its magnificence, the worthy little abode of the minor arts of the eighteenth century. This temple will be Luciennes, built in three months, as if at the command of an enchantress, by the architect Ledoux, whom Madame du Barry thanked by getting him into the Academy.[2]

[1] "Anecdotes about Madame du Barry." 1775.
[2] "Secret Memoirs of the Republic of Letters." Vol. VII.

Madame Du Barry

It will be a palace-boudoir in which everything will have the finish and the preciousness of a jewel. The industry of the time will seem to have employed there, even in nothings, the invention, the patience, and the taste of a thousand little genii. The slightest ornaments will be unique, exquisite, and *recherche;* and, from room to room, the masterpieces of handicraft will display there the supreme effort and the delicious refinement of elegant designs and excellent implements. The carved woodwork, the flowerings, the acanthus-leaves, the laurel-branches, the birds pecking in the intertwined myrtles, will be carved and re-carved and, so to speak, perfected by chiselling. There will be in the gildings and the overgildings of the furniture so many leaves of gold and so many touches of the burnishing stick, such an exhibition of care and pains, that the gilder will ask 5,915 livres for the bed.[1] And it will be by Gouthiere that the bronzes will be wrought in amorous fashion.[2] He will

[1] See in the Appendix the detailed description of this bed made, in the beginning, for the mansion at Versailles.

[2] Gouthiere claimed, after Madame du Barry's death, 756,000 francs. The carving in bronze of a single pedestal was fixed at 50,000 francs; the mounting and adjustment of the ornaments of this pedestal at 46,000 francs; the gilding at 63,000 francs; the placing of the pedestal, in which was included the journey of the three workmen, at 5,000 francs. The three other pedestals were reckoned up at 420,000 francs. Although he consented to reduce his bill to 640,000 francs, keeping certain articles not finished and not delivered, Gouthiere was not paid by the Government, was obliged to ask for admission to an almshouse, and died in want.

His son having entered a protest as against the indemnity which was paid to Madame du Barry's legal representatives, under the law

shape the flames, arms, locks, sash-fastenings, and door-handles which will lose nothing by their proximity to those little bronzes preserved by the Museum of Naples as the most charming things transmitted to us by the art of former days.

Luciennes was a small square edifice with five windows on each side, which had in front a peristyle of four columns with a pediment showing a Bacchanalian group of children carved in bas-relief by Lecomte.

The peristyle opened on a vestibule leading into the dining-room; and we have this dining-room at Luciennes, all animation, all filled with guests, all alive, so to speak, in the clever water-colour of the younger Moreau, now in possession of the Museum of the Louvre.[1] In the middle of the ceiling, at either side of which were gilt tumbrils, there are floating clouds of Olympus and sportive Cupids. The white marble walls are cut by Corinthian pilasters with capitals, bases, and stems of gilt bronze. Between the capitals, bas-reliefs, framed in gold, display Loves, the portrait of Louis XV. and the united arms of the King and

[1] This water-colour, exhibited in No. 1196, has on the back, with the arms of Madame du Barry, this manuscript note: "*Fete given at Luciennes, December 27th, 1771.*" With this drawing of Moreau and Villiers's description it is easy to rebuild the palace-bijou of the Favourite.

of April 25th, 1825, a judgment of the Tribunal of First Instance in Paris declared the protest effectual to the extent of 80,000 francs, and the legal representatives were held liable to pay 32,000 francs to Gouthiere Fils. (*Gazette de Tribunal*, February 28th, 1836.)

Madame Du Barry

Madame du Barry. Four galleries, where Madame du Barry's musicians repeated, on each occasion of returning from the chase, the sound and the dying echo of the horn, are full of women leaning on the balcony rails, and fanning themselves. Throughout the apartment, all white and gold, a vapour of light seems to rise from the lustres hanging in front of the mirrors between the columns, shedding on them flashes to which other flashes respond in other mirrors, handfuls of flame which fling into the air four figures of women carved in marble by Pajou, Lecomte, and Moineau, and standing on marble socles with golden wreaths. Around the table, surrounded by curious lookers-on, behind the round backs of the armchairs and the clubs of the chattering guests' perukes, the attendants, the servants, the persons carrying dishes, keep coming and going rapidly, some in yellow straw livery, others in crimson velvet coats with facings, with blue collars and wrist-bands, with white boot-tops and white gaiters, three-cornered hats on their heads and swords by their side. You see even little Zamore in a turban with feathers, a rose-coloured vest and breeches, gliding towards a lady who has, doubtless, left some bon-bons on her plate. The crystal, the silver, the structure resembling an opera-scene which rises above the table-cloth, the *cordons bleus,* the diamonds, the smiles on the faces of the guests, all keep the table in a glow; and in the brilliant light shed around there is seen by the side of Madame du Barry's pretty countenance the handsome, noble face of Louis XV.

Madame Du Barry

The dining-room opened on the square salon where the view from the windows embraced Saint Germain, the Vesinet, Saint Denis, the Seine in all its windings, and, there below, Paris. This salon, the arabesques of which had been sculptured by Metivier and Feuillet, was decorated with a cornice with a console in which Gouthiere surpassed himself; and the spaces above the doors exhibited the gayest touches of brilliant colourings from Fragonard's brush, given by Drouais to Madame du Barry.[1]

Two parlours communicated with the large salon. The one at the right presented, in a series of four big pictures by Vien, a symbolic history of love in young girls' hearts. It had tables of precious marble, and two marble figures by Vasse represented, the one of them Love, the other Knavery holding his mask. At the left, the oval parlour, where Briard had painted on the ceiling the charming allegory of love of the country, was all full of mirrors, which reproduced the superb mantelpiece of lapis-lazuli in the form of a tripod with a prodigious wealth of bronze.[2] Nothing was lacking in this enchanted palace. There was even, as in one of Veronese's illustrations of a fairy tale, a familiar negro-boy, something like a human chimera, to carry the trays with refreshments, to hold the parasol and to roll himself on the carpets. He was one of those pretty little monsters whom that age of grotesques loved so much,

[1] "Miscellanies of Literature and History." Published by the Society of Bibliophiles.
[2] "Manual of a Traveler in the Neighbourhood of Paris." By Villiers. Paris X. Vol. I.

a two-legged pug, whom the Prince of Conde christened Zamore. It seems to me that I can see him in this sketch which I have under my eyes, in this drawing of the very amusing coxcomb, Portail, with his tuft of white and red feathers, his silk head-dress from which escape at the temple and at the neck locks of hair, with his big white eye, his flat nose, his mouth like a pomegranate, his ear wearing a pearl, his big waistcoat, his fine coat, his proud frill and his ruffles, a bush of lace from which issues an ebony hand. Zamore and Luciennes! They were so well adapted to each other, the chateau was so suitable a cage for the negro-boy, that, on one evening of folly, the King gave Zamore, who was playing at his feet, the management of the chateau and the grounds of Luciennes, with a salary of 600 livres.[1] Luciennes! should we not speak of it as the palace of one of those funny sovereignties such as the books of the eighteenth century show us in those *Turkisms*, in which, subjected to the whims of a favourite odalisque, the erratic good-pleasure of a capricious sultan holds sway?

For such extravagant expenditure, for this rain of gold poured out on all the arts and all the industries, for so much money flowing daily from the two open hands of the Favourite, there was needed a bottomless chest, a banker always ready to pay. Madame du Barry had found the banker in the Controller-General, the chest in the coffers of the

[1] Does the Royel warrant really exist? I have made a minute examination of the registers of warrants in the National Archives from 1769 to 1774 without being able to find it.

State. This Terray, this species of priest, this lugubrious joker,[1] this pale Satyr,—for all the statesmen grouped around the Du Barry are of a bilious mould: Maupeou is green, D'Aiguillon is yellow, Terray is livid,—this Terray, in his complaisances towards the Favourite's caprices so peculiar to fast women, showed a baseness, a laxity, a shamelessness, which have no parallel in the history of any minister of finance in any other country. In the commencement of Madame du Barry's vogue, at the moment when the mistress had as yet only an allowance of 30,000 livres a month, he got this allowance doubled by persuading the King that there would be an economy in suppressing the lady's little notes and private money-orders, which were unlimited. When the allowance was doubled, it may well be doubted whether the little notes and the private money-orders did not go on as in the past.

On New Year's Day, 1770, he obtained for her as a New Year's gift the " Nantes Lodges," with a revenue of 40,000 livres.

In 1771, on the death of the Comte de Clermont, he suggested to the King that it was necessary to think about Madame du Barry, who had until now been solely occupied with the task of pleasing His Majesty, and therefore had no thought on her means, so that she found herself in a

---

[1] The Abbe Terray's joke about the fetes on the occasion of Marie Antoinette's marriage is well known. When Louis XV. asked him what he thought of the fetes, the Controller-General, with his clouded face, replied: " Sire they are *beyond payment.*"

precarious state. And he proposed, without in any way disarranging the plan of economy which Louis XV. had imposed on himself, to give 100,000 livres a year for life to the Favourite out of the 300,000 of which the Comte de Clermont's death had caused the extinction.[1] Some time afterwards, he got for the Favourite, on the renewal of the lease for gunpowder, a good-will of 100,000 livres, a good-will which bad tongues accused the Abbe of having, in the beginning, stipulated for getting on his own account.

But these gifts, these good-wills, however enormous they were, had their limits, and they did not amount to very much in comparison with the immense and unknown sum of money which came into Madame du Barry's hands through the shameful acceptance by the Abbe Terray of bonds of Madame du Barry as *bonds of the King,* so that Madame du Barry drew, without counting, from Choisy, from Trianon, on Baujon the banker of the Court, to whom she gave orders for payment of any sum she wished, leaving him to settle accounts with the Controller-General. And do we not know that Madame du Barry's bonds on Baujon since 1769, the first year when she occupied the place of Favourite, to 1774, the year of King Louis XV.'s death, amounted to the sum of 6,427,803 livres?[2] All the policy, all the science,

---

[1] "Memoirs concerning the administration of Finances under the Abbe Terray, Controller-General. London, Jolin, Adamson, 1776.

[2] M. le Roi, in his elaborate study of curious information, has made an estimate of the sums spent by Madame du Barry. Here it is as he has given it:

all the labour of the Abbe Terray to sustain himself consisted in never letting Madame du Barry be in want of money.

---

1. Furniture given by the King to Madame du Barry on her marriage..................   30,000*l.* —*s.*   *d.*
2. Sums paid for Madame du Barry by Baujon. banker of the Court, from the year 1769 to the year 1774 ....   6,427,803*l.* —*s.* 11*d.*
3. For the purchase of her mansion at Versailles by Monsieur, brother of the King, October 24th, 1775 ....   224,000*l.* —*s.* —*d.*
4. For the exchange of 50,000 livres of a life annuity for 1,250,000 livres delivered by the Royal Exchequer by the King's decree of April, 1784 ....   1,250,000*l.* —*s.* —*d.*
5. Madame du Barry enjoys 150,000 livres of a life annuity out of the city of Paris, the States of Burgundy and the Lodges of Nantes, from the year 1769 to 1784, which gives a total of........................   2,400,000*l.* —*s.* —*d*
6. From the year 1784 to 1793 she has no more than a life-annuity of 100,000 livres, which gives a total of......................   900,000*l.* —*s.* —*d.*
7. The enjoyment of the Chateau of Luciennes and of its numerous dependencies, the Chateau and the construction of the Pavilion may be estimated at a revenue of 50,000 livres a year, making from 1767 to 1793...   1,250,000*l.* —*s.* —*d.*

The general total of all these sums is...   12,481,803*l.* —*s.* —*d.*

IX.

In the midst of the complete satisfaction of her hatreds, her passions, her tastes, her caprices, and her fancies, the favourite sultana had her existence and her nerves worried by the insulting disdain of the Dauphiness. In those salons of Marly, of Choisy, of Versailles, of Fontainebleau, in those salons, now humbled and reverential, Madame du Barry had to endure the silence of the haughty little red-haired beauty[1] and all that the latter conveyed by such silence. In spite of the maternal orders of Maria Theresa, who took the preliminary steps to obtain Louis XV.'s forgiveness for the partition of Poland,[2] in spite of the letters of Prince Kaunitz, in spite of the objurgations of Mercy-

---

[1] Madame du Barry called Marie Antoinette "the little *rousse*," and the future Louis XVI. "the little ill-bred boy."

[2] Maria Theresa writes to Marie Antoinette: "It is sufficient for the King to distinguish such a woman or a man for you to owe the person respect without sifting their merits."

Madame Du Barry

Argenteau, the Empress-Queen's ambassador, Marie Antoinette could not conquer the insurmountable repugnance which she felt for " the most silly and impertinent creature imaginable." [1]   Nobody had the power to compel the young Princess to hold conversation with the Favourite, to make her address to Madame du Barry in society one of those commonplaces which would be the pledge and the mark of the acceptance of her person amongst the ladies of the Court.   Madame du Barry, thus wounded publicly every day, kept wearying the King with her complaints, with her despairs, with her tears, asking his intervention as a father-in-law in order to put a stop to this cruel state of affairs, so that in the month of July, 1771, at Compiegne, Louis XV. conveyed to Mercy-Argenteau his desire to have an interview with Maria Theresa's confidential adviser.   The Duc d'Aiguillon, the bearer of the message, gave him a rendez-vous the next day but one, after his return from hunting, at the house of the Comtesse du Barry informing him that Louis XV. wished to say he was not housed at Compiegne in a way to receive him suitably, and therefore wished him to call at the Favourite's abode.   The step was a delicate one, the greater number of foreign ambassadors having up to this time refused to visit Madame du Barry.   However, Mercy-Argenteau obeyed the King's orders.

Mercy-Argenteau called at the Favourite's house at seven

---

[1] Letter of Marie Antoinette to Maria Theresa, published in " Maria Theresia und Marie-Antoinette." By Arneth, Vienna, 1865.

144

MARIE ANTOINETTE

To face page 144

o'clock. The Duc d'Aiguillon informed him that the King had finished dressing, and, under the pretext of examining a picture, he brought away the ladies who happened to be in the salon, and left the Empress-Queen's ambassador alone with Madame du Barry, who made him sit down beside her.

The Favourite seized the opportunity to say to Mercy-Argenteau that she was very glad the idea of the King speaking to him at her house had put it in her power to make his acquaintance, and that she wished to take advantage of it to talk to him confidentially about a painful subject which greatly affected her. She was not unaware that for some time past people had been busy in poisoning the Dauphiness's mind against her, and that, in order to succeed in so doing, *the had recourse to the most atrocious calumnies,* daring to attribute to her remarks by no means respectful with reference to the Princess. Madame du Barry protested that this was utterly without foundation, that even far from having to reproach herself with such an enormous offence, she had always been on the side of those who bestowed well-merited praise on the charms of the Archduchess. She declared that, though this Princess had constantly treated her with rigour and a species of contempt, she had never indulged in complaints against her Royal Highness, but only against those who inspired her with these feelings of aversion. Madame du Barry added that, when there was a question of some object which the Dauphiness appeared to desire, as, on a former occasion, a demand for payment for that princess's house, she had made it her business to represent to the King that *he could not shrink from complying with the wishes of the Dauphiness."*

At this stage of the conversation the King arrived by a little staircase, and the Comtesse withdrew.

" Till now you have been the Empress's ambassador; now I beg of you to be my ambassador, at least for some time," said the King, as he entered, to Mercy-Argenteau. Then, with a certain embarrassment, he talked to him about Marie Antoinette, saying to him that he loved the Princess with all his heart, that he thought her charming, but that she was young and lively, " and that having a husband who was not capable of guiding her," it was impossible that she could avoid the snares which were directed against her by intrigue. He remarked with displeasure that she gave herself up to prejudices, to hatreds, which did not enanate from her, but which had been suggested to her; that she treated badly and even with affectation the ladies whom the King admitted into his intimate circle. Louis XV. ended by repeating several times to Mercy-Argenteau: " See the Dauphiness often: I authorize you to say to her anything you wish on my behalf. She is badly advised, and she should not follow such bad advice."

In consequence of this interview, Mercy-Argenteau placed Marie-Antoinette in this dilemma: either she wanted to indicate by her conduct that she was aware of Madame du Barry's role with the King, in which case it was due to her dignity to insist on the Comtesse being excluded from the Court circle, or else she wanted to appear ignorant of the Favourite's position, in which case she should treat her like every other woman who had been presented at Court.

Next day the Dauphiness informed Mercy-Argenteau that she would speak once to the Comtesse du Barry on the first opportunity.

A few days later Mercy-Argenteau intimated to the Dauphiness that Madame du Barry would be joining the Court circle on the following day accompanied by the Duchesse de Valentinois. Marie Antoinette promised to speak. It was agreed that, when play was over, Mercy-Argenteau should approach the Favourite and enter into a conversation with her, while the Archduchess, in the act of taking her usual turn, should address some remark to Madame du Barry. Mercy-Argenteau, delighted with his victory, left the Dauphiness, making her give her word of honour not to tell the royal aunts about this little arrangement. So next day the Comtesse du Barry, accompanied by the Duchesse de Valentinois, was in the Court circle. Play was nearly finished. Mercy-Argenteau had been sent by the Dauphiness to sit down beside Madame du Barry, who felt quite happy, as she saw Marie Antoinette advancing towards her ready to speak, when Madame Adelaide, who was in the secret, suddenly raising her voice, said:

" It is time to go! Come! Let us wait for the King at my sister Victoire's." And the Dauphiness followed Ma-

dame Adelaide without having had time to address a word
to the unhappy and humiliated Favourite.[1]

Madame du Barry had another annoyance in her life—her
brother-in-law. There had been since the beginning of her
regime as Favourite demands every day for money and for
notes to appease creditors, " to lift him out of the depths of
the tomb," as the Roue tragically wrote.[2] In order to get
out of the depths of the tomb, a moment before Terray's accession to office, the Comte Jean had conceived the brilliant idea of overthrowing the Controller-General, Maynon
d'Invau, and replacing him by a friend of his, by one of his
" pals," Guenee de Brochau, *Procureur-General* of Requests
at the Hotel. Guenee de Brochau once Controller-General, it
would mean the Comte Jean's hand in the public exchequer.
Unfortunately the plot was found out; Brochau was put into
the Bastille, and the Comte Jean got orders to travel for
the good of his health—always at the expense of the Comtesse du Barry. Still, if the Favourite had been tormented
merely by Jean du Barry's need of money, it would have

[1] " Secret Correspondence between Maria-Theresa and Mercy-Argenteau." Published by the Chevalier Arneth, 1875. Tome I.

[2] Letter from Jean du Barry without any date, published by the
Revue de Paris in the year 1836. Tome XXXV. Hardy, in his " Manuscript Journal," relates that in the month of December, 1769, Jean
du Barry had been driven from Court, and forbidden to reappear
there. On this point a story was told that the Comtesse, having asked
for 600,000 livres to pay her debts, and the King, having applied for
this sum to the Controller-General, the Duc de Choiseul procured
incontestable proofs that this money was destined for the brother-in-
law, and submitted them to the King.

Madame Du Barry

been well enough; but he was continually harassing her, persecuting her with his advice, with his plans of conduct, with his monitions, wishing to make her profit, according to his own phrase, " by the flashes of his genius."[1] How-

[1] Letter of the Comte du Barry, published in the *Revue Retrospective,* 3rd Series, Vol. I. The letter deserves to be cited as the letter of a rascally pimp, of an intriguing politician:

" M. Jame has not left me ignorant, my dear sister, that it was at the bottom of your heart he found the best advocate of my cause. Would to Heaven that this heart had never yielded to the suggestions of those who were interested in disuniting it from mine! How many misfortunes we might have spared each other! There remains for you at your age a long career to enjoy: the decline of mine may still shed on it some advantage by making use of my experience and of the position in which at this moment I find myself.

" M. Jame can inform you of some of my views for the purpose of being useful to you in my turn, and I would be ungrateful for the first time in my life if when I owe to you the facility of appearing in my own city with honour, I did not on my return sacrifice my time and my attentions to serve you. This may be and will be so, my dear sister; you will still profit by some flashes of my genius. They have often lighted up your path. I repeat to you, they will light it up still. . . . You and he (M. Jame), my dear sister, are the only friends I know. I have been repulsed with arms of brass by persons whom blood and gratitude ought to render inviolably attached to me: you alone will have the merit of having set me up again on the top of the wheel. I am not laying a tax on the extent of the service you have promised to render me. I shall receive with thankfulness what will come from you. It is the last service of this sort I have asked from you, and if there were within my reach any negotiable bill or any article of furniture that could be sold, be sure I could not have asked you for anything. It is with tears in my eyes, I repeat to you, that I see you forced to deprive yourself of your capital in order to assist me to get out of the abyss in which I am, for I am firmly convinced that you are just as destitute of money as I am myself; but I have nothing except a life-mortgage, and if I

ever, in spite of his debts and of his creditors, the Comte
Jean lived in great style. He gambled in the most desperate
fashion, kept five mistresses, married the sultana of his
harem to a Chevalier of Saint-Louis, for whom he got a
pension of 2,000 crowns so that he might have the usufruct
of it to himself. He held under the baptismal font a child
of Beauvoisin whose baptism cost, in sugar plums and in
presents, 25,000 livres. Installed for a little while in the
chateau of Triel, where he had around him all the gamblers
of France, he lost 7,000 louis at one sitting, and he boasted
when rising from the table that he had got to his fifth million. The Comte Jean appeared as a product of rotten civili-
zation, one of the decadents of his time, as a type in which
seems to exhibit itself in its shamelessness, in its cynicism, in
its scandalous contempt for every human religion, the moral-
ity of a " Rameau's Nephew."[1] It was the Comte Jean who
said, when people spoke of his losses at play, " Don't worry,

[1] An allusion to Diderot's remarkable work, " Le Neveu de Rameau," in which the vices of a parasite in the days of pre-Revolution-
ary France are ruthlessly gibbeted.—TRANSLATOR.

die without having repaid by some service that which you render me,
you and I know that it is to no purpose.

" I do not insist on appearing at Luciennes on account of the peculiar reasons you mention. I do not see, however, why you should
not make an appointment in Paris at the house of M. Darnet, or
elsewhere; perhaps an hour's conversation would be instructive and
profitable.

" May Heaven preserve you, my dear sister: I have been told that
it has taken care of your freshness and your figure. I thank it for
doing so."

my friends; 'tis you'll have to pay for all this." It was the Comte Jean who, with reference to a money-order refused by the Abbe Terray, went shouting all over Paris that he would blow up the Controller-General, that he would blow up D'Aiguillon, that he would blow up the ministry. It was the Comte Jean who came to demand from the Farming Committee for his friend Desaint the directorship of Paris, and, when he was told that the post had been already given to the Sieur Chomel, cried out against it :—" As if everyone did not know it was he who had the honour to give a mistress to the King . . . and let them take care not to put him into a temper! "[1]

The scandal this time was too marked and too public. He was advised to go and spend a few months in his marquisate at Lisle in order to learn, as Madame du Barry put it to him, to "turn his tongue seven times in his mouth before speaking." He left in a state of dissatisfaction at not having been sustained by his sister-in-law against the ministers; he returned home in a very bad temper at not having seen his exile abridged by having credit given to him, and, as a sequel to two or three scenes which he had with her, the Roue launched against his former mistress the cruel ballad which he composed or inspired:

> " Woman of shame!
> Why are you so proud with me?
> My Royal Dame!
> Whence comes all your dignity?

[1] Horace Walpole says of Du Barry (Memoirs of the Reign of George III., Vol. II., p. 200) : " He seems to have been a consummate blackguard."—TRANSLATOR.

Madame Du Barry

If you ever get faded, and have to climb down
    In the street,
    You will meet
Some kind " pals " of yours on the town.
    Woman of shame, etc.

  " When the monk, your sire, said,
    Mass to buy you a crust,
And your mother got bread
    By the wages of lust,
You were humble and meek,
    And just as you should be :
Then no more of your cheek
    When you're dealing with me !
Now listen ! be just your old self,
    Or some day you may find yourself sold ;
And, though I love you better than pelf,
    Let me show I can kick, as of old.
    Woman of shame !
Do you think I am broken at last ?
    My Royal Dame !
Don't forget what you were in the past ! " [1]

The fêtes [2] were not discontinued at Luciennes, where around this spring table of the King, who at first had at either side of him only the Maréchale de Mirepoix and the Marquise de Montmorency, came to sit down in succession all the ladies of the Court. In the beginning there were the Duchesse and the Vicomtesse de Laval, then that Comtesse of Choiseul, whose husband was the personal enemy

[1]   original of the ballad, " Drôlesse," is couched in much stronger language than the translation here given of it.—TRANSLATOR.

[2] The " Secret Memoirs " refer to a fête given in March, 1773, by Madame du Barry, at which there were four spectacles and a hundred comedians, singers, and dancers from three theatres. At this fête an armed Cupid came forth from an egg.

of the Duke, then also Mesdames de Valbelle, de Nesle,
d'Avaray de l'Aigle, d'Harville, and that Madame de Crenay
who had been lampooned in some verses:

> " Crenay is a coquette,
> And on light toe she trips,
> And so plump is her waist that she often slips:
> Then Fenelon lifts her in excellent style,
> And each guest applauds with a ringing cheer;
> She is fair and fat and as round as a sphere,—
> But she dances all the whole." [1]

The Duchesse de Mazarin with the Princesse Kinski consented to be half admitted,[2] and, so to speak, remained on
the threshold of the little palace, ready to be replaced by
more illustrious ladies. And so with other and older names
in France. For with time they were *all* bound to " hop " to
the *fetes*. Would the news not go round one day that
Madame de Forcalquier, she who was known as the " Bel-
lissima," was at Choisy, which was the antechamber to
Luciennes? " To see in a grated box the new actress in the
comedy? " " No, madame, she must be supping there."
" Supping! Ah! I'm quite sure she's not. I know what she
thinks, and I'll bet on it against anyone who likes." " Do

[1] " Crenay fait la coquette,
Et veut encore danser,
Sa taille rondelette souvent la fait glisser,
    Notre Fenelon la releve en cadence,
Chacun s'ecrie a l'unisson
Elle est bien grasse, elle est bien ronde
    Mais toujours va qui danse."

[1] Letters of the Marquise du Deffand to Horace Walpole." Paris,
1812. Tome II.

not bet, Madame! There can be nothing more certain."[1] In fact the Duchesse de Forcalquier, who grew indignant, not more than three months before, at being suspected of such infamy, had allowed herself to be enrolled amongst the list of *ladies who supped* with the Du Barry.

For these fine ladies, will Luciennes be what Bellevue was? Will Versailles find in the enchanted palace noble pleasures, charming amusements. No, the Court will meet there only the broad and unrefined diversions of a commonplace household. The mistress of Luciennes will not invoke Racine and Tragedy to distract the ennui of a King's old age. She will not have recourse to the piquant comedies, to the refined operas, to the delightful inventions of Madame de Pompadour. She will not awaken the echoes of Bellevue's past, and the memory of those charming ballets, of those felicitous allegories, of those pretty verses, of that light, lively, warbling music. But she will give dressing-room suppers—bachelors' suppers, where ceremonial, wit, epigrams, improvised couplets, and fashionable recreations will be replaced by noisy mirth and the risky jests of Courtille, from which nothing will be lacking save Ramponneau's face. The Du Barry will have plays acted before the King not by ordinary comedians, but by the comedians of the Boulevard du Temple.

The Du Barry will inaugurate at the Court the repertoire

[1] "Complete Correspondence of Madame du Deffand." By M. de Sainte-Aulaire, Paris, 1866. Tome II.

of the theatre of one Guimard. And the merriest of Colle's comedies, the one that shows least regard for public decency, " Truth in Wine," will afford her the satisfaction of seeing the fine ladies of Versailles blush. Then, during supper, there will be sung by Larivet and his wife such gay couplets that they will embarrass even the Favourite's own female friends. After " Truth in Wine," after the shameful suggestiveness and broad jokes, the Du Barry will introduce the delights of Audinot's " Penny Show," which will one morning astonish all Paris by the unexpected announcement:

" His Majesty's booth comedians will to-day give no performance at the theatre as they are going to Court." And the most vulgar play in Audinot's choice repertoire will end with the " Fricassee," that loose country-dance which the common people dance in public-houses.[1] Vile, ignoble laughs, which will teach the language of the streets, the fashions and the accent of " forest fetes " to this corrupt Court, which as yet had, however, preserved all the graces, and, if we may say so, all the decencies of corruption.

Enboldened by their license, the Du Barry, abandoning through familiarity her fine airs and the position in which good-fortune had placed her, shook off the mask she wore as Favourite, became " La Lange " of former days, and

[1] " Secret Memoirs of the Republic of Letters." Tome VI. At this representation, which took place on the 8th of April, 1771, Madame du Barry amused herself infinitely and laughed with her breast exposed."

from her mouth burst forth the language of her *protegee,*
Madame la Loque, the fishwoman. And the roofs of Versailles, astonished and filled with shame, had to listen to a
woman addressing a King of France in the language of the
gutter. Here was the great evil produced by the King's
intrigue with Madame du Barry: she ruined (deplorable
ruin!) the respect for royalty. In this scandal lay the sin
—that is too light a word—the crime for which Louis XV.
had no remorse, of which the Du Barry's conscience could
not realize the shamefulness, and of which the monarchy
had to endure the penalty. Dreadful and lamentable sample
of the law made for Kings and which condemns them not
to have it in their power to descend to the appetites of their
pleasures, or to compromise the familiarity of their hearts,
without compromising in their persons the human religion
which they represent, the principle of which they are the
image, the dignity which they betoken, royalty itself.

Indeed, by contact with the Du Barry, everything around
the King was debased and invisibly crumbling. The discipline of Versailles was lost, while the curiosity of Paris grew
bolder. The sanctuary of the royal majesty flew open, and
showed the alcove of which the fair Bourbonnaise sportively
drew the curtains.

The people lost faith and illusion when this gay wanton,
excited by champagne, was heard smashing the glass of the
" Oeil de Bœuf." Everywhere in the midst of this royalty,
still standing and almost entire, Madame du Barry works
evil by following her vocation and obeying her instincts as

Madame Du Barry

a courtesan. She is that charming instrument of destruction,—a pretty mistress in a great heritage; and in her philosophy of nature, in her laughter which treats everything familiarly, in her insolent spirit of camaraderie, in her mischievousness and romping sluttishness, so brazen-faced, ingenuous, and charming, in that intolerance of all hierarchies, in that deprecation of all grandeur, in those aggressive outbursts of contempt for the men and women of the Court, there is the groundwork and the fatal vengeance of every woman of pleasure—that curious tendency, like the wantonness of a dreadful child breaking the things with which it plays. One day when, after sipping punch out of a ladle, she put it back into the bowl, the King reproached her for compelling everybody to drink her spittle, and did she not give this reply: " Well, I want everybody to drink my spittle? " [1]

Involuntarily and by her nature she discredits everything that approaches her, everything that touches her. Whether she pushes Zamore's fingers into the Chancellor's peruke, or with her throat in the air gets the Papal Nuncio to present her slippers to her while jumping out of bed in her chemise, she always plays this part of scoffing at, lessening, and lowering to her own tone and her own level, the institutions, the traditions, the qualities, and even the State measures of the French Monarchy. Barriers, venerations,

---

[1] Extract from the " Memoirs of Horace Walpole on the Reign of George III." (year 1771), given in the " Letters of Horace Walpole," published by the Comte de Baillon. Didier, 1812.

the prestige and the solemnity of the representation of the will, of the love even of the King, everything that places the King above humanity even while he is brought into close relations with it, sinks under the follies and caprices of the last of the Royal Favourites. " Let some years pass away, and the crown will be no more," said an Englishman, " than the nightcaps of two lovers." This throne around which Louis XIV. had maintained the etiquette of adultery, this throne in which Madame de Pompadour sat with some remains of decency, will resemble, under the insults and insolences of the Du Barry that cord of Saint Louis on which the courtesan Lacour made the old Duc de la Valliere spit!

And the idea occurs to you to ask yourself whether this daughter of the people who introduces Billingsgate into Versailles was not predestined to be the portress of the revolution in the palace of our Kings, and to open a way for the bloody work of October.

X.

Madame du Barry's Qualities as a "Good-natured Girl of the Town."—Her Family.—Her Daughter, Madame de Boissaisson.—Marriage of the Vicomte Adolphe.—Fresh Attempts of the Favourite to Get into Marie Antoinette's Good Graces.—The Ear-rings worth 700,000 livres.—Project of a Dissolution of the Du Barry's Marriage by the Pope.

BUT, if, by the fatality of her nature, the Favourite did all this injury, if she was guilty of being a courtesan and of involuntarily using her instincts for the ruin of the monarchy, the woman redeems herself by the easy virtues " of a good-natured girl of the town "—we must have recourse to this popular phrase; it is the only one which paints with one touch Madame du Barry. Madame du Barry loved neither vengeance nor spite; and even the books of the Revolution rendered her this much justice: " she did not humiliate even those whom she might have ruined."[1] She compromised with the pamphlets; she punished her enemies merely with roguish tricks. She did not silence people with *lettres de cachet;* she did not send epigrams to the Bastille.

---

[1] " The Gallery of French Dames to serve as a Sequel to the Gallery of the States-General." London, 1790. Madame du Barry is there represented under the name of Elmire.

Madame Du Barry

The mystifier who parodied her just as she was, dressing his mistress as Comtesse du Tonneau,[1] knew beforehand that he did not risk martyrdom. It is she herself who asked pardon for Sophie Arnould, at whose hands she had been subjected to a calumnious attack.[2] Her reign had only one Latude, a Latude in the enjoyment of freedom—Theveneau de Morande, whom she did not insist on having *drowned* or *suffocated,* but whom she bought with a large sum of money.[3] Her resentments and her angers were only out-

[1] " The Countess of the Cask."

[2] " Secret Memoirs of the Republic of Letters." Tome V.

[3] Theveneau de Morande, the author of the *Breast-plated Gazetteer,* had in 1774 forwarded to Madame du Barry from London, where he had taken refuge, the prospectus of a book of which 6,000 copies were printed and which was entitled: " Secret Memoirs of a Public Woman, or Essay on the Adventures of the Comtesse Dub—from her Cradle to the Bed of Honour." 8vo. London. 4 volumes. Two negotiations, conducted by Bellanger and Preaudeau de Chenilly, failed. The Duke determined to send Beaumarchais to treat with the pamphleteer. Beaumarchais had an interview with Theveneau de Morande, who agreed to suppress every edition on the condition that he would receive 32,000 livres in cash, and that a pension of 4,000 livres would be secured to him, of which half would revert to his wife on his death. Every copy was consumed in a brick-kiln in the neighborhood of London, save one, of which the leaves were cut in two, and each half was to remain hidden in the hands of Beaumarchais and of Theveneau de Morande so as to provide against a new publication of this work, in which case the conditions of the agreement were to be null and void. This was the story told to Dutens by Beaumarchais, who declared that the " Summary," the " Anecdotes," in short, all the other books which appeared about Madame du Barry, had no connection with the book of Theveneau de Morande. Had the book been really quite destroyed? (" Memoirs of a Traveller taking a Rest." By Dutens. Bossange, 1806. Tome

burst of childishness which subsided, like her resolutions, like her obstinacies, like her refusals of permission to go to Chanteloup, under the mockery, the laughter, and the pretty sayings of the Marechale de Mirepoix.[1] She was generous as grandly, as foolishly, as a courtesan who is not avaricious. She gave and allowed to be taken everything around her, working with her purse for the advantage of those who had known, served, or pleased her. She had in her heart the devotedness of the people, their natural attachments, the sentiment of the family. She went, every fortnight, to spend a day with her mother, whom she addressed as the Marquise of Montrable,[2] to whom she had given quarters in the convent of Saint Elizabeth as well as a carriage, a country-house, and a little farm-house called the Maison Rouge[3] near Lon-

[1] The story of the whip given by Madame du Barry's chambermaids to the Marquise de Rosen, her former *darling,* who had abandoned her, if the anecdote is true, is but a joke in very bad taste.

[2] The Marquise de Montrable had learned very little of orthography in her new position. Here is a receipt truly curious for a quarter of the pension which her daughter allowed her: "J'ay recu de madame la comtesse du barry par les mens et de denier de monsieur buffants la somme de trois cent livres pour un quartier de la pension quelle a bien voula ma cor det. Le dit quartier echu du 1er Juillet, 1777." Catalogue of Autograph Letters of the 21st of January, 1856.

[3] We find in the accounts of Madame du Barry, who had re-entered into possession of this little estate after her mother's death, a lease of the property entered into with M. and Madame Morgan, commencing the 1st of April, 1792. This is the Morgan denounced by Greive for his counter-revolutionary intrigues.

II.) The "Secret Memoirs" speak in May, 1773, of another book printed at Strasburg, with obscene prints and forming a sequel to the

jumeau. On her mother's death, on the 20th of October,
1788, she assigned for the benefit of the Sieur Rançon de
Montrable, her mother's husband, a life annuity of 2,000
livres, to *recompense* Rançon *for his kind conduct* towards
his spouse. She gave a pension to Madame Quantiny, her
mother's sister; she obtained posts for and pushed on four
of the latter's children. She took with her the last comer, a
little girl, whom she brought up as her daughter, and whom
the public believed to be her child. This was the child christened "little Pierrot" or again "Betsi," whose roguish
face Drouais painted above the door of Luciennes. As long
as her life lasted, we find Madame du Barry in familiar and
helpful relations with her family. A very affectionate letter
of the 24th of August, 1788, dated from Metz and written
by a niece married to the Marquis de Boissaison[1] invites
Madame du Barry, while her husband will be *under the cov-
ering* of the camp, to come and spend some days with her.
She promises her fresh butter, eggs from her hens, sends
her delicious preserves, and ends her letter by saying that
her little Hercule—a name which recalls Brissac—does not
let a day pass without asking her: "When are we going to
return to Luciennes?" But would not this niece be a

---

[1] Revolutionary Tribunals: The Du Barry's "Dossier." National
Archives W' 16.

"Porter of the Carthusians." This book, which entered into details
as to the amours of the King and the Du Barry, would have been
seized, with its printed sheets, engravings and the manuscript, and
nobody would have possessed a copy of it.

daughter of Madame du Barry? No book of the period, I am aware, affirms positively that Madame du Barry was never a mother; and yet M. d'Allonville declares that Madame du Barry had a daughter without knowing who was the father, that she married her with a dowry of 100,000 francs to a nobleman possessed of no means. He declares that in 1838 this daughter and a granddaughter of Madame du Barry resided in Munich, while the grandson (Hercule, without doubt) was a major-general in Russia. M. D'Allonville even mentions the name of the nobleman who was the husband of Madame du Barry's daughter, who appears to have been the Marquis de Boissaisson, an *emigre* during the Revolution.[1]

The injuries done by the Roue to his sister-in-law, Madame du Barry's just resentment, the distance from her person at which she kept him, did not prevent the Comte Jean from recommending himself in some suppliant letters to the Favourite in the name of the past, from soliciting her " good heart " and her credit for the purpose of getting a wife for his son, the Vicomte Adolphe, who had first been a page of the King, then an officer in His Majesty's regiment of infantry, then cornet of Light Horse of the Guard, with the rank of campmaster of cavalry, and who boasted of having in his pocket a commission as first equerry of the King which he had carried off by assault from MM. de Coigny and de Polignac.[2]

[1] " Secret Memoirs." By the Comte D'Allonville. Werdet, 1838. Tome I.
[2] The Vicomte Adolphe had only the promise of the post. The ap-

Madame Du Barry

Many attempts to get the Vicomte Adolphe settled into a great family had already been made by Madame du Barry. At one time, she had taken it into her head to marry him to Mlle. de Bethune; she had been stopped by Louis XV.'s cold reception of this proposal, perhaps because he considered it insolent pretension on the part of the Du Barrys to seek to form an alliance with the Sully family. Then the Favourite fell back on a natural daughter of the King known under the name of Mlle. de Saint Andre; but the negotiations for this marriage were broken off owing to the firmness and plain-speaking of the tutor before they were already far advanced.

It was in consequence of this rupture that the Comte Jean, in a letter which he asked the Favourite to read in her residence at Luciennes, as "in a sentimental conversation," denuding himself for a moment of all prepossessions in her regard, dealt with the important question of his son's marriage. "I have sought," he wrote, "in good faith and with the utmost desire to succeed amongst the girls of rank at the Court. You have partly seen the mortifications which I have experienced." He next avowed that, in spite of his aversion to the girls of the commercial class, he had just as fruitlessly cast his eyes on some opulent families. Then he

---

pointment was prevented by this remark publicly made by the Dauphin: "If he gets this position I will give him something with my boot in the face the first moment he takes off his boots on his arrival." ("Historic Memoirs of Stephanie Louise of Bourbon-Conti." Paris, Floreal, Year VI. Tome I.)

came back to the two matches which had been broken off; he reproached his sister-in-law, after the marks of satisfaction shown by the King to the Abbe Terray and to Bertin, when they spoke of the alliance with Mlle. de Bethune, with not having to give immediate results to these overtures, and with having thereby herself provoked the coldness which had subsequently come over Louis XV. He next spoke to her about Mlle. de Saint-Andre, the daughter of the King, and about Morfil, Boucher's model, " who, on losing the hope of becoming Madame du Barry's niece, had even abandoned the desire to please by denying herself every sort of finery in the interior of the convent." He expressed keen regret for the loss of this match, which would have brought 24,000 livres a year and an estate of the same value, and all the more because " although it might have been, as a fortune, over that which she saw in the Rue de la Jussienne and below that which he might have got in the Rue Neuve-des-Petits-Champs, his position did not permit a dismemberment on his part in order to make a brilliant career for his son by marrying him." Finally, the marriage with Mlle. de Saint Andre had this further advantage, that she was the only person, wrote the man anxious about the future, who could *preserve for them a corner of modesty* in the Dauphin and prevent that Prince from one day yielding to the impulses of hatred.[1]

Madame du Barry, who at heart was interested in getting

[1] Letter of the Comte Jean du Barry, published by the *Revue de Paris,* year 1836, Tome XXXV.

her nephew married, in propping herself up by an alliance with a great family, in feeling that she had beside her in that world of the Court a young woman on whom she could count, set out on a quest, passed in review the matches of Paris and Versailles, announcing her intention to do something for the bride. She had not succeeded in finding anything when her sisters-in-law " Chon " and " Bitschi " discovered a young lady in Tournon. She belonged to the family of Du Vivarais, which happened to be in very poor circumstances, as there were a great number of children, but it was well-connected and related to the Soubises, and the daughter was exceedingly beautiful. The marriage was approved by the father and the son, and the marriage-articles were drawn up. By the first, second, third, fourth, fifth, and sixth articles, the Comte Jean made a gift to his son of the county of Lille Jourdain and the forest of Bouconne. By the seventh article, the Comte and Comtesse de Tournon settled a sum of 60,000 livres, as a dowry on their daughter.[1] By the fourteenth article the Comtesse du Barry made, as well to Mlle. de Tournon as to the Vicomte Adolphe, to the exclusion of the children to be born, a gift of the sum of 200,000 livres to be invested for their benefit in the acquisition of landed estate or in mortgages or preference shares.

[1] The suit of the Comte du Barry with the Comtesse de Tournon, containing the notes of the evidence on both sides. Amsterdam, 1781. The dowry was never paid, the Comte states in his note, which goes so far as to say that on her marriage the bride was without everything, and that he had to supply linen, clothes, and effects.

Madame Du Barry

The marriage was celebrated at Saint Roch.[1] After leaving the church the married pair had lunch at the Controller-General's, and immediately started for Compiegne, where the presentation was to take place. This marriage took place, at the moment when Madame du Barry, always full of the idea of disarming Marie-Antoinette and given up to the

[1] This union ended in a tragic fashion. In 1778 the Vicomte went with his wife and his sister-in-law, Mlle. de Tournon, to Bath. He had determined to accompany Lord Rice, an Irish nobleman, with whom he had for eight years been on terms of intimate friendship. The Vicomte du Barry and Lord Rice had been on the most friendly footing when, one night, after midnight, they were both seen rushing out of the house, followed by the Vicomtesse, who, having vainly attempted to reach them, called out to them with loud shrieks. A carriage conveyed themselves and their seconds outside the city, and it was agreed, while waiting for daybreak, that the two adversaries, placed at a distance of twenty-five paces, out of which they were not to move, armed with their two pistols and their swords, should advance towards one another, should use their weapons so that it was to be understood the victorious combatant might finish his adversary, even when he had fallen on the ground. At daybreak the Vicomte jumped down from the carriage, fired first, and pierced Lord Rice's thigh. The latter responded with a pistol-shot, which passed through the Vicomte du Barry's breast, and advanced upon him, sword in hand. The Vicomte exclaimed: " I ask for life from you." " I give it to you," replied Lord Rice, who saw him at the same moment sink on the ground and vomit forth a torrent of blood and expire. The seconds were not informed of the motives for the duel. Lord Rice, when questioned by Dutens, gave two or three different versions of the cause of the quarrel; the general opinion was that the Vicomte du Barry had been jealous of Rice. On her return to France, the Vicomtesse du Barry got permission from the King to erect into the barony of Tournon some fiefs which she acquired in Corsica, and changed her name. At this insult, Du Barry, the Roue, wanted her to take his name—her husband's name. She replied by a rather sad note, in which she said she did not know at first the

167

dream of a reconciliation with the future Queen of France, in spite of continual disappointments, pursued her object with obstinate determination, with the tenacity of a self-willed child whom nothing can repulse. She was impelled at the same time by a certain sentiment of respect, rather fantastic in its contemptuous nature and by a natural fear of the future and by the necessities of her present situation. In view of the King's ennui, the incurable, splenetic ennui, which had poisoned his whole life, and which was becoming, in the summer of this year 1773, blacker than ever, Madame du Barry felt that she no longer brought sufficient dissipation to her royal lover; she wished, fearing the worst, to distract Louis XV. with the youthfulness of her two daughters-in-law, with the animation and gay laughter of the Dauphiness, which she knew amused the old King. So Madame du Barry had appealed to Mercy-Argenteau to induce the Dauphiness to testify to Louis XV. the desire she would have to accompany the King in the little trips he was accustomed to make to his country houses. Before attempting this step the Favourite had assured herself of the friendly

---

role that Madame du Barry filled with Louis XV., accused her husband of having inherited his father's vices and his love of play, which had ruined him, and attributed his death to a scuffle the result of an uncertain combination which had not turned out lucky, and for which one of the parties to it demanded satisfaction from the other through anger at having been baulked in his desires. Then in order the better to get rid of her name she married again. "Memoirs of a Traveller taking a Rest." By Dutens. Vol. II. "Summary of the Memories of the Mlle. de Tournon, Widow of Viscomte du Barry, in response to that of her father-in-law, the Comte du Barry."

disposition of the Comtesse de Provence,[1] and in concert
with D'Aiguillon she had gained over to her projects a lady
who ruled Madame Adelaïde and would have a powerful influence in counteracting the devout antipathies and irreconcilable hatreds of the Royal aunts for "the clique."
Through the influence of Madame de Narbonne, to whom
the Mayoralty of Bordeaux had been promised for her son,
and an interest in the approaching renewal of the lease of
the farming rights for herself, Madame Adelaïde was led
to treat Madame du Barry better, and was likely by her example to drag the Dauphiness in her train. Thus, beguiled
and turned round all of a sudden, Madame Adelaïde had already written a letter to the King, in which she assured him
of the efforts which she was going to bring to bear on the
minds of her children in order to please him in everything,
a letter to which the King replied that he was grateful to the
Princess for the marks of her affection and submissiveness,
but that he counted little on this attempt with the Dauphin,
who " showed an estrangement of the most marked character towards the fair sex." Chon, the sister-in-law, the po-

---

[1] As the attitude of Marie Antoinette towards Madame du Barry
was dignified, so that of Madame was basely temporizing. The Comtesse de Provence spoke to Madame du Barry at her table, at her
presentations, had received her in the interior of her apartment at
the fete given to her by the Comtesse de Valentinois, paid attentions
to her, in short, encouraged in those meannesses by Monsieur, with
whom Marie Antoinette, in the liveliness of her indignation, could not
avoid making scenes over her duplicity and her lack of dignity, vainly
striving to get rid of the "infernal household of D'Aiguillon and the
Du Barry."

litical Maitre Jacques of the cabal, having become hostile to the Duc d'Aiguillon, laughed at all these *shufflings,* and never ceased repeating in every tone, with the bantering irony peculiar to her, that, by her incessant and clumsy persistence, Madame du Barry would only irritate the Dauphin and the Dauphiness, and would end by being[1] more badly treated by them. On the first step being taken by Madame Adelaïde towards a reconciliation with Madame du Barry, the Dauphin made a display of temper, the gentle Madame Victoire openly revolted against Madame de Narbonne's negotiation, and the diplomatic Comtesse de Narbonne abandoned the Favourite by ill-treating her. In view of the attitude of the royal family, Madame Adelaïde, confused and a little ashamed, acknowledged that she had been deceived, led into error, and declared that she would prevent the Comtesse de Narbonne from ever speaking to her on that subject.

Thereupon d'Aiguillon got enraged, declared that he had been betrayed by everybody, and the Favourite fell into deep dejection at seeing, as a consequence of the ill-success of her little intrigue, the presentation of the Vicomtesse, her niece, adjourned and showing very little prospect of being accomplished.

In fact, the presentation of the Vicomtesse Adolphe, which ought to have taken place on the 25th of July, was put off till the following Sunday, the 1st of August, in the hope of finding some means of obtaining a favourable reception

[1] " Secret Correspondence between Maria Theresa and the Comte Mercy-Argenteau." By Arneth. Didot, 1875. Tome II.

for the person making the presentation, and for the person presented.

At last, on the 1st of August, in the afternoon, after the salutation, the Comtesse du Barry, accompanied by the Duchesse de Laval and the Comtesse de Montmorency, presented her niece to the King. Then, in the midst of an immense concourse of people, who had come to Compiegne in order to see and compare and contrast the beauty of the niece with the beauty of the aunt, a crowd making it almost impossible to pass through the ante-chambers, the Comtesse and the Vicomtesse du Barry went up to the Dauphin's apartments. The Prince was in the embrasure of a window, chatting with somebody, *playing the devil's tattoo* on the panes. At an announcement from an usher of the chamber, the Prince turned his head round, seemed not to have noticed the two women, and continued his conversation and his drumming without giving the embrace.[1] Marie Antoinette made a slight bow to the Favourite, to the young bride, and to the ladies who accompanied her, but did not speak to anyone. It was the same way in the evening at play, where it was the etiquette that the women who had been presented should attend. It was the same way next morning at the toilet, where it was still the etiquette that the women presented should pay their court. In the evening no more than in the morning[2] did the Dauphiness

[1] "The English Spy." London: John Adamson, 1784. Tome I.

[2] Marie Antoinette, in the apprehension of some scolding from her mother, tried to obtain pardon for her silence in a letter which she

address a word to any of the women. Marie Antoinette
pushed things further; although all the ladies who were
introduced and who danced were admitted as a matter of
right to the Dauphiness's ball, the Princess never wished
her lady-in-waiting to have permission to call the Vicomte
Adolphe.

The Roue, who had been refused admission at the Comtesse's door, had only obtained permission to spend two days
at Versailles. He was only to see his sister-in-law one moment during the second day of Louis XV.'s small-pox.

After such a complete humiliation, so many affronts, it
might have been supposed that the Favourite would give up
the task of attempting to overcome the Dauphiness's aversion. No; it was nothing of the kind; on the contrary, the
unhappy Favourite clung more and more to the illusion of
making herself one day agreeable to Marie Antoinette, of
obtaining at last, through her own lips, that precious
exchange of words so humbly and so obstinately solicited.
She did not see that by this incessant and continual persecution she rendered the Dauphiness more hostile, less tractable,
as her sister-in-law Chon was constantly saying. In Septem-

wrote on the 3rd of August: "My dear Mother,—The presentation
of young Madame du Barry passed off very well. A moment before
she came to see me I was told that the King had not said a word
either to the aunt or the niece; I have done likewise. But, moreover,
I can well assure my dear mother that I have received them very
politely; everybody who was at my house has agreed that I had
neither embarrassment nor eagerness in seeing them go away. The
King has surely not been dissatisfied, for he has been in very good
temper with us all the evening."

ber, 1773, on the occasion of the harsh letter addressed by the King to the Dauphiness soliciting the recall of the Comtesse de Gramont,[1] when the news was brought to the Comtesse du Barry that Marie Antoinette believed the letter inspired or dictated by her, she immediately sent for Mercy-Argenteau. In this interview, she declared with the greatest warmth that she had no knowledge of the request for the recall, she even offered to use all her authority with the King to procure the Comtesse's return, asking as a recompense only the assurance of the good-will the Dauphiness would feel towards her. The mind of the Favourite was yoked to a single idea, was perpetually in search of a means, an invention, a stratagem, to make the Dauphiness abandon her estrangement from her person. In the month of November, she imagined that a letter of the King might make an impression on the Dauphiness and conquer her prejudices. The letter was waived on the suggestion of Mercy-Argenteau that the Dauphiness would be annoyed when she had no doubt of the pressure exercised over her feelings, and the Favourite sought a new combination. The Favourite was not to be discouraged by

---

[1] Here is the letter of the King to the Dauphiness, as Mercy-Argenteau reports it: "You are very ill advised, my dear daughter, in asking for the return of Madame de Gramont. This can only be suggested to you by the Choiseul party, by the members of which you are surrounded. The access which you give them does not agree with the wise counsels which you receive from the Empress; therefore, what I believe it is best to do for you with regard to your request is not to speak of it to anyone."

coldnesses, or disdains, or repulses, or the exclusion of the Vicomtesse du Barry from the King's carriages while hunting, or the sad reception quite recently given to Mlle. de Fumel.[1] A softening in the glance, a trifling lack of hospitality in the attitude, a less severe treatment than usual, made the poor woman return to her *fad*. She said to herself that now the Dauphiness abstained from talking about her in a mortifying fashion, she strove to rob her contempt of the character of aversion, and finally discovered in the *negative treatment* of Marie Antoinette, according to the expression of the Empress-Queen's ambassador, a vague pledge of future reconciliation.

And, in order to arrive at the realization of her secret dreams, did not the Du Barry's imagination and tact as a courtesan suggest to her in January, 1774, this corrupting device? A jeweller possessed ear-rings formed of four brilliants of extraordinary size and beauty estimated to be worth 700,000 livres. Knowing the Dauphiness's passion for precious stones, Madame du Barry persuaded the Comte de Noailles to look at the marvellous diamonds, and to tell Her Royal Highness that if they pleased her, she need not be embarrassed either about the price or the payment, because the means would be found to get the King to make a present

[1] There was a proposal for a marriage between Elie du Barry, the youngest of Du Barry's three brothers, with Mlle. de Fumel, a wealthy lady of high position. "On her presentation," says Mercy-Argenteau, "the reception given by the Dauphiness, as at the presentation of the Vicomtesse Adolphe, was very cold and silent."

of them to her. The Dauphiness simply answered that she had no idea of increasing her store of diamonds.[1]

The Abbe Terray remained the cashier, with coffers always open, and money always ready for the whims, the fancies, the extravagant expenditure of the Favourite. He gave the Comte Jean money for play, for keeping his mistress Madame Murat in luxury, for a dowry to her son the Vicomte Adolphe; and in the scarcity of the Exchequer he found money continually for all the Du Barrys in the world. Destitute of every great political idea, without a higher view of humanity, the Abbe had only the ambition to accumulate honours, prerogatives, and ministries. It was necessary for him to add to the office of Controller-General the post of *Director and Orderer-General of Buildings, Gardens, Arts, Academies, and Royal Manufactories*, and when he had snatched this immense governing authority from the Marquis de Merigny, he wanted again to carry off the *small things* from the Duc de Richelieu. Insatiable, he kept mining under the Duc d'Aiguillon, whom he laboured to place on terms of coldness with the mistress, and openly coveted the seals. In order to obtain all he wanted, he saw himself obliged to grant everything. And even his poor imagination devised plans for securing the attachment of Madame du Barry, for making her the docile instrument of his incessant claims through a gratitude still greater than that which money creates. It was thus that he took up the idea, that

[1] "Secret Correspondence between Maria Theresa and the Comte Mercy-Argenteau. By Arneth. Didot, 1875. Tome II.

he gave a body to the chimera presented for a moment by the Chancellor and the Duc d'Aiguillon to the Favourite's fancy[1]—the dissolution of her marriage with the Comte and a marriage of conscience with the King.[2] He drew up in writing a consultation of which this is a resume:

" Madame du Barry represents to His Holiness that, little acquainted with canonical rules, she only ascertained, since the celebration of her marriage with the Comte Guillaume du Barry, that it was forbidden for a woman to marry the brother of a man with whom she has lived. She confesses with all the sorrow of a *repentant soul* that she had weaknesses for the Comte Jean du Barry, her husband's brother; that she had happily been warned in time of the *incest* which she was about to commit, and that her *conscience, now enlightened,* did not permit her to live with her new spouse; that, therefore, the crime has not yet been committed; and she supplicates His Holiness to be kind enough to relieve her of such a *scandalous* alliance."

By amusing and luring with this fantastic dream the credulous creature, and by talking to her about interviews with the Nuncio, the ironical Abbe entered into the Favourite's intimate confidence, and saw himself already the directing minister—the Minister of all the Ministries—a species of Choiseul.

[1] The Memoir of Linguet for " Simon Sommer, Carpenter, Landau," by discussing whether the divorce could be legitimately allowed, was a means of feeling the pulse of public opinion, perhaps an attempt to get a general law passed, of which Madame du Barry ought to have taken advantage.

[2] " Memorial concerning the Administration of Finances under the Abbe Terray." London, 1776.

XI.

Intrigues of Women Seeking to dispossess Madame du Barry of the King's Heart.—Madame Louise, the Carmelite.—The Chancellor passing over to the Devotee Party.—The Physique of Old Louis XV. —The Remark of the Surgeon, La Martiniere.—The Lent of 1773.— Men Struck Dead by the King's side.—Louis XV. falls ill at Trianon. —The Intrigues of the Aiguillonists and the Anti-Aiguillonists around the Death-Bed.—Dismissal of Madame du Barry.

THE possession of Louis XV.'s heart was not a tranquil possession. Madame du Barry had to be protecting herself every moment against the jobberies of the antechamber to supplant her, the subterranean plots of very illustrious pimps, shameless plans making a courtier's fortune depend on the accession of a new mistress.

In 1771 Hardy speaks of the negotiations to give the Princess of Monaco to the King; in default of her, a young lady named Smith; and lastly a third person the secret of whose name is guarded.

A very pretty and very graceful creature, the wife of a musician of the King's bed-chamber, Madame Beche, created for some time very serious obstacles in the Favourite's path.[1]

[1] "Secret Correspondence, Political and Literary." London, John Adamson. Tome I.

Madame Du Barry

Another lady, a Dutchwoman, Madame Pater, who had become Countess of Newkerke, and whose beauty had, ten years before, caused a revolution in Paris, was pushed forward by the Duc de Duras,[1] a gentleman of the bed-chamber, who, it was said, received from Chanteloup instructions from his friend the Duc de Choiseul. The intrigue was skilfully and secretly carried on. The marriage, according to the Protestant rite, of the Pater was dissolved, and she was to be united to the King by secret nuptials. And when the Du Barry was warned, what hand did she find? The hand of D'Aiguillon drawing up and sketching instructions for the Dutchwoman in her intimate relations with the King, instructions in which is found a little of the Machiavellism of the " Dangerous Liaisons." A scene followed, in which Madame du Barry, with the vivacity of speech which was natural to her, reproached her ally, her lover, for his treason. She recalled to him that she had pushed him into the ministry in spite of the general reprobation, that she had maintained him in the office of Foreign Affairs, in spite of the King, saying after the partition of Poland: " If Choiseul had been there, it would not have happened," that she had in fact *saved him from the executioner*.[2] However, Madame du Barry had now, in all the feminine ambushes prepared

---

[1] Madame du Barry put the Duc de Duras outside the door of her apartment, saying that he had not only presented the Pater to His Majesty, but *had held the candle*, and for that reason she begged him no longer to put his foot in her abode.

[2] " The Annals of Louis XV." A. Villefranche at the Widow Liberty's, 1782. Second Part.

against her, the surprise of finding behind women her best
friends. The Abbe Terray himself, the man who appeared
the most attached to her fortune, had placed near the Favourite one of his bastards, Madame d'Amerval, whose
youth, giddiness, and childishness amused Madame du
Barry. It was at the moment when the Abbe exhorted the
Favourite, while awaiting the dissolution of her marriage, to
follow the example of Madame de Pompadour, to yield to
the physical caprices of the King, softly urging her to put
La d'Amerval into the bed of Louis XV. But Madame du
Barry had the instinct that, under the cloak of a passing
fancy, the minister Bonneau was slyly raising up a rival
against her.[1] Finally, in her own family, in the person of
her niece, the beautiful Madame Adolphe du Barry, she had
to fear an instrument of ruin worked by the Comte Jean,[2]
who, always ambitious of governing the kingdom, believed
that he was more easily master of his daughter-in-law than
of his sister-in-law. And there again did not Madame du
Barry find herself associated in the Roue's plans with the
Comte d'Aiguillon, whom people accused to the aunt of infidelities with the niece?[3]

[1] "Memoirs concerning the Administration of Finances under the
Ministry of the Abbe Terray." London, 1786.

[2] When people spoke to Madame du Barry of the plans of the
Comte Jean and of the impression made on the King by the beauty
of Mlle. de Tournon, the Favourite said gaily that "the office of
the King's mistress would not pass at least out of the family." But
at heart she felt very uneasy.

[3] Of infidelities the Duc d'Aiguillon was very capable, but of machinations to overthrow the Favourite it is far less credible that he

Madame Du Barry

But more than all the light women of the Court and the city there was to be dreaded on behalf of Madame du Barry a more dangerous woman: this was Louis XV.'s daughter, Madame Louise the Carmelite, who, under the mantle of Saint Theresa, sent to her for the occasion of making her vows,[1] wanted to rule France from the depths of her cell—Madame Louise, with whom the Chancellor, deserting Luciennes, went every eight days to communicate.

The great friendships between the *cousins* had grown cold. The Favourite had not been able to obtain from the Chancellor the pardon of the bankrupt Billard, the nephew of Billard du Monceau. Then Maupeou had not been without knowing of D'Aiguillon's secret attempts to re-establish the Parliament on the assurance of the Princes that he would be *whitewashed;* he was not ignorant of the support given to these attempts by Madame du Barry up to the day when she saw that the King, glad to be rid of the " black robes," determined to keep near him the man who had delivered him from them.[2] The result was coldness and almost hostility between the Minister and the Favourite. But, apart from any little grievances which he

---

[1] "Life of Madame Louise of France." By the Abbe Proyart Perisse Freres. 1860. Tome I.

[2] "Anecdotes about the Comtesse du Barri." London, 1775.

---

was guilty, and very slight credit is to be given to those stories, which are belied by the courageous attachment of the Duke to the Du Barry when she had fallen into disgrace.

LOUISE-MARIE OF FRANCE

To face page 180

could have against the mistress, Maupeou was above all
driven to withdraw from her and from her party by
his knowledge of humanity, by the presentiment that
in the Bourbon growing old religion was quite ready
to reappear. And he thought that, at the present
moment, it was more useful to him to be on the side of
the confessor than on the side of the mistress. So the Chancellor played the devotee, denouncing now the ministers
who were dragged at the feet of this woman of loose morals,
who lived only with comedians, singers, jugglers, all people with talents which brought them ill-repute and reprobation. Sustained by the Chancellor, Madame Louise assumed
more authority every day. The King often came to see her,
and at each of his visits Madame du Barry trembled. At
the beginning of 1772, the two of them, Madame Louise and
the Chancellor, had even arranged a marriage between the
King and the Archduchess Maria Elizabeth, sister of the
Emperor, she who had said that she would never marry the
King of France. And on the 25th of January, Madame du
Barry, seeing the King starting for Saint-Denis, flung herself at his feet, said to him that she knew her ruin was determined upon, that she preferred to receive her *conge* from
the mouth of the King than to have the humiliation of receiving it from the Black Cabal, that the Chancellor and the
Archbishop were knaves,[1] and prevented by this scene the

[1] " Journal of Events as they came to my Knowledge." By Hardy.
National Library. Manuscripts. French Supplement, 6680.

visit of the King. Later on, it was again Madame Louise
and the Chancellor, who, playing upon a caprice of the King,
filled Louis XV. for a moment with the desire to marry the
Princess de Lamballe, and drew on Madame du Barry, when
she jested with the King about the report of this marriage,
the severe rejoinder: "Why, I might do much worse."

The proposed marriages did not take place, but the action
of the Carmelite on the King remained powerful, and became greater as the years accumulated on Louis XV.
There was, above all, each year, an epoch which was
always a critical time, Easter week, when every effort
was made in order that, according to the expression of
Madame Louise, "the good God should take possession
of her father's heart[1] in order that the King should be
induced to go to Communion." In vain did the Favourite
make the gay remark, "Well, if His Majesty makes his
Easter duty, I'll make mine."[2] She spent no less than an
entire fortnight in a state of mortal apprehension.

The King was growing old; and age, years, the fatigue of
life, the weariness of the soul, in place of appeasing his passions, only irritated the capriciousness of his desires. That
physical obsession, which takes possession of certain old
men, made its prey of Louis XV. with advancing years. The
love which had filled his head and his body was no longer

---

[1] An expression of Madame Louise's letter when she learned about
the Du Barry's dismissal from her father's bedside.

[2] "Anecdotes about the Comtesse du Barri." London, 1775.

more than an appetite and a brutality of his heart; and he seemed no longer to have living within him anything but furious and half-dead desires. . . . For a moment, however, after Madame de Pompadour's death, the King entered into a sort of Platonic *liaison* with a charming woman, the Comtesse de Seran, whose tastes he gallantly consulted by having a suite of apartments furnished for her use in blue.[1] For some months there was a discreet, respectful relationship, an interchange of polite language, pleasant chats which had all the charm of familiarity, court paid to the lady with those graces and those courtesies so natural to Louis XV. when he wished to please. It might be said that a rejuvenescence took place in the King's thoughts, a return to his first amours[2] with the Comtesse de Toulouse; and the Court believed that this was the commencement of one of those liaisons which border on love without quitting friendship, one of those tender, delightful kinds of intercourse which make even an old man's soul amorous. But this Platonism of Louis XV. was quickly killed by the Du Barry's caresses, those caresses of the brothel, attacking only the physical side of love and leading into the rut of animalism. Unsatiated, the King went from Madame du Barry to others, and from caprice to caprice, exhausting love without exhausting temptation, tormented, restless, burning, trembling, and interrupting his pleasures only to throw him-

[1] "Memoirs of a Father." By Marmontel. Paris, 1804. Tome III.
[2] Nous revenons toujours a nos premiers amours.—TRANSLATOR.

self into religious acts which he made his female flatterers share in. In this fever, wine, punch transported by Madame du Barry from London drawing-rooms to the supper of her own rooms in the palace,[1] every stimulant, was used by the King, sustained him, lent him the energy to keep him from growing old. Between the mistress and the lover there was no longer any bond save that of habit and sensuality, stripped of every bond of mind, stripped of even all the decent coquetry and all the modest elegance that had attached the King to Madame de Pompadour. And just picture to yourself, Madame de Pompadour with her shepherdess's costume, her straw hat, her ribbons, her beauty in fitting attire, her charming veils; then see the Du Barry in the costume which restores youthfulness to the King, in her disguise as a Bacchante,[2] half-naked under gauze, and her neck brazenly exposed,—you will have a representation of the two amours of the King.

In the meantime, the King was more than sixty years old. These amorous excesses had produced in the case of the old man ailments the nature of which he communicated to his principal surgeon, La Martiniere. Louis XV. went to his consultations, conformed with his prescriptions, even made him sleep for several months in his own bed-room. And one night in the month of May, 1773—of that month the whole

[1] " The Breast-plated Gazetteer or Scandalous Anecdotes of the Court of France." Printed a hundred leagues from the Bastille, at the Sign of Liberty, 1781. " The Breast-plated Gazetteer " goes further.

[2] " Anecdotes about the Comtesse du Barri." London, 1775.

of which Louis XV. would not see next year—Madame du Barry's elderly lover, talking about the sad decay of his faculties, ended by saying with a sigh: " I see that I am no longer young, that I must put on a break." " Sire," replied La Martiniere with his plain-speaking, " you will do better to unyoke."

The Lenten sermons preached by the Abbe de Beauvais at the Court during the Holy Week of the year 1773 made a deep impression on the King's mind. Suddenly there fell, in this chapel of Versailles, on those lost fine ladies, on those pandering courtiers, the bold language of an obscure man, who flagellated everybody's turpitudes, who dared to mount up to the King's person, assigning to Louis XV. and his concubine this courageous Biblical allusion: " In short this monarch (Solomon), sated with sensual indulgence, tired from having exhausted with his withered senses every sort of pleasure that surrounds a throne, ended by seeking for a new sort in the *vile remains of public license.*" To the indignation of the courtiers, to the complaints of Madame du Barry so pitilessly pointed at, Louis XV. contented himself with answering that the Abbe de Beauvais was doing his business.

Another sermon had a more decided effect on Louis XV., returning day and night to his terrified imagination. It was a sermon on Death, at which the young preacher protected by Madame Louise, reducing to nothingness that list of centenarians which had just been given by the editor of the " Gazette de France " in order to fill the King with illusions, and to make him believe in a far greater longevity in his own century than in past centuries, brutally destroyed the security brought by this lying adulator, showed the King the Death of the Eighteenth Century leaning over the bedside of the men of his age. Then he brought back and recalled to the King's memory the death of the Duke of Burgundy, the death of the Dauphin, the death of the Dauphiness, the death of the Queen, the deaths of beings who had been dearest to him, of his mistresses whom he did not name, but whom he recalled as having been carried off in the flower of their age, letting him understand that his turn had long since arrived, and stamping and driving into the brain of this Bourbon, haunted since youth by the disturbing dream of nothingness, the fixed thought of an approaching end.[1]

Thus penetrated and beset by those words, by those recollections, by those menaces, by those predictions of death, the King also reflected with a sense of dread that he was in his sixty-third year, a time regarded as a climacteric date fatal to old men.[2] Then there happened to take place around Louis XV. a succession of startlingly tragic deaths. The ambassador of Genoa, Sorba, whom he was accustomed to see every day, died suddenly. D'Armentieres followed

[1] For a moment it was said that the Abbe Beauvais had fallen into disgrace. The contrary happened. The Abbe de Beauvais was nominated Bishop of Seney, and, in the Lent of 1774, when he again preached at Court, His Majesty laughingly challenged him to fulfil the engagement he had made to preach at Court in the Lent of 1776, although he was a Bishop.

[2] "Secret Anecdotes about the Comtesse du Barri." 1775.

Sorba very closely.   The Abbe de la Ville, the instrument of
Choiseul's ruin, coming to thank him for the place of Director of Foreign Affairs, was struck with apoplexy under
the King's eyes.   Lastly, one evening, when Louis XV. was
playing picket with Madame du Barry, and the Marquis de
Chouvelin, that old friend and former associate in his pleasures, sat propped up against the back of his arm-chair,
Madame du Barry, raising her eyes, said: " What a grimace
you are making, Monsieur de Chouvelin," whereupon the
King turned round: Chouvelin fell dead at his feet.[1]

The Lent of 1774 came round, and a remark which fell
from the terrible mouth of the Abbe de Beauvais agitated
the King's mind like a summons from God.   The young
preacher had just hurled against the walls of the chapel of
Versailles, the menace of the prophet: " Forty days more,
and Nineveh will be destroyed! "[2]

On her side, Madame du Barry, superstitious like all
women of pleasure of her kind, was devoured by vague
anxieties and secret presentiments, so that she several times
allowed this remark to escape from her before her intimate
friends: " I would be glad if this nasty month of April
had passed."   This was the month when the Almanac of
Liege for the year 1774 announced that " a great lady who
played a role at a foreign Court would cease to do so."

---

[1] " Secret Memoirs of the Republic of Letters."   Tome VII.

[2] In the " Conversations of the Other World," Louis XV., speaking to the Prince of Conde, says: " You know well, cousin, that it
was that cursed sermon of Maundy Thursday that killed me."

Madame Du Barry

The King now spoke about his sickly state of health and the possibility of his death, and sometimes, at the end of his remarks, about " the frightful account we would have to render to the Supreme Being for the employment of the life which he has bestowed upon us in this world."[1] The politicians, foreseeing the approaching entrance of the confessor on the scene, under the pretext that the Abbe Maudoux's sight was very weak, strove to replace that ecclesiastic, who was opposed to intrigue and devoted to Marie Antoinette, by a more pliable confessor.

The Favourite, of whose dismissal before six months D'Aiguillon himself had given an intimation to Mesdames,[2] the Favourite, who realized the instability of her position, and who knew that she could only hold her own by dragging the King's mind out of the blackness of his thoughts, set her wits to work to find voluptuous distractions for him. She had triumphed in the Lent of 1773 by giving orders for the performance of an erotic opera. She tried to kill the action of the Lent of 1774 on the remorseful feelings of the King by organizing a little pleasure-trip to Trianon in the closing days of the month of April.

On the 27th of April, the King, who had arrived the previous night at Trianon, felt unwell, he could not follow the

[1] " Secret Correspondence between Maria Theresa and the Comte Mercy-Argenteau." Didot, 1875. Tome I.

[2] " Complete Correspondence of Madame du Deffand." By Sainte Aulaire. Levy, 1866. Tome —.

chase on horseback, and when he alighted from his carriage on his return complained of a violent headache.[1]

He retired to Madame du Barry's apartments, imagining it was indigestion; but his illness grew worse, and in the night he sent for Lemonnier, his principal physician. Lemonnier found the King feverish, but no symptom of a nature to cause uneasiness. Madame Du Barry, dreading the weakness of the King's mind, that *terror of the devil* which was now awakened in him by every attack on his health, sought to prevail on him to get nursed at Trianon without giving notice to the Royal family, and she was aided and sustained in her desire by the Duc d'Aumont, the first gentleman of the Bed-chamber. The King's indisposition was known during the day at Versailles. The Royal family did

---

The story of the passing fancy to which the King's death was attributed is told in these terms by the Abbe Beaudeau: "During the last days of April, the King was at Trianon with the Du Barry. While out walking he saw a little girl gathering grass for the cows she was minding. He saw that she had very fine eyes. He came over to her, and lifted up her head-dress and her hair. When she had been cleaned up, the King thought she would be 'charming' if she were dressed as a fine lady. 'Well! let us dress her.' Here is their little peasant dressed like a lady with rouge and patches. She is truly 'charming.' 'Let us make her sup with us. Her embarrassment will amuse us.' Meanwhile, her brother died of smallpox; next day she caught it, and died of it on Saturday. And there is the tale or the history." Let us say that nothing is less proved than this story of the King and the little cowherdess, as Beaudeau pretends. Voltaire informs us that there was at this time an epidemic of smallpox in the neighbourhood, and the King might very simply and very naturally have fallen a victim to it.

not run the risk of coming to see the King, but the Dauphin despatched to his grandfather the surgeon La Martiniere, an enemy of the Du Barry, who had exercised a certain influence over the King's mind since those occasions when he slept in Louis XV.'s bed-room the year before.

La Martiniere, having reached Trianon on Thursday, April 28th, had no trouble, with his imperative and abrupt style of speaking, in triumphing over the invalid's vacillating disposition. He prevailed on the King to set out as soon as the carriages had arrived. He himself watched the preparations for the journey; and the King, swathed in his morning-gown, was put into a carriage and conveyed at a walking pace to Versailles into the midst of the Court, within reach of the Church.

The King, on his arrival, was carried up to bed, received the Royal family, but only for an instant, and sent them away, telling the Dauphin not to come back till he sent for him. Then he spent the rest of the evening with Madame du Barry.

The night of the 28th was bad. The King had fever and some hallucinations; he began to be frightened by his condition. The doctors, Lemonnier and La Martiniere, decided on the morning of the 29th that the King should be bled, and asked the patient to let other doctors be brought in, with a view to opening a permanent consultation. The King, at Madame du Barry's suggestion, named Bordeu, the Favourite's doctor, and Lorry, the Duc d'Aiguillon's doctor.

The news of the bleeding produced a great impression

at Court. The antechamber was filled with courtiers, who entered the patient's bed-chamber along with the doctors summoned for the consultation.

The doctors, still ignorant of the King's malady, announced that there would be a second bleeding in the afternoon and a third bleeding during the night or on the following day, if the second did not free the King from his headache.

"A third bleeding," said the King; "but in that case it must be some disease. . . . I would be glad if they could avoid doing it to me."

A third bleeding was not only for the King a sign of a grave malady; it was a promise of victory for the Choiseul party, a promise of defeat for the Du Barry party. The *anti-Aiguillonists,* the *anti-Barryites,* began to have hopes for their political views of a return to God through the terror inspired by this bleeding; the *Aiguillonists* and the *Barryites* began to fear that it would lead to the mistress's expulsion,—so much so that D'Aiguillon, Richelieu, and the Duc d'Aumont circumvented Lorry and Bordeu and got them to put aside all question of the third bleeding.

The second bleeding, in which four great basins of blood were taken from the King, left him quite prostrated.[1] About

---

[1] To this bleeding has since been attributed the bad course of the King's malady and finally his death, as it had been effected in the beginning of the eruption. The doctors were put on their guard against the idea of small-pox by an eruption on the skin, which the King had in his youth at Fontainebleau, and which had been described as small-pox.

five o'clock, nevertheless, the King sent for his children,
and kept them for half an hour without uttering a word.   It
was not a good evening with him ; the fever increased.   The
Duc d'Aumont wanted to send for Madame du Barry ; but
an altercation broke out between the Duke and the doctors,
who were opposed to the admission of Madame du Barry.
The Duc d'Aumont did not venture to go any further, and
Madame du Barry had to be satisfied with a conference
with the Duc d'Aiguillon.

On Saturday, the 30th of April, the King, having been
carried for the sake of the convenience of those around him
from a large bed to a small one, a doctor happened to draw
close to Louis XV.'s face a wax-candle, which brought into
full view on his forehead and cheeks red spots in which
pimples were already seen to have gathered.   There could
be no doubt about it any longer.   It was small-pox.

The doctors, as if relieved at having their uncertainty
ended, announced the disease almost gaily, saying that the
King was wonderfully prepared for it, and that all would go
well.   And the Court was reassured, believing it meant eight
days' confinement to bed, in spite of the menacing response
of Bordeu : " By Jove . . . small-pox at sixty-four,
with a constitution like the King's, is a terrible disease ! "

In the pestiferous apartment Madame Adelaide, Madame
Victoire, and Madame Sophie had been shut up with their
father. . . . Louis XV. had sunk into a state of extreme exhaustion, mingled with an anxiety which could not
be calmed.   He no longer spoke.   His eyes were at the same

MADAME LA DUCHESSE DE CHÂTEAUROUX

To face page 192

time haggard and fixed. The party of the Du Barry began
to get frightened, and pushed into the King's chamber
the woman whom he loved in order to awaken in the dying
man a little of the sensual life, and in order to have it repeated out of doors that the favour of the mistress still continued. As a consequence of some strong words exchanged
between the Prince of Beauvau, Choiseul's friend, and the
Duc d'Aumont, it was La Borde, valet of the quarter, who
was in the pay of the Du Barry party, who *gave the order*
in the King's room. So, every evening, La Borde sent out
everybody, went to look for the Favourite, and led her to
the bedside of the King, who showed in his weakened condition little gladness at seeing her.[1]

Meanwhile, the *anti-Aiguillonists* and the *anti-Barryites*
cried out against the scandal, demanding that the sacrament
should be administered to the King, urged the pious M. de
Beaumont to imitate the example of the Bishop of Soissons,
who in 1771 drove away from the side of the King the
Duchesse de Chateauroux. And it so happened (strange
fact!) that " in this jobbing and this trafficking in the conscience of the King"—this is the expression of Cardinal de
Luynes—the party of the devotees and the Jesuits banded
themselves in a league to prevent the King from receiving
communion, while the Choiseul party, the party of the philosophers and of the sceptics, entered into a league to impose

---

[1] " Memoirs of the Baron de Besenval." Baudouin Freres, 1821.
Tome I.

this communion on the temporisings of the Archbishop of Paris.

On Sunday the 1st of May, there was a fresh consultation of the doctors, and an official announcement of the Archbishop's visit.

On the 2nd of May, the Archbishop of Paris, though suffering from the stone and passing blood,[1] came with the sacrament and with the intention of demanding *a notorious and anterior expulsion of the concubine.* But there was secretly in M. de Beaumont's breast, between his zeal and his conscience, a sense of gratitude for the signal services which Madame du Barry had rendered to the party of which he was the chief ecclesiastic by the overthrow of Choiseul, the elevation of D'Aiguillon, and the annihilation of the Parliaments.

Before the Archbishop's arrival, a conference took place between Madame du Barry, D'Aiguillon, Richelieu, and Fronsac, in which it was agreed that in order to get the visit to come off in the presence of the Duke of Orleans, it should be one of simple politeness, and that nothing should be said about the sacrament. Even Madame Adelaide, on whom the doctors of the Du Barry party had imposed the idea that the question of eternity was perhaps premature, and might give the patient his death-stroke, was won over to this combination. When, therefore, at eleven o'clock in the morning, the Archbishop presented himself at the door of

[1] " Secret Correspondence, Political and Literary." London, 1787.

the King's antechamber, Richelieu rushed forward to meet him, and implored of him not to cause the King's death by a *theological proposition;* then, with the cynicism of his graceful manners, he proposed that the prelate should listen to some pretty little sins of his own, swearing that he would hear some the like of which he had never heard since he became Archbishop of Paris. And passing from these remarks to seriousness, he represented to the Archbishop, that to send away Madame du Barry was to prepare the way for Choiseul's triumph, to injure the woman who was a friend in order to serve the enemy. Finally he flung at the prelate by way of peroration what the Favourite had said to him the night before: "Let the Archbishop leave us alone, and he shall have a Cardinal's hat; I will take care of that and will answer for it."[1]

The Archbishop entered the King's room, remained there a quarter of an hour, and went away without speaking about confession. The King, as if revived by the Archbishop's silence, had Madame du Barry quickly sent for, and kissed her beautiful hands with delight.

The Choiseul party turned to another man, Cardinal de la Roche-Aymon, a nature ambitious and deceptive, who, currying favour with the two parties, said that he could not openly propose the sacraments, but that he would watch and seize hold of the first opportunity. However, the fervent and the enthusiastic amongst the clergy grew impa-

[1] "Historical and Political Memoirs of the Reign of Louis XVI." By Soulavie. Treuttel and Wurtz. Year X. Tome I.

tient. The Bishop of Carcassonne, showing his pectoral cross to Cardinal de la Roche-Aymon, appealed to him in the name of that cross not to let his King, the most Christian King, die without being anointed, called on him to act in such a way that the King should show *an example of repentance to France, to Christian Europe, which he had scandalized.* To the intimidations of Richelieu, and the threats of Fronsac to throw him out of the window if he spoke of confession to the King, the cure of Versailles replied: " If you do not kill me, I will re-enter through the door, for it is my right." [1]

During this tumult, these divisions, these comings and goings, whilst the Eucharist was wandering through the corridors, the King's disease was growing towards nausea, and his body was covered with that leprosy which would torment his agony with the fear that the pus of his pimples might mingle with the Host.[2]

On the 3rd of May, the doctor's bulletin announced that the King had been delirious during the night, and the Duc d'Aiguillon thereupon made a scene with the doctors at the King's door, the noise of which reached Louis XV., who asked what was the matter. And the minister came in to the King, who spoke to him in the most tender terms about his mistress, even asking to have her brought to him that evening by La Borde.

[1] " Memoirs of the Marechal de Richelieu." Buisson. 1793. Tome IX.

[2] The decomposition of Louis XV.'s body was such that the night-men of Versailles had to be asked to put it into the coffin.

Madame Du Barry

During the day, a conversation had taken place between the King and the Archbishop, who had taken up his quarters in the Lazarists' house at Versailles. . . . In the evening, when Madame du Barry entered, still radiant after the words of the morning, the King made her come over near his bed, and said to her in a low voice: " Madame, I am sick ; I know what I have to do ; I do not want to begin over again the scene at Metz ; we must part. Go to Ruel, to M. d'Aiguillon's ; be sure that I shall always feel for you the tenderest friendship." And he pushed her away in a last dismissal.

Scarcely had Madame du Barry left when Louis XV. asked for her again, stammering in a voice which was beginning to become delirious: " Ah ! she is gone . . . then we must go, too—at least we must pray to Saint Genevieve." [1]

---

[1] This account of Louis XV.'s death is taken, to a great extent, from the two narratives given by Soulavie on the subject in the " Memoirs of the Marechal Duc de Richelieu " and in the " Historical and Political Memoirs of the Reign of Louis XVI." The information with which the historian supplies us as to the end of the King he got from M. de la Borde, first valet of the King's Bedchamber, who had communicated to him his " Memoirs of the Court of Louis XV.," hitherto unpublished ; from the Abbe Dupinet, Canon of Notre Dame, who repeated to him the conversation he had on this subject with the Archbishop of Paris ; lastly from Cardinal de Luynes, from Madame d'Aiguillon, from the Duc de Brissac, and from the Marechal de Richelieu. It is time to lift Soulavie out of the contempt in which he has been held, and to assure him his proper merits as an authority for the facts of history. He had the good fortune to see passing through his hands the most curious and most authentic

XII.

The Nothingness of the Du Barry's Historic Role.—The Patronage of Art conferred on Chasers of Bronze, on Carvers in Wood, on Embroiderers, and Dressmakers, etc.—*Lettre de Cachet* which exiles the Favourite to Pont-aux-Dames.—The Disbandment of the Du Barrys.—Purchase of the Estate of Saint-Vrain.—Madame du Barry playing a Twelve-Sous Piece and Losing 90,000 Livres.—Return to Luciennes.—Love-letters of the Du Barry.—Picture of Luciennes before the Revolution.—The Beauty of Madame du Barry at Forty Years.

The reign of Madame Du Barry was finished.

There was in the Greek anthology this epitaph on a young woman:—" May the earth be light on her! She weighed so little on it!" So we might say of the Favourite:—" May Posterity be light on her! She weighed so little on History." In fact, this reign of Madame du Barry is the reign

---

documents of the eighteenth century. I shall only cite as an example the " Autograph Correspondence of Mademe de Chateauroux," published by us from the originals in Rouen in the " Duchesse de Chateauroux,"—a correspondence which he certainly consulted, and of which even the smallest detail agrees so perfectly with Richelieu's biography. I shall recall also as a proof of the esteem to which Soulavie's information is entitled the two conversations of Madame de Pompadour with the President of Meinieres, the first of which has been lately republished by the Faculty of Bibliophiles from the manuscript of the President.

of a King's mistress which was peculiar and without a parallel; it is neither a tyranny nor a government. It is an omnipotence without being a domination, a caprice without being an initiative. It is power without the will, without the personality, of power. The unconsciousness and irresponsibility of a dream are its attributes, as they are the excuses for it. Examine, study the character of Madame du Barry as a favourite: nothing of what emanates from her belongs to her position. She does not possess in herself a single idea, nor has she a single enemy. She plays a part in the great historic events of the time without either desiring or comprehending them. Brought into the King's bed by passions and interests which are unknown to her, she is kept there by favourable circumstances which she allows to operate without observing them. She is devoted to friendships and to individuals without having the least idea of devotion to a cause, a system, or a party; and she is protected by the providential course of affairs, without having to encumber herself with an effort, an intrigue, or a recompense for favours received. The exile of Choiseul, the exile of the Parliaments, the sudden political changes, the revolutions of the Palace, pass through her hands; they pass neither through her heart nor through her head. Without having to pursue good-fortune herself, the time raises her to a remarkable position, surrounds her with servitors, leads successively to her feet the Duke of Orleans, the Prince of Conde, the Duke of Chartres. That secret rivalry between the Chancellor and the Abbe Terray, which puts these two men at the mistress's feet, which renders them the slaves of her whims and her squanderings, all those divisions of the ministry and of the Court which deliver up ambitions and consciences to her, are kindled underneath her and without her. The seductions of women who compete against her for favour, the beauties lying in ambuscade, the fascination of a Baroness of Newkerque, of that beautiful Madame Pater, demand, so to speak, from Madame du Barry neither a care nor an effort for the purpose of self-protection: the attempts, the temptations, miscarry of their own accord through the conflict of opinions and the warring interests of the plotters. Thus flows along softly and without a struggle the favour of this spoiled child, who, without affections, without hatreds, repeating what she is taught to say, wishing for what she is taught to wish for, without aim, without interest, without passion,[1] forms the singular contrast with Madame de Pompadour of a Favourite who reigns and does not govern.

Madame du Barry does not even keep, of the domination of the woman who came before her, the part which is the easiest to exercise control in, and the lightest to carry,— that patronage of literature and art of which a King's mistress can make herself so great and so charming a distributor. Even the sway of good taste is not exercised by

[1] "Letters of the Marquise du Deffand to Horace Walpole." Tome II.

Madame Du Barry

Madame du Barry; and, as she did in political matters, she abandons herself to her time in artistic matters. She follows the fashion, and in nothing does she figure as a leader. Her patronage descends, with her pleasures and her tastes, which were those of a grisette, from the opera to the couplet, from painters and sculptors to workers in bronze and carvers in wood, from the Encyclopedie to La Morliere and from Montesquieu to Audinot. The *clientele,* the persons whose society is cultivated by her whom Voltaire calls " Égerie," are not by any means artists, philosophers, or poets. They are the gods of the lower empires—the mimics, the buffoons, the dancers, the comedians. She forgets herself with them to the extent of downright familiarity; she enters into their affairs; she negotiates their promissory notes; she meddles in and soils her fingers with their passions. And how great would have been the amazement of those poor ambassadors of dying Poland who came to implore the Favourite's aid in saving their country if they had been able to read the real object of her brain's solicitude at the moment! All her thoughts were about Dauberval, who threatened to go to Russia, or about Chasse, who had refused to sing before her, or about Raucourt, of whom she wished to make an influence, or about the old woman Dumesnil, the old woman whom she thought of dressing, or about Mademoiselle Dubois, whom she wished to marry to Dauberval, who did not want her![1] Amongst the celebrities

[1] " Secret Memoirs of the Republic of Letters." Tomes VI and VII.

Madame Du Barry

of her time Madame du Barry had only one artist at her little levee: the painter Doyen, who owes this favour less to his talent than to the pungency of his blackguard, filthy, *obscene* conversation.

Madame du Barry, having started from Versailles on Tuesday the 5th of May at three o'clock, surrounded still with some remnant of Court-grandeur, and sustained and consoled by Madame d'Aiguillon, persisted in taking a hopeful view of things, still placing confidence in that succession of carriages which encumbered the road between Versailles and Ruel. On the 10th, a thunderbolt told the Favourite everything: the King had died at two o'clock. And on the 12th a messenger from Versailles brought Madame du Barry the following letter:

"VERSAILLES, May 12th, 1774.

"I hope, Madame, that you will not have any doubts as to all the pain I feel at being obliged to announce to you that you are forbidden to appear at Court; but I am obliged to carry out the orders of the King, who wishes me to impress on you that his intention is not to allow you to come there till there is a fresh order made by him. His Majesty, at the same time, is kind enough to permit you to go and see your aunt in the Abbey of Pont-aux-Dames, and I am going for that reason to write to the Abbess in order that you may not experience any difficulty in the matter. You will be good enough to acknowledge the receipt of this letter through the person who brings it to you, so that I may be

LOUIS XVI

To face page 202

Madame Du Barry

able to assure His Majesty of the fact that I have carried out his orders.

" I have the honour to be, with respect, Madame,

" Your very humble and very obedient servant,

" THE DUC DE LA VRILLIÈRE."[1]

Madame du Barry was, at first, overwhelmed, in spite of the mildness of the terms of the " lettre de cachet "; then, regaining her powers of displaying anger in the presence of the messenger who had brought her the unlucky news, she indulged in the language of the street-walker: "A nice . . . reign, that starts with a *lettre de cachet!*"[2]

With the dawn of the new reign, all the followers, all the relatives of the Favourite dispersed like a flock of adventurers. Removal from the Court, exile, flight, fear, shame, executed justice on the entire family.[3] No more Du Barry!

---

[1] Letters sent from the King's residence. National Archives, O' 416. All the other *lettres de cachet* given of this period in the old biographies as well as in the recent biographies are false. Madame du Barry's aunt, spoken of in this letter, who had retired into Pont-aux-Dames is, without doubt, Madame Quantiny, her mother's sister. Here is the account which Hardy gives of her departure: " Friday, May 13.—It is understood that the Comtesse du Barry started last night from the village of Ruel in obedience to a *lettre de cachet,* to go to the Abbey of Pont-aux-Dames with the severest prohibitions against seeing anybody there or writing to anybody. She was seen in her carriage with six horses, accompanied by only one chambermaid, and followed by a second vehicle in which were two individuals, one of whom is an ' exempt.'"

[2] The words omitted are certainly "the language of the gutter."— TRANSLATOR.

[3] On the 12th of May, the day when Madame du Barry received the letter which relegated her to Pont-aux-Dames, the Vicomte

They fled, hid themselves, or exhibited all the signs of conscious degradation. A marquis's lady, Mademoiselle de Fumelle, was seen to make the servants under her wear grey surtouts, to conceal through a sense of humiliation her livery and her name. Du Barry, the Roue, "Mohammed" Du Barry, threatened with the fortress of Perpignan, quitted in hot haste his four mistresses—La Thevenet, La Morance, La Dubois, and La Breba—and this pavement of Paris into which he boasted that he had, since his sister-in-law's accession to the post of Favourite, flung eighteen millions of francs. He hurried into Switzerland and did not take breath till he arrived in Lausanne.[1] And what hootings

[1] Eighteen months after his flight, the Roue wrote from Brussels (November 4, 1774) to M. de Malesherbes, a heart-rending letter of which we have already quoted some fragments. In this letter he complains of his life of wandering from country to country, of the harshness of his creditors, who, not satisfied with the sale of his chattels, of his pictures, which had realized a sum of over 400,000 livres, demanded from him a still greater sum. He asked leave to spend some days in Paris in order to see his creditors, oculists, and doctors, and implored as a last favour that he should be allowed to go and recruit his shattered health in some province in the South. He obtained permission to return to Toulouse. In Toulouse he got married again; he built houses; he bought pictures;

Adolphe du Barry received this letter from De la Vrilliere: "It is with much pain, Monsieur, that I fulfil the orders which the King has just compelled me to transmit. His Majesty has wished me to impress on you that you are not to appear at Court until there is a fresh order made by him. You will be good enough to acknowledge the receipt of my letter through the person who brings it to you, so that I may be able to assure His Majesty of the fact that I have carried out his orders.—I have the honour, etc." (Letters sent from the King's residence.) National Archives. O' 416.

there were at this skedaddle—this escape? What furious
delight the public displayed at his deliverance! His losses at
play, his efforts in disposing of damaged goods at the highest price in the market of Venus, were recalled to the minds
of those who knew his history. People spoke repeatedly
about his insolences and about his indecent familiarity in
addressing the King as " Comrade."[1] The public contempt
took its revenge. Ironies and witticisms were launched
against this flight and general smash-up—the vengeances

[1] " Frerot." The word is equivalent to the Socialistic word
" Comrade." It was applied in the thirteenth century to certain sec-
taries who rejected the idea of private property.—TRANSLATOR.

---

he gave invitations to dinner; he went to bed; he got up: " It is a
very monotonous life for a man accustomed to *high intrigue*." And
in 1784 we find the Comte Jean in Paris, this time trying to make
some capital out of his wife—a young, pretty, and virtuous woman
whom he had voluntarily familiarised with vice, whom he had
deliberately depraved, and who, introduced by him into the house of
the Controller-General, does now, after driving out the Vicomtesse
de Laval, the honours of M. de Colonne's table. Then, when his
big plans had utterly failed, the Comte Jean decided on returning to
Toulouse, where he resumes his career as a gambler, and continued,
during the first years of the Revolution, to fatigue Madame du Barry
with his applications for money, as the following letter annexed
to Madame du Barry's " Dossier " testifies: " Levignac, October 20,
1790.—Far be from me, my dear sister, every reproach and every
repetition of the past. You know whether it is in a great measure
through my attention that my last journey has been worth 500,000
livres to you. You may remember your promises; you may recol-
lect having claimed 20,000 livres which I received as a slight instalment. Is it fair that you should enjoy everything and that there is
left only to me the remembrance of a journey as ruinous to me
as it was profitable to you? . . ."

which the witty world of Paris can extract from a humiliation of France. The joke of the hour was: " The coopers
will be very busy now: all the *barrels* are leaking:"[1] or else
the story of the Roue asking the advice of his friend Guys,
the well-known buffoon, as to the best expedient to have recourse to: " Faith! my dear boy, the jewel-case and the
post-horses; " and when the Roue did the indignant: " Oh!
well, then, the post-horses and the jewel-case! "[2] And
while the effigy of the defaulting Du Barrys was thus
dragged in the gutter,[3] the mud covered at Toulouse the
forehead of the husband, the face of the Comte Guillaume.

Pont-aux-Dames was a sad dwelling after Luciennes.[4]
The old buildings almost in ruin, that convent thrown by
the Carlovingians like a savage Saint-Denis into the midst
of the woods—what a change! and what a sad penitential
retreat for this Favourite so soft and so much attached
to her ease that during the King's agony she sent for her
bed to Luciennes at Ruel![5] In the first months, the Favourite's immurement was nearly complete, as is shown

[1] " Secret Correspondence, Political and Literary." Tome I.
[2] " Secret Memoirs of the Republic of Letters." Tome VII.
[3] On the 30th of September, 1770, Paris was filled with the report
of a secret execution by torchlight of Du Barry the Roue. Hardy's
Manuscript Journal.
[4] In a satirical print entitled " France Saved." the draughtsman
represented Louis XV. in the tomb, the Chancellor flying pursued
by justice, Louis XVI. radiant, and in a corner the Du Barry knock-
ing at the gate of a convent.
[5] "Journal of Abbe Baudeau." *Revue Retrospective.* Tome III.

by this letter emanating from the King's abode permitting her as a favour to see her jeweller every time she would consider it necessary for her affairs:

" August 6th, 1774.

" I have, Madame, as you desire, addressed to the Sieur Aubert, jeweller to the Crown, a letter for the Abbess of Pont-aux-Dames, by which I give her notice to let him enter the convent every time that you deem it necessary for your affairs, and that he presents himself there.

" I learn with pain that your health is not perfectly good. I implore of you to be well persuaded of the real interest I take in it, and that will be always as at all times. I hope this indisposition will not have any consequences, and I sincerely desire it. I have the honour to be[1] . . ."

Madame du Barry submitted to the order " forbidding her to speak or write to anybody." She accustomed herself to her imprisonment, to those hard natures, to those severe walls, to those gothic roofs, to her dingy abode, to the service of her only chambermaid. The agreeability, however, of the Abbess softened for her the first harshness of this abrupt change, and the shock of a life so different. She let herself be distracted by the curiosity which all the sisters, young or old, displayed at seeing her and approaching that mythical personage, a King's mistress! Her eyes were

[1] Missives, National Archives, O'416. We may notice the tone of this letter of La Vrilliere. The Abbe Terray had been more brutal, he refused money to the Favourite in the last days of the King's malady.

amused and tickled by the pretty dress of the Bernardines. Soon Mlle. du Barry and Mlle. de Tournon, the wife of the Vicomte Adolphe du Barry, got leave to come and reside at Pont-aux-Dames and brought to the exile the resource of their society, the animation of their gaiety, courage, and patience. Then, with time, seclusion lost some of its rigorousness. Madame du Barry almost resumed the train of her past life. Her servants were let go back to her; her women, some cooks, and an officer returned to her; and, at her request, the King authorized her to summon to Pont-aux-Dames the architect of Luciennes, Ledoux, who added to the Abbey a wing in which Madame du Barry found once more a souvenir of her dear palace.[1] Friendships came to her; she charmed the whole convent by her politeness, her amiability, her kind words to the credulous sisters, the promise of an abbess-ship and a prioress-ship to another, as soon as she returned to Court; finally, by a thousand little presents scattered around her with the graciousness she showed in giving; and she ended by making herself popu-

---

[1] Hardy gives these details: " Friday, June 3.—This day, it is rumoured that the Comtesse du Barri lives happy and content in the Abbey of Pont-aux-Dames, that she received visitors there, that three ladies connected with her, viz.: the Marquise du Barry, the Vicomtesse du Barry, perhaps the Dame de Montrabe her mother, formerly known by the name of *Manon Giroux,* are keeping her company, that she has had an addition made to the building in order to have more accommodation, that, finally, she has given a general and special power of attorney to the Sieur Lepot d'Auteuil, notary in Paris, to manage her affairs and pay all her debts, after the examination and liquidation has taken place."

lar in Pont-aux-Dames, where the good nuns were at her feet as in a family where she was a welcome guest.[1]

There was not enough of depth in Madame du Barry's soul to make her remain overwhelmed very long at her fall. She scarcely knew how to measure it. It was an awakening which did not arouse her indignation. Her disgrace revealed in her a simple and entirely natural philosophy which some of the greatest hearts and greatest minds cannot attain. She lost power as she had possessed it—giddily. Her first outburst of despair took the form of low language; her regrets merely took the form of pouting. Through her solicitations, through the support of friends whom she had still at Versailles, Madame du Barry at length got permission to quit Pont-aux-Dames, but on condition that she should reside ten leagues away from Paris and the Court. It was then that with the purchase-money of her house in Versailles, which she had sold to Monsieur, she bought the estate of Saint-Vrain near Arpagon, which, as it happened, was found to belong to M. Duval, that ex-clerk in the Ministry of Marine for whom she had conceived the first of her youthful attachments. The park, one of the first parks in France laid out in the English fashion, with its thickets of green trees in the Italian style, pleased the prisoner of Pont-aux-Dames the first moment she saw it. The Duc d'Aiguillon, whose quite recent disgrace was due very largely to his persistent attachment to the Favourite, and who in a

[1] "Secret Correspondence, Political and Literary." London, 1787. Tome I.

lively conversation with Louis XVI. had declared to him
that independently of the personal debt of gratitude he owed
the woman, he was obeying the orders of the late King, who
on his death-bed had recommended his mistress to him, installed the new proprietress in her estate of Saint-Vrain, before setting out for his exile in D'Aiguillon.[1] On the 24th
of June, 1775, she was completely settled there, and Madame
du Barry sent round a circular letter in which she informed
the nobility of the neighbourhood that she would have a
table of twenty-five covers every day, and that she would
be perfectly delighted if they came and dined there.[2]

Madame d'Aiguillon spent the entire summer with
Madame du Barry, who was beginning to find the house
dreadful and the park tiresome. Ere long she saw only a
solitude in this picturesque piece of ground. More free, but
more alone, more out of her element again in the country
than in a convent, she regretted her friends, her habits, society, the fashionable throng, and above all, her dear Luciennes. Thereupon, she was pursued to Saint-Vrain by the
troubles of her entangled affairs, the embarrassment and

---

[1] "Secret Memoirs of the Republic of Letters." Tome VIII.
Madame du Barry, in the summer and autumn of the year, made
two journeys to the estate of D'Aiguillon which the Duke could
not prevent. However, Madame du Barry rendered a money-ser-
vice to the Duke: she lent him 200,000 livres which the Duke did
not pay back till the 13th of August, 1784.

[2] "The Conversations of the Other World on that which takes
place in This, or Dialogues, Grotesque and Picturesque." London,
1784.

tiresomeness of her twelve hundred thousand livres of debts[1]
and so inconstant was her mind, of so little consequence did
the next day seem to her, that she no sooner left than she
was importuned by the noise her stewards made around her
as to her most pressing debts. The most beautiful resolutions passed through her mind; she thought of reforming,
reducing her expenditure. She wished to diminish her staff
of servants, to cast aside her train of attendants, to establish
order, to practise economy,—fine promises with which she
satisfied herself every night, and which took flight at dawn!

Money, expenses, went rolling on in the most large-
handed fashion. She gave orders, she made purchases, foolishly, as in the past, without caring about payment; and
every moment she got the greatest surprises at being as-
sailed by claims of tradespeople—or by demands for payment on account before beginning some work. At last, owing to the growing insolence of merchants, she determined
to open her eyes and to look into the figures; alarmed, she
attempted to negotiate the sale of the Lodges of Nantes, and
found she could not carry it out. Almost about the same

---

[1] Madame du Barry was also beginning to have the weariness and
the annoyance of pamphlets which spoke by no means sympathet-
ically about her. The "Historic Summary" made its entrance
into France in December, 1774, the "Anecdotes" appeared in October, 1775, and their success led to this letter being sent from the
King's residence to Albert, Lieutenant of Police: "I have known
for some time, Monsieur, the very poor book of anecdotes about
the Comtesse du Barry. It is really a matter of some moment to
prevent the publicity of it, and you cannot take too many precautions
to attain that object." (Missives, National Archives, O¹417.)

time, in this brief spell of panic and of reason, she decided to make greater sacrifices. Here is a list drawn up for her notary, Lepot d'Auteuil, of all the beautiful things of which she wanted to denude herself, so as to turn them into money; it contains the best and most precious things in her museum at Luciennes. In addition to the Polembergs, the Ostades, the Teniers, the Jacob Xaverys, and the pictures bought in Rome by M. de la Borde, there are the " Four Hours of the Day," by Vernet, the two large pictures of Casanova, the four large pictures of Vien decorating the oval salon of Luciennes, and Greuze's well-known pictures—the " Child Caressing a Spaniel," the " Child in his Shirt playing with a Dog," a " Woman in a Polonaise," a " Woman in Her Chemise," the " Broken Pitcher," and the sketch of the " Prayer to Love; " then the " Children " of Drouais; then four beautiful Gobelin tapestries fabricated by Cozette, and again the marble figures on gilt pedestals in the salon, and the porphyry vase with ormolu bas-reliefs in the central drawing-room, and the four white marble candelabra in the dining-room.[1] When she was free from these annoyances Madame

[1] List of pictures, statues, groups, and other articles forming the mass of the objects for sale. " Manuscript accounts of Madame du Barry." National Library. French Supplement, 8157 to 8158. The objects were given up to be sold to the highest bidder, but only in 1777. The sale, which was a collective sale, and in which Madame du Barry's name does not appear, took place at the Hotel d'Aligre on the 17th of February, 1777. A " Village Interior," by Ostade, coming from the Choiseul collection, was sold for 7,250 livres; a " Public-House," by Teniers, coming from the collection of M. Lempereur, for 6,500 livres; a vase by Jacob Xavery, for 803 livres; a " Venus

Madame Du Barry

du Barry fell back again into the melancholy existence of Saint-Vrain. With autumn, the few visitors from the surrounding chateaux who came to see her deserted her. Fevers arose out of the marshy meadows of the park.[1] In the chateau, Madame du Barry killed time as best she could. A document preserved in the National Archives shows her to us a slave to her attendants, rushed about between the perpetual indigestions of one of her chambermaids and the continual confinements of the other, carrying indulgence and kindness so far as almost to live without the two invalids and get an additional servant. Age and disgrace had no more matured her than they embittered her. She remained at Saint-Vrain what she was at Versailles. She had, in this sullen exile, the follies, the vanities, the modes of amusement, and the obstinacies of childhood. She spend days, she tries to pass a small portion of the night, at cards, at nine-holes, playing without any calculation, losing foolishly with friends discreet enough not to claim the

[1] "Historic Memoirs of Jeanne Gomart de Vaubernier, Comtesse Du Barry." By Favrolle, Year XI. Tome III.

Asleep" by Polemberg, for 240 livres; the Greuzes realizing the highest price. The "Child in his Shirt playing with a Dog," taken from the Choiseul collection, was sold for 7,200 livres; the "Child Caressing a Spaniel," for 2,612 livres; the "Prayer to Love," a smaller copy of a picture of which the original belonged to the Duc de Choiseul, for 1,950 livres; the "Woman in Her Chemise," for 2,599 livres; the "Woman in a Polonaise" was withdrawn at 500 livres. Finally, two pieces of tapestry, after Boucher, by Cozette, under glass (H. 48 inches, L. 70 inches) reached the figure of 2,660 livres. The pictures by Vien and by Drouais, the porphyry vases, and the white marble candelabra, were not put up for sale.

money they had won. One day, she plays a piece of a dozen sous, and undertakes not to lose more than the sum of six livres. Before dinner, she has lost more than twenty thousand livres, and from revenge to revenge, stubbornly continuing to play with the impatience of a young girl, determining with every fresh game to play better than her opponent, finishes by losing one night 90,000 livres.[1]

The day after this foolish loss (November 6th, 1775) Madame du Barry started for Luciennes, to which, thanks to Maurepas, she had obtained leave to go back. This first permission had only been granted provisionally, and during the absence of the Court from Versailles, only a little while afterwards, she was allowed to resume definite possession of her dear Luciennes.[2]

In this sweet exile, in this enchanted retreat of her disgrace, Madame du Barry is no longer the child of yesterday, the female gambler of Saint-Vrain,—she is the woman, the amorous woman whom we are going to find, and luckily it will not be necessary to have recourse to witnesses, or to stories which are often false, in order to paint her: a bundle of little love-letters will open for us the secret recesses of her heart, and it will be sufficient for us to read over her shoulder in order to penetrate to her inner depths.

This romance of Madame du Barry has the most tedious

---

[1] "Memoirs of the Chevalier de Langles to justify himself for having won at play 90,000 livres from Madame du Barry and for having sought to reconcile her with the Duc de Choiseul." National Archives.

[2] "Secret Memoirs of the Republic of Letters." Tome VIII.

and most commonplace commencement in the world. A friend of Madame du Barry, Lord Seymour,[1] the English Ambassador in France, has a daughter who is ill. Madame du Barry is interested in the sick child, and writes to the father:

"I am much touched, monsieur, at the cause which has deprived me of the pleasure of seeing you at my house, and I sympathize most sincerely with your daughter in her illness. I am sure your heart is sick, too, and I share in your sensibility. I can only exhort you to take courage, since the doctor reassures you as to the danger. If the interest I feel in your trouble can in any way mitigate it, you should be less agitated.

"Mlle. du Barry is as sensitive as I am as to everything which concerns you, and asks me to assure you of the fact on her part.

"Our journey has been very happy. Cornichon does not forget you, and speaks of you incessantly. It gives me great pleasure to know that the little dog can amuse your daughter, even for a moment.

"Accept, monsieur, the assurance of the sentiments I feel towards you.

"Luciennes, Saturday, 6 o'clock."

[1] The only historical evidence of this *liaison* of Madame du Barry with Lord Seymour is this phrase of the Abbe Georgel: "On the dismissal of the Comtesse du Barry, in the moment of her disgrace, she appeared to console herself for her past grandeur with an Englishman, Lord Seymour." (Memoirs to serve for the History of the Events of the End of the Eighteenth Century.)

Then the letters became more caressing. These are the first stages of the tender passion—attentions and little kindnesses.

"It has long ago been said that little kindnesses preserve friendship," is the first line of one of those letters.

Soon come the pretty acts of thoughtfulness, the sending of "a piece of money wasted very foolishly on a little game of loo; it is of the time of Louis XIV. M. Seymour is a great admirer of this age so fruitful in marvels; and here is a little one sent him by the ladies of Luciennes. It is with delight that they show their desire to honour him. They deprive themselves of things belonging to them because they are well aware that M. Seymour will realise the cost of the sacrifice, and will be satisfied that the ladies would be glad to find occasions more essential to mark their affection for him."

The day comes when love grows strong and breaks out, abandoning itself, surrendering itself altogether, oozing forth in avowals and passionate words, intense, luring, and sweet.

"The assurance of your affection, my dear friend, make the happiness of my life. Be sure that my heart finds these two days very long, and that, if it were in its power to shorten them it would have no more pain. I expect you on Saturday with all the impatience of a soul entirely yours, and I hope you will have nothing to desire. Adieu! I am yours.

Madame Du Barry

" This Thursday at two o'clock."[1]

When the last letter was written, Lord Seymour's love was dead. Madame du Barry writes to him:

" This Wednesday at midnight.

" It is useless to speak to you of my tender and sincere affection: You know all about it. But what you do not know is the pain I feel; you have not deigned to reassure me about what affects my soul. So I believe that my tranquillity and my happiness touch you very little; it is with regret that I speak of it to you, but it is for the last time. My head is all right; my heart is sick. But with much care and courage I shall succeed in conquering it. The work is painful and grievous, but it is necessary; it is the last sacrifice which remains for me to make: my heart has made all the others. It is for my reason to make this. Adieu. Believe that you alone occupy my heart." [1]

[1] We find in a catalogue of autographs (February 5, 1855) a dis-

[1] Autograph letters of Madame du Barry communicated by M. François Barriere. We give the little feminine touches with their orthography in those love-letters; but this specimen seems to us sufficient, and we shall give the other letters with an intelligible orthography.

tracted letter forming part of this amorous correspondence of Madame du Barry, and written, without doubt, a very short time before or a very short time after the one which we have read: " My heart is yours without division, and, if I failed to keep my promise, my debts are responsible for it. I have been very much upset since you left me, and I assure you that I have only the strength to think of you. Adieu, my kind friend, I love you, I repeat to you, and I feel happy in doing so. I embrace you a thousand times, and am yours. Come early."

Madame Du Barry

What an unexpected tone there is in this correspondence! Does it not seem to impart into this courtesan's life the un-dreamt-of charm and the restrained emotion of the history of Madame Michonin in Richelieu's memoirs? And how another Du Barry is revealed to you in the shadow, behind the popular Du Barry of the pamphlets and romances! It is no longer the courtesan; it is no longer the Favourite; it is a loving woman. What astonishment! What an expia-tion! Those humilities of a grisette, those timidities and almost modesties, those effusions, those tears, those resigna-tions, those stifled sighs like groans, those regrets which possess the nobility of self-sacrifice! And what a light it throws on the woman and what forgiveness it wins for her, so full of love as she was and so charming in her sincere avowals of affection!

Time and Madame du Barry's levity of character cured her of this love, of this wound, and left in her heart only a tender memory. She recovered from it, and found a calm happiness in that Luciennes which exile had made still dearer to her; and there, without plans, without intrigues, without that agitation which usually accompanies disgrace, she lived in choice company,[1] in the midst of many friends. She received with respectful kindness the illustrious stran-gers and the Princes of Europe who were anxious to carry away from France the recollection of a visit to Luciennes.

[1] Amongst the women whom she received at her house, the "Gal-lery of the States General" says she showed her appreciation of gallantry as much as of prudery.

Madame Du Barry

The affairs of Madame du Barry were now disentangled; her debts were paid off;[1] she kept a fastidious equipage, and had indulged in splendid luxury. The future seemed to her to be no longer menacing; she now enjoyed peace, the devoted attachment of those who were left around her as well as the affection of the new friends who were brought into close contact with her and learned to understand her, and the sympathy and consideration which her philosophy and the propriety of her new existence won for her.[2]

Meanwhile, the years went by, and gradually and almost insensibly the woman was forgotten by her contemporaries. Foreign sovereigns, on a visit to our country, no longer took the road to Luciennes, and only the ambassadors of Tippoo Sahib thought themselves still obliged to present their homage on bended knees and in embroidered muslin robes to the ex-mistress of Louis XV. The solitude of the

---

[1] In reality, Madame du Barry was scarcely free from the worry of her debts before April, 1784. At this date Louis XVI. settled on her 60,000 francs a year in exchange for the sum of 1,250,000 livres, which had been handed over to the Exchequer.

[2] Metra relates that in the month of January, 1779, Madame du Barry had a desire for marriage, a *fancy for a sacramental union* with an American whom she had met in the country at the house of the celebrated player Sormanni. This American, whose name was Bellanger, was a sort of young fool, very rich, son of a merchant in San Domingo, who subsequently acquired a certain notoriety by driving over a woman in Nantes and beating the substitute of the Procureur-General of the Parliament of Brittany. But an order of the King commanded her intended to leave France, and His Majesty advised Louis XV.'s former mistress not to be so sensitive in the future to the attractions of conjugal love.

Madame Du Barry

little chateau was scarcely ever troubled now with visits, and in 1785 Madame du Barry was almost reduced to the society of Madame Souza, the wife of the Portuguese Ambassador, the Marquise du Brunoy, and her neighbour, M. de Monville. And there were many days when, in summer as well as in winter, the chilly little mistress of the chateau, clad in a dressing-robe of cotton cambric or white muslin, spent the entire day carrying her memories of the past through the park or beyond it.[1] There were now some evenings when, very often reduced to a single listener, to a Madame Lebrun who was painting her portraits, the Favourite, with her feet on the fender, spoke about Louis XV. and the old Court, but with reserve, indulgence, freedom from resentment, discretion, in language in which the vividness of her recollections and the boldness of her former habits of speech were toned down—and as if she were speaking of a past far, far, far away.

The Comte d'Allonville, who saw her, during these years, while staying at the house of the Duc de Brissac, gives expression to his astonishment at the decency of her behaviour, at the distinction of her manners, at the modest tone of the new woman who had been formed in the house of Madame

---

[1] She often went to visit the unfortunate, the sick, and the women in confinement in the neighbourhood. Madame Lebrun tells how she saw Madame du Barry in a passion at finding that the linen, wine, and soup she had ordered for a poor woman who was about to have a child in the district had not been brought to her, and how on her return home she made a scene with her servants, pushing them out with a bundle of linen, and claret, and soup.

du Barry, and with whom no fault could be found save that
she still pronounced her words in a ridiculously childish
fashion out of place in a woman of her age.

"It was in this dining-room," said Madame du Barry
one day to Madame Lebrun, as they were having a cup of
tea together, "it was in this room that Louis XV. did me
the honour to dine." And, after a moment's silence, she
added, as if talking to herself: "There was a stand overhead for the musicians when they played and sang. . . .
There, in that Luciennes, persons and things had begun to
resemble a dream. And, in the midst of this country district, in which the old straggling engine of Marly could be
heard emitting mournful groans in the distance, the little
chateau, silent and ruinous, with its deserted galleries, in
which were heaped together pell-mell, vases, columns, the
rarest marbles, the most precious furniture, while in some
corner lay stretched on a sofa that Royalty had once occupied a man enjoying a siesta,—the little chateau assumed
the vague aspect of those palaces, buried in a deep sleep
by a fairy's wand. The man, sleeping in broad daylight,
was the Duc de Brissac, who since Louis XV.'s death had
lived in Luciennes as a sort of husband-lover of Madame
du Barry, and his passion for his fair mistress seemed to
grow stronger each day.

Madame du Barry, in fact, was always beautiful, and, in
a fashion, more charming than ever. A portrait which Cosway[1] painted of her on the occasion of her journey to Eng-

[1] Painted by Cosway, engraved by Conde.

land, and which was engraved in London after her death, has preserved for us the most adorable image of her that is left to us. With her head softly thrown back, her shoulders lowered, her arms hanging freely, her hair loose and flowing in wanton curls over her shoulders, she lets fall from her coquettish laughing eyes, veiled in languor, sparkling with desire, one of those sweetly beaming glances which seem like light seen through vapour. Her little nose quivers; a half-smile plays round and tickles her curving lips. And, looking at this enchanting visage, this oval amorously rounded by the years, it seems to us that we behold in his portrait the voluptuousness of the eighteenth century—a Bacchante of Greuze.

Madame Lebrun confirms the truth of this portrait by her souvenirs of 1785 and 1789, saying that the face of Madame du Barry was still charming while admitting that her complexion was beginning to spoil.[1]

[1] "Souvenirs of Madame Vigee-Lebrun." Fournier, 1835. Vol. I.

XIII.

THE year 1789 arrived, and then came the taking of the
Bastille, with reference to which during the cannonade
which the wind brought to Luciennes, Madame du Barry,
sitting opposite Madame Lebrun, repeated many times:
" If Louis XV. were living, surely this would not have been
so!"

Then, immediately followed the anxieties caused by the
articles in the Revolutionary newspapers, the printing of
the " Livre Rouge," the publication of the " Vies Privees,"
the attempts at blackmailing, like that contained in this letter from Avignon dated the 12th of November, 1789:

" Madame,—Some days ago I learned that there has been
printed here a pamphlet which interests you personally. I
have taken all the necessary steps for verifying the fact, and
by means of some money which I gave the printer who
worked off the first copy, I was able to procure the opening

pages of this document which I have the honour of sending you. It is a tissue of lies which are devoid of all foundation, but which human wickedness might interpret differently. It may be seen, from the plan of this libel, that the author would like to induce the National Assembly to destroy your income for the benefit of the State, alleging as a reason that Louis could not give you an estate which did not belong to him. To secure the success of his bad design, he must send or bring a copy of it gratuitously to each deputy of the National Assembly, and afterwards sell five or six thousand copies of it in Paris and throughout the rest of the Kingdom, for all these wickednesses have for their object to gain money. . . . It is essential that it should not appear in public, especially at this moment of fury and of rage, when the least pretext is sufficient to make the populace rush into horrible excesses."[1] . . . From that day forth, there were continual alarms about her fortune up to the moment when apprehensions were beginning to be felt for the lives of the beings who were dearest to her heart. Nevertheless, it must be recognized that Madame du Barry

---

[1] Revolutionary Tribunals: The Du Barry's "Dossier," National archives, W[1] 16.—The correspondent signs his letter "M. Dupin, Hotel de Lamoureux, Rue Verte, Faubourg Saint-Honore, Paris." We read on this letter: "Letter threatening the Du Barry with a pamphlet which is found in the hands of the Citizen Vouland." Could this pamphlet be the "Life of the Comtesse du Barry," published in 1790 and followed by her letters and her amorous and political intrigues, from the *Court Printing-office,* containing a portrait with verses commencing thus:
   "The Messalina whom you see." . . .?

did not seek to purchase pardon by a base desertion of the persons connected with the Court, even by a certain craftiness of conduct. Madame du Barry had in her nothing of the virtues of prudence or of audacity which are the means of safety in times of revolution. She was incapable of hiding her riches, of deceiving people as to her expenditure, of feigning privation and suffering, of making herself miserable to escape jealousies and denunciations. She lacked, moreover, that force of will, that energy of fear, which tears you away from your country and from familiar habits, and makes you take refuge abroad. In order to fly, she would have had to quit that French life which was the life of Madame du Barry; she would have had to separate herself from Luciennes, which she could not leave.

She was, in short, in the highest degree, improvident, thoughtless, babbling, *crack-brained,* incapable of restraining herself from talking, as is shown by those curious recommendations, which seem to come from some of the upper servants in the chateau, to whom the mistress allowed a familiar tone of plain-speaking:

" Does Madame la Comtesse not forget any necessary papers? I recommend to her much forethought. In everything she must not speak if she can help it. In every moment of life, silence is good, and it is a matter of absolute necessity in the present circumstances. Every one around us has ears interested in listening to everything.

" Madame la Comtesse is not careful enough about what belongs to her. She must keep her money and her jewels herself. I recommend Madame la Comtesse, in short, to be not merely beautiful and amiable but a woman of *character*, and one who is mistress in her own house." [1]

And, at this time, a great danger of this nature was to break out, to scatter aloft its indignations, to deliver up to hostile ears both its horrors and its upheavals, with its heads cut off and exposed to public gaze, with its crimes of a revolution born in blood. Her lax-mindedness even made her impervious to fear. She did not conceal the portraits of Louis XV. and of Marie Antoinette. [2] She subscribed to the aristocratic pamphlets and newspapers. [3] Finally (mortal im-

[1] Revolutionary Tribunals : The Du Barry's "Dossier." National Archives, W' 16. I believe they are the recommendations of Morin. Madame du Barry's confidential man, who speaks at the close like a philosopher of the cultivation of his garden,—that garden in which he must have buried a portion of his mistress's jewels and silver-plate.

[2] Morin, in his deposition of the 24th Frimaire (December 14th, 1793) declares, that it was only after she had been several times advised not to leave in evidence any pictures which might *fatigue* the sight of the Federates that he had, with the aid of Dehaut, the floor-cleaner, concealed between the window and the blind of the dining-room a portrait of Louis XV. and a portrait of Marie Antoinette, which Madame du Barry does not seem to have relegated to her dressing-room until later.

[3] In the "Dossier" of Madame du Barry we find a statement of her subscriptions to the newspapers ;

Subscription to the "Gazette de Paris" from January 1st, 1790, to May 1st, 43 livres.

Subscription to the "Actes des Apotres," 36 livres.

Subscription to the "Logographe," 21 livres, 12 sols.

Subscription to the "Gazette Universelle," from June 1st to September 1st, 12 livres.

Subscription to the "Correspondence Politique," 12 livres.

prudence!) Madame du Barry could not refuse pity. She would tender the humble homage of her services to that Marie Antoinette whom, in the days when she was the Favourite, she treated harshly as a rival: her devotedness would only grow the bolder in proportion as that unhappy Queen's misfortunes increase. She would confide to her intimate friends all her zeal to serve Marie Antoinette; and when, after October, in those fatal days which brought the wife of Louis XVI. for the last time into close relations with the mistress of Louis XV., the Queen would thank Madame du Barry for her attentions to the Life Guards, who were brought to Luciennes all covered with blood, Madame du Barry would reply in this letter which should make all feel indulgent to her memory:

"These young wounded soldiers have no other regrets than that they have not died for a princess so worthy of all homage as Your Majesty. What I have done for these brave fellows is much less than they deserve. I console them, and I respect their wounds, when I reflect, Madame, that without their devotion, Your Majesty would, perhaps, no longer exist.

"Lucienne is yours, Madame; is it not your benevolence which has restored it to me? All I possess comes to me

---

On this statement we find this note:
"Proof that she subscribed to all the aristocratic newspapers. As "soon as the 'Gazette de Paris' and the 'Actes des Apotres' had "ceased publication, she throws herself on the 'Gazette Universelle' "and the 'Correspondence de l'Ami Dupan.'" National Archives, W¹ 16.

from the Royal family; I have too much gratitude ever to forget it. The late King, by a sort of presentiment, forced me to accept a thousand precious objects before separating me from his person. I have had the honour of addressing to you this treasure of the time of the notables; I offer it to you again, Madame, with all my heart. You have so many expenses to meet and favours without number to distribute! Allow me, I implore you, to give to Cæsar what is Cæsar's." [1]

But love still more than devotedness was destined to compromise Madame du Barry, and her *liaison* with the Duc de Brissac ought not to be forgotten in the fatalities which pointed her out for death and led her to the scaffold.

Not the least of the adventures in Madame du Barry's adventurous life was this conquest, the triumph of her beauty, which relieves and ennobles in its closing pages the chronicle of her life.

The spoiled child of love, she ended by winning the adoration of a true knight, the last of the chivalry of France. The Governor of Paris, the man with the greatest escutcheon in France, the Captain-Colonel of a hundred guards of the King's Guard, this splendid nobleman, who bore so great a name in the train of the pages and the carriages accompanying him, this hero of another time, whose soul, like his dress, belongs to the days of Louis XIV., this type, this superb and venerated relic of honour and chivalry, *this soldier*

---

[1] "Secret Memoirs from 1770 to 1830." By the Comte d'Allonville. Paris, 1838. Vol. I.

Madame Du Barry

since his birth, the inheritor of the masculine virtues of old France, as well as of its most polished and most noble gallantries, this fine old man, the last courtier of women, this son of Brissac, brought up in the religion and the traditions of his family, in the world, and almost in the language, of the high sentiments and refinements of tenderness of Clelie and of Astree, . . . Louis-Hercule-Timoleon de Cosse-Brissac, became the lover, the adoring and respectful lover of the Comtesse du Barry. And truly there will be seen in the attachment of M. de Brissac such a gift of himself, such delicate attentions, such eager forethought, such deep worship, something so piously tender, that it disturbs and staggers our judgment about the woman whom he deemed worthy of so beautiful a love. It seems that in M. de Brissac's eyes Madame du Barry appears in that bright light in which M. d'Allonville saw her, with that decency of tone, that distinction of manners, that demeanour equally removed from pride and humility, from license and prudery, that face which was sufficient to refute all the pamphlets.[1] So open was Madame du Barry's heart that it was impossible it should not be profoundly touched by M. de Brissac, and that it should not let itself in fact be penetrated by this love, this self-immolation, these hourly tendernesses. In the Duke's letters to Madame du Barry there are no expressions save those of the most caressing adoration:

[1] "Secret Memoirs from 1770 to 1830." By the Comte d'Allonville. Paris, 1838. Vol. I.

Madame Du Barry

"Adieu, my heart." "Come, my *dearest heart.*" "A thousand loves and a thousand thanks, my dear heart." "Yes, it is my happiness to be loved by you." "It is you alone that can touch my heart." "My only happiness is to think of you and on the eternal sentiments I have vowed to you." "Your heart and mine are but one for ever." The only things spoken about in these impassioned letters are the beauty, the goodness, the *magnanimity* of Madame du Barry, above all "that perfect evenness of temper which constitutes the charm of her habitual society." And what a pretty expression of the feelings of a loving old man we find in this end of a letter: . . . "I have not got my spectacles, so I write to you one single line, which comprehends everything: I love you and for life."[1]

The sentiment of the old Duke was so true, so entire, so old-world that it disarmed the malignity of the public.[2] Society was not ignorant of the Duc de Brissac's passion, and was indulgent to this passion. There is even a curious testimony to the knowledge of it by the Court. At the time of the project of the flight to Varennes, the Duc de Choiseul, the Minister's nephew, wished to communicate the fact confidentially to M. de Brissac, but Louis XVI. refused, saying that he could not avoid speaking about it to Madame du Barry. The Duc de Choiseul gives another proof of

[1] Revolutionary Tribunals: Madame Du Barry's "Dossier." National Archives, W[1] 16.

[2] This amorous sentiment of the Duke went back far. In 1772, Madame de Cosse, tiring-woman to Marie Antoinette, being invited

the profound and inexplicable attachment of the Duc de Brissac to Madame du Barry. The decree disbanding the King's Guard, as well as that under which its commander was impeached, had been delivered at one o'clock in the morning. Choiseul hurried to the Tuileries to give notice of it to the King and Queen, who had gone to bed. They sent him immediately into Brissac's apartment to persuade him to fly. On the announcement being made to him that the decree would be without doubt proclaimed before two o'clock, the Duke, refusing to effect his escape, got up out of bed merely to write a letter—a long letter to his mistress— which he had forthwith despatched to Luciennes by his aide-de-camp, Maussabre.[1]

The Duc de Brissac was arrested and brought to Orleans. And Madame du Barry, whose anxiety had reached

[1] *Revue de Paris,* 1829. Tome IV.

---

to sup by M. de la Vrilliere with Madame du Barry, refused. M. de Cosse, according to the expression of Mercy-Argenteau, entirely given up to the Comtesse du Barry, received bitter reproaches for it. He was asked to use his authority with his wife. Not knowing how to get out of the affair, the Duke thought of telling the Favourite that his wife had acted according to Marie Antoinette's orders. And thereupon the Duke wrote a letter to his wife—a very strong letter— in which he exacted from her that she should show every sort of attention to the Comtesse du Barry and should not refuse to do anything that would please her. The Duchesse de Cosse, who had been appointed, it is true, at the request of the Favourite, replied, that in taking possession of her charge, she had gone to pay a visit to the Comtesse du Barry, but that, after this step, she had decided not to do anything which should make her be regarded as a person associating with the Favourite, and that she preferred to send in her dismissal.

its highest pitch, received on the 2nd of June, from Maussabre, the Duc de Brissac's letter reassuring her and adding
for her information that " he had reached the place of his
destination without the slightest incident having happened to
him." Already an object of suspicion owing to her *liaison*
with a servant of Royalty, already denounced, Madame du
Barry imports an element of bravery into her devotion to
her lover. Every day her postilion Augustin was on the
Orleans road bringing letters from the ex-Favourite and
bringing back replies from the prisoner. Of this correspondence of love carried on thus in the antechamber of death,
two letters, one from the mistress, and the other from the
lover, have been preserved for us and are found in the
" Dossier " of the guillotine.

Here is Madame du Barry's letter: " I was seized with
a deadly fear, Monsieur le Duc, when M. de Maussabre was
announced to me. He assures me that you are well, that
you have the calmness of a pure conscience. But this does
not suffice for my interest in you. I am far from you; I
am ignorant of what you are going to do; you tell me that
you do not know yourself. I am sending the Abbe to know
what is happening, what you are doing. Why am I not near
you? You would receive from me the consolation of a tender and faithful friendship. I know you have nothing to
fear if reason and good faith reigned in that Assembly.
Adieu, I have no time to write to you more. The Abbe has
come into my room. I want to send him off quickly. I shall
not feel easy till I know what has become of you. I am

quite sure you have acted regularly on the question of the formation of the King's Guard. So I have nothing to fear for you on that head. Your conduct has been so pure since you were at the Tuileries that nobody can impute anything to you. You have done so many acts of patriotism that I do not know what fault they can find with you. Adieu. Tell me all the news about yourself and never doubt all that I feel.

" This Wednesday at eleven o'clock."

And this is the letter written by the Duc de Brissac in the month of August :

"Orleans, 6 o'clock in the evening.

"I received this morning the kindest of letters and the one which has given most delight to my heart. Yes, you shall be my last thought."[1]

And this was not a commonplace phrase. The Duke spoke truly, for, almost at the same time that he wrote this letter, he made on the day following the death of Royalty his will, in which we find this injunction to the Duchesse de Mortemart, his daughter :

" I recommend to her ardently a lady who is very dear to me, and whom the misfortunes of the times may place in the greatest distress. My daughter will have a codicil from me, which will indicate to her what I direct on this subject."

[1] At the foot of the letter we read : "*Ne varietur,* this 9th day of Brumaire, the year II. of the Rep." with the signatures of Voulland, G. Jagot, Du Barry. Revolutionary Tribunals : " Dossier " of Madame du Barry. National Archives, W¹ 16.

Madame Du Barry

This codicil is thus expressed:

" I give and bequeath to Madame du Barry of Luciennes, over and above what I owe her, a life-annuity of 24,000 livres a year, free and exempt from all deductions, or else the usufruct and enjoyment during her life of my estate of La Rambaudiere and of La Graffiniere in Poitou, and the household goods attached to it, or else again a sum of 300,-000 livres paid all in one sum of money, the whole at her own choice, so that, after she has made her election of the aforesaid three legacies, the two others will be null and void. I beg of her to accept this feeble proof of my sentiments and my gratitude, of which I owe her all the more inasmuch as *I have been the involuntary cause of the loss of her diamonds,* and if ever she succeeds in getting them back from England, those which will remain missing or the expense of the different journeys which the search for them rendered necessary, as well as that of the premium to be paid, will rise to the level of the actual value of this legacy. I entreat my daughter to make her accept it. The knowledge that I have of her heart assures me of the exactness she will show in paying it, whatever may be the charges with which my estate will find itself burdened by my will and codicil, my will being that none of my other legacies may be paid till this has been entirely satisfied.

" This 11th of August, 1792.

[Signed:]

"Louis-Hercule-Timoléon de Cosse-Brissac." [1]

[1] "Madame du Barry." By I. A. Le Roi, Versailles, 1858.

Madame Du Barry

This presentiment of his approaching and tragic death, all those who were attached to the Duke had at the same time as himself. They gathered in deep alarm around Madame du Barry; and the mistress and the house of Luciennes were plunged into the most cruel apprehensions.

Bernard d'Escourt, that ex-captain of cavalry, who made himself, as it were, the knight of honour of the former Favourite, having been sent to Paris to see some deputies on the reception of the news that the prisoners had been transferred from Orleans to Versailles, wrote to Madame du Barry on the 6th of September, 1792: "The prisoners from Orleans arrive to-morrow in Versailles. . . . We must hope that *they may arrive safe and sound, and that they may gain time to save their lives.* . . . There have come to my hands ten letters from Orleans for actual deputies intimating beforehand that misfortune threatens those unhappy persons believed to be in Orleans, that they will be murdered on their arrival here:—Madame de Maurepas, enlightened by the transfer of the Duke, wanted to go at once to the Assembly; she was prevented from doing so. She has written to Danton and to the Abbe Fauchet. Madame Flammarens and I have carried the letters; they [have] deeply interested the Abbe Fauchet.

"My soul and body are overwhelmed, and I shall not feel at peace till I know that the Duke is in Versailles. If we can pass, I will send there; if I cannot go, send there on your own account, but above all be careful to avoid any steps

235

which might become public and do you harm, and injure both one and the other." [1]

The day after that on which this letter was written, the 8th of September, in accordance with the sad anticipations of the Chevalier d'Escourt, the Orleans prisoners met with the assassins of the prisons on reaching Versailles, and were massacred. The Duc de Brissac, armed with a knife *à la d'Estaing,* sold his life dearly.

The grief and horror of this death break out in this letter of Madame du Barry:

" Since that cruel day, monsieur, I am in a state of grief which it is easy for you to conceive. There you see consummated that dreadful crime which renders me so unhappy and delivers me up to eternal regrets. In the midst of the horrors which surround me, my health keeps up. We do not die of sorrow. I am sensibly touched, monsieur, by your interest; it will soften my pains if I cannot feel them at every moment. I have to-day heard from your wife. I think she will soon come to see me. I expect her with impatience. It is such a consolation to be with persons who share in our sentiments that I regret every instant I spend without seeing her." [2] Madame du Barry returned to the

[1] Letter presumed to be from the Chevalier d'Escourt. Revolutionary Tribunals: Madame du Barry's " Dossier," National Archives, W^1 16.

[2] Autograph letter of Madame du Barry. National Archives, W'16. This letter and the greater part of the documents forming portion of Madame du Barry's " Dossier," which are in the National Archives, were published as having previously been unpublished by M. Dauban in " La Demagogie in 1793 "; they had been already pub-

Madame Du Barry

subject of this death in a letter addressed to the Duc de Brissac's daughter, the Duchesse de Mortemart:

"Nobody has felt more than I, Madame, the extent of the loss you have had. I flatter myself that you have not misunderstood the motive which has prevented me from paying you sooner the sad compliment of mingling my tears with yours. The fear of increasing your first grief will prevent me from speaking to you about it. Mine has reached its highest point. A destiny that ought to have been (so) beautiful, so glorious, what an end, great God! The last wish of your too unhappy father, Madame, was that I should love you as a sister. This vow is too agreeable to my heart for me not to fulfil it. Accept the assurance of it, and never doubt the sentiments which attach me to you for the rest of my life."[1]

[1] Madame du Barry's "Dossier" contains a letter, dated September 30th, from the Duchesse de Mortemart, who expresses herself in these terms: "The last wish of him whom I loved and will always regret is that of my heart; I will love you as a sister, and my attachment for you will only end with my life." In a previous letter, dated the 5th of June, and sent, I believe, from the waters of Aix-la-Chapelle, she said to Madame du Barry that "she was greatly afflicted and that she believed she had compromised her father by re-entering France with her husband who was an *emigre*," and she added: "Can we make it a crime for a woman who is an invalid to have gone to take the waters and to make it rebound on her father?" Finally, in another letter sent as usual from abroad, and dated June 20, the Duchesse de Mortemart, speaking always of her father, wrote, almost reassured, to Madame du Barry: "I

lished in 1803 by M. de Favrolle (Madame Guenard) in the "Historical Memoirs of Jeanne Gomart de Vaubernier, Comtesse Dubarry."

XIV.

The Theft of the Night of January 10, 1791.—"Two Thousand Louis to Gain: Diamonds Lost."—Madame du Barry's Three Journeys to England.—Madame du Barry's Letter on the Jams of Luciennes.—Announcement of the Arrest of the Proprietress of Luciennes by the *Courrier Français.*—Madame du Barry interrogated by the Abbe Fauchet, President of the Committee of General Safety.

THIS blood of Brissac, which the Revolutionary Press cast in the Du Barry's face, marked her out for death. And yet death was going to have so much work to do that perhaps Louis XV.'s mistress would have been forgotten amongst the crowd of victims were it not for a theft which had occurred on the night of the 10th or 11th of January, 1791, during one of her sojourns at the Hotel Brissac.[1]

[1] It was not the first time that Madame du Barry had been robbed. On the 20th of April, 1776, three thieves, one of whom wore the Cross of Saint Louis, made their way into her presence, and, threatening her with a pistol, stole from her a rich jewel-case. In a letter

render you a million thanks, madame, for the news you have had the goodness to send me. As your letter has been delayed, I have only received it with news of my father from his own hand, which has given me great pleasure; I have learned since that he had been interrogated and was not any longer *au secret*. Here is as tolerable treatment as can be expected for a prisoner. In spite of his well-known innocence, I am afraid the proceedings will not be long." . . .

Madame Du Barry

This robbery brought about the denunciation against her
on account of her wealth; it inflamed the resentments of the
"Revolutions of Paris" against the pomp of the ex-courte-
san and her contempt for the rights of man.[1] It directed

[1] "Since the Revolution, the Dame du Barry had not ceased to
employ all the ascendency given her by great riches, acquired we
know how, in making misunderstanding prevail between the inhabitants of the neighbourhood of Luciennes and the Swiss of Courbevois. Her secret intrigues, concocted with the principal officers,
have not had all the success desired; on the contrary, we have had
such unfavorable accounts of the mistress of the chateau of Luciennes, that we do not hesitate to raise doubts as to the reality
of the theft of the diamonds. The considerable reduction with which
the said lady's income has been threatened has given rise in her
mind, it is said, to the idea of rendering herself interesting by representing herself as the victim of a grievous event and procuring for
herself a claim to the indulgence of an inexorable National Assembly.

from her niece, Madame de Boissaisson, dated August 24, 1788, there
is a reference to a big theft of linen carried out by some thieves
who must have been thoroughly acquainted with the people of the
house. As to the theft of the night of the 10th or 11th of January, 1791,
here are the details given by Morin in his examination in Frimaire,
Year II. (December 18, 1793): A Swiss dressed in red had to
keep guard without during the entire night and a gardener had to
sleep in the antechamber, according to "the orders" given by Madame du Barry. Nevertheless, by reason of the difficulty of putting
up a bed in this antechamber, Morin had exempted the gardener
from the necessity of sleeping there, saying to him: "We must hope
that nothing will happen this night." And with the aid of the porter
Girardin he took a ladder used by masons, left against the window
of Madame du Barry's dressing-room, and brought it across to the
ornamental pond. Some inner shutters fastening with brass hasps,
freshly settled by the upholsterer and left to be closed by the floor-
scrubber, were intact. It was only the outer blinds which were
smashed with a paving-stone.

public attention towards so much riches, the existence of which had been unknown. It fixed on all the dead walls of Paris this placard: " Two Thousand Louis to Gain: Diamonds Lost "—this placard giving particulars of all the stolen articles, which imprudently displayed before want, before envy, before Revolution, the list and the fascination of all these diamonds, all these sapphires, all these emeralds, all these sardonyxes, all these engraved stones, these strings of two hundred pearls, these brilliants with ten heads,

"However this may be, her conduct, in the position in which she presents herself, is scarcely such as will gain her sympathy. The said lady gave a very good salary to a Swiss soldier to serve as door-keeper at Luciennes. The actual caretaker was a young man of eighteen with a kindly and very honest face. On learning about the removal of her jewels, the first step of the mistress of the chateau was to drive in a carriage with four horses to the barracks of the Swiss commander at Courbevois. She had no difficulty in making him despatch to her house fifty grenadiers, who came at once, but with regret, to take into custody the young Swiss, who was generally esteemed and liked by all his comrades. He was conveyed to one of the prisons in Ruel, where orders were at the same time given to put him in fetters in the darkest of the cells.

"We have all these facts from the lips of a Swiss from Courbevois, a candid young man, who informs us at the same time that all the prisoner's company, when freed from the restrictions of military discipline, proposed to take the Dame du Barry aside and to call upon her for a just reason for the violence exercised at her entreaty on the person of a soldier at most only suspected. The theft of the diamonds of Golconda would not justify this blow at the rights of man and of the citizen; and, besides, is it an offence sufficiently grave to be put in fetters on the mere suspicion of a woman who is still proud of having been for a time the first courtesan of the empire?" This Swiss confessed, a few days after, said the "Feuille du Jour," that individuals whom he did not know had made him drunk in a public house.

twenty heads, a Golconda inventory which the cupidity of the passers-by spelled out at the street-corners.[1]

And here we soon find the exaggerations of popular stupidity unchained. . . . Rapacious ambitions, furious and ill-concealed covetousness rise up everywhere around the house, around this estate which sounds hollow under the wooden shoe of the patriot and lets him guess what a fortune lies hidden in its bowels—this mine of gold coffee-pots, sacks of double gold louis, porcelain jars mounted with gold, bracelets of antique gold, washhand-basins and water-pots of rock-crystal, gold cups with coral handles, gold knives ornamented with diamonds, and statues and miniatures. The prey was too beautiful not to tempt a Republic which had been accustomed to coin money in the Place de la Revolution.

Finally this unfortunate theft led to Madame du Barry's four journeys to England—journeys which were destined to get her accused of being an *emigree,* of being there on a secret mission, of understandings with the enemies of the Republic.

Thirty-five days after the theft of her jewels, February 15th, 1791, Madame du Barry received intelligence through a courier from London to the effect that the thieves had been arrested.[2] Madame du Barry, whose weak brain was

[1] See in the Appendix the placard of Madame du Barry's lost diamonds and trinkets.

[2] Favrolle (Madame Guenard) thus describes their arrest from the report of an English newspaper of February 20, 1791: "When they had reached London, five in number, and had put up at a tavern in the city, these gentlemen asked for a single room, which

unhinged, and who, since her loss, had spent a good deal of her time with fortune-tellers, started, in a state of wild delight, the day after[1] the lucky news reached her. She left with Maussabre and D'Escourt, who were to accompany her in her first three journeys. She took with her Pretry, her valet, a man-servant named Marechal, and her chambermaid, Roussel. She had the following letter despatched to Morin, her confidential man: " The diamonds, my dear Morin, have been found, and Madame la Comtesse is starting to-morrow for Boulogne to go and identify them. Forth has arrested the thieves, and has apprised Madame du Barry of the fact. She entreats of you, my dear Morin, to be doubly careful and to keep a watch around the chateau at

[1] Note of Madame du Barry, preserved in her "Dossier." National Archives, W¹ 16. " I started the next day, the 16th (February) ; I embarked at Boulogne on Sunday, the 20th, and remained in London till the 1st of March, when I left again for Luciennes, where I arrived on Friday, the 4th."

seemed a surprising thing. They ordered a good dinner, and as their equipage did not create a favourable impression, they said to their host that their money had not yet been changed, but that next day they would have an abundance of it. Having made this confidential statement they went to the establishment of M. Simon, a rich lapidary, and asked him for nearly one-sixth of the value of the jewels. The lapidary at first bought the portion of them which he had for fifteen hundred pounds sterling. He inquired of these individuals whether they had any more of them, and on getting an affirmative answer, he went to give information about the matter to the Lord Mayor. This magistrate got the entire gang arrested. A search was made, and though they had hurriedly thrown the large diamonds into the fire, the most important part of the stolen articles is in safe custody. The person who acted as interpreter is an Englishman already well-known in connection with a great number of robberies."

night." The diamonds had, in fact, been found. They were shown to her. She identified them, declaring on oath that they were her property.

But the legal proceedings were far from being terminated, and, in place of bringing them away with her, she had to leave her diamonds deposited with Messrs. Hamerleys and Morland, bankers, sealed with her own and with the bankers' seal. And the lady who had been robbed returned to France, after this first journey undertaken too precipitately and in too adventurous a spirit.

She set out again on the 4th of April,[1] bringing along with her the jeweller Rouen,[2] and returned home on the 21st of May. In spite of her activity, in spite of the persons of

[1] Note of Madame du Barry: "I left Paris on the 4th of April, and arrived in London on the 9th. I remained there thirty-eight days, that is to say, till the 18th of May, when I left for home. I reached home on Saturday, the 21st."

[2] Madame du Barry says in her secret examination that for her three first journeys she had passports from the minister Montmorin. Here is the passport for the second journey:

"IN THE KING'S NAME.

"To all officers, civil and military, charged with watching over and maintaining public order in the different departments of the Kingdom, and to all others whom it may concern: Greeting. We command you and order that you have to let pass freely *the Dame du Barry going to London with the S. d'Escours, Knight of S., Rouen, jeweller, two women and a valet and two couriers.* Without placing or allowing to be placed in her way any obstacle, the present passport to be valid only *for three months.* LOUIS.

"Given at Paris, April 3rd, 1791."

Note of Madame du Barry. National Archives, W⁹ 16. "I have been obliged to start for London again on Monday, the 23rd, having received a communication on the night of my arrival informing me

great influence who interested themselves in the celebrated woman, in spite of all the money she spent, her case, with the tediousness of English legal procedure, did not finish. The matter had, in reality, been clumsily initiated and more clumsily conducted, as this tail-end of a letter dated June 30th, 1791, testifies: " I begin again to be convinced that this business will be so costly that it will ruin the divinity. It has been so badly conducted that one must not be astonished if everything goes badly."[1] And the Du Barry came back without her diamonds on the 25th of August, 1791.

During her stay in London, a letter of Madame du Barry, relating to Luciennes and to the details of her home life, paints for us the woman in her inconsistent nature, in her light spirit, in her childish interest equally divided between the most menacing and the most paltry things. We see her occupying herself quite as much with her jams, which were always *too much cooked* at her house, as with the precautions that should be taken against the pillage of the rest of her property. Here is an example in this letter addressed to her confidential man, Morin:[2]

[1] The Du Barry "Dossier." National Archives, W'16.

[2] Morin had been for twenty-five years in the service of Madame. The son of a vinedresser from Auteuil, after having been a servant to many ladies in Paris, he entered the Comte du Barry's service by a mere chance on the 5th of June, 1768. Since that time he had always been attached to the house of Madame du Barry, in the capacity of a lackey for four years, and the rest of the time in the capacity of a valet in the special service of Madame du Barry. (Examination of Morin, on the 24th Frimaire. Year II. December 14, 1793.)

that my presence was absolutely necessary in London, where I remained till the 25th of August, when I returned."

Madame Du Barry

"Morin will go to the Mayor, the Commander-in-Chief, and the Justice of the Peace, to thank them on my behalf and to tell them that I count on their zeal and their interest, that I believe they will, in conjunction with my people, defend what is left of my property if it should be attacked by brigands. I flatter myself that we shall not be obliged to come to this extremity and that peace and tranquility will be restored. I am already rather unhappy at being separated from my house, from my friends, and in a country, whatever people may say, not as good as France before the troubles which agitate it.

"I approve of Morin's plan for putting my effects beyond the reach of thieves, and he is to consult the Duke about it. But good care must be taken that nobody suspects it.

"I do not know why Maisieu[1] always wants to be a ridiculous man, it is only by perfect agreement that we can mutually serve each other, and render the efforts of the wicked useless.

"I have given instructions to Fiston to go to Luciennes to assist Salenave in making the jams for the supplies of my house. I do not know why he has not been there, for I find that they are not well made in my house; they are always too much cooked. Morin will say to Mademoiselle Roussel to put all my laces which are in the cupboard of the chapel, into a trunk out of reach of any sort of attack, as

[1] I have retained Madame du Barry's bad spelling of a well-known word in her own language. Unless she misspelled this word through caprice, she here shows gross illiteracy.—TRANSLATOR.

they are susceptible of being stolen or burnt. I hope that we shall not be reduced to this sad extremity, but it is really necessary to anticipate everything. I see with mortal pain that I must still remain here up to the 14th of August, because the rascals who robbed me will not have their trial finished before the end of this month.

" THE C'TESSE DU BARRY.

"London, July 4th."[1]

After Madame du Barry's return to France, the Legislative Assembly replaced the Constituent Assembly; the National High Court entered upon its functions at Orleans; the new mode of beheading prisoners sentenced to death, called " Guillotine,"[2] was adopted; Brissac, the commander of the King's military establishment, was ordered to be impeached; the 10th of August succeeded to the 20th of June; a National Convention was formed; the King and Royal family were imprisoned in the Temple; the prisoners in the Abbey were murdered; the Orleans prisoners were massacred; and, what we have not yet said, Brissac's head was flung on the table of the salon at Luciennes.[3]

And when a portion of her lover's body was so ferociously exhibited under her eyes, Madame du Barry had not enough

---

[1] Signed autograph letter. The Du Barry "Dossier." National Archives, W¹ 16.

[2] The guillotine was so called from Dr. Guillotin, a member of the National Assembly, who introduced it as the swiftest and most merciful mode of carrying the death punishment into effect.— TRANSLATOR.

[3] *Courrier Français*, No. 259, September 15, 1792.

PRINCESSE DE LAMBALLE.

To face page 246

of leisure to give herself up entirely to her grief. She was forced to think of herself; it was necessary for her to think of defending her liberty, her life. She had to struggle against the mistrusts and the suspicion and the espionage which had for months been watching the incessant goings and comings, when Brissac was, day and night, either galloping on his own horse, or making his aide-de-camp, Maussabre, gallop on his horse towards Luciennes. The growing unpopularity of Brissac had slowly and noiselessly enveloped the mistress of the chateau. The Revolutionists saw in Madame du Barry the accomplice of the aristocrat who had recruited that Constitutional Guard of the King with which he fondly hoped to fight the last battle of the monarchy, so that, on the day when Brissac quitted Orleans to come to die at Versailles, this article appeared in the *Courrier Français,* which made all Paris believe that his mistress had been arrested and imprisoned :—

" The justice of the people strikes equally the traitors who conceal themselves behind gilded wainscotings. Madame du Barry has been arrested at Luciennes, and has just been brought to Paris. It has been noticed that this heroine of the old *regime* was continually sending emissaries to Orleans. It was thought with reason that these frequent embassies had some other object besides gallantry, to which Madame du Barry must at length be quite a stranger. Mistress and confidante of Brissac, she formerly shared his treasures and his pleasures; she shares perhaps to-day his counter-revolutionary ambition.

Madame Du Barry

"It will be fun for our young people to learn that Madame du Barry was arrested almost at the very time that the statue of La Pucelle was demolished at Orleans; this arrest was made on the night of the 30th or 31st, at two o'clock in the morning." [1]

Madame du Barry sent her friends to carry on the campaign, and D'Escourt wrote to her:

"I have found the editor of the *Courrier Français,* who will retract to-morrow the falseness of the article which refers to you; I have promised him a recompense if the new article is well done." [2]

The *Courrier Français* did not contradict the statement it had published, and Madame du Barry remained under the impending stroke of the announcement which she was every moment expecting to see realized.

During all these months of 1792 spent in France, Madame du Barry's life is only one continual alarm, one succession of violent deaths around her. To-day it is Brissac; yesterday it was Maussabre, who was torn away from the room where she concealed him at Luciennes, and who said as he was going that *if they sent him to Paris he would be massacred* [3] After the death of Maussabre and the death of

[1] *Courrier Français,* No. 246, September 2, 1792.
[2] Letter presumed to be from the Chevalier d'Escourt. Du Barry "Dossier," National Archives, W^1 16.
[3] Here is the account of Maussabre's death as it is to be found in "My Thirty-eight Hours' Agony," by Jourgniac Saint Meard: "The Abbey, September 3rd. Eight o'clock in the evening. I had formed a peculiarly close friendship with the Sieur Maussabre, who has only been arrested because he had been M. de Brissac's aide-de-camp. He

248

Madame Du Barry

D'Angremont, the first person guillotined during the Revolution and with whom she had had business relations, led to her being summoned before the Committee of General Safety of the Convention. She underwent an examination, in which she answered in a way that satisfied the members

---

had frequently given proofs of courage; but the dread of being assassinated had strained his heart. I succeeded, however, in somewhat dissipating his anxieties when he threw himself into my arms saying: 'My friend, I am lost; I have just heard my name pronounced in the street.' In vain did I say to him that perhaps the persons he heard were interested in him; that, moreover, fear would cure nothing, and that, on the contrary, it might only destroy him. It was all no use. He lost his head so that, not being able to conceal himself in the chapel, he went up the chimney of the sacristy, where he was stopped by gratings which he had even the folly to try to break with his head. We asked him to come down; after many difficulties he came back to us; but his reason did not come back. This is what caused his death, of which I will speak in a moment.—THURSDAY, SEPTEMBER 4. ONE O'CLOCK IN THE MORNING. Jourgniac Saint Meard was led to the wicket, lighted up by two torches, facing Maillard, who *stood* leaning against a table on which we saw papers, a writing-desk, pipes and bottles. They began to question him:—"When the attention they showed in listening to me, and which, I confess I did not expect, encouraged me, and I was going to make a *resume* of the thousand reasons which caused me to prefer the *Republican regime* to that of the Constitution, I was on the point of repeating what I said every day in M. Desennes' shop, but at that moment the door-keeper entered quite scared to give notice that a prisoner had escaped through the window. The President said they should have him fired at with pistols, but that, if he escaped, the jailer would be answerable for his head. It was the unhappy Maussabre. Some musket-shots were fired at him, and the jailer, seeing that this device would not succeed, lighted some straw. The smoke made him feel half stifled. He was despatched in front of the wicket-gate.

249

of the first committee, in which there was still a little humanity left. And the Abbe Fauchet who presided at the Committee, struck with pity for the woman, said to her that it was dangerous to have her name found compromised in the examination of this villain, and, with the assent of his colleagues he took up a pen, and erased in her presence a few lines of D'Angremont's deposition.[1]

[1] Manuscript Deposition of Blache, the eighth made which does not mention the oral deposition before the Revolutionary Tribunal. Du Barry's "Dossier," Archives, W^1 16.

XV.

Letter of Madame du Barry to Lebrun with Reference to her Four Journeys to London.—Dinner in London with the Duc de Choiseul.—Seals put on Luciennes, during her Absence.—Greive, *Factionist and Anarchist of the First Order, and Disorganizer of Despotism in the Two Hemispheres.*—His Denunciation of Madame du Barry, whose Arrest is suspended by Boileau.—Greive's Address to the Convention. —Arrest of Madame du Barry, who is released a few days later.—Letter full of Hysterical grief from Madame du Barry to the Administrators of the Department of Seine-et-Oise.—Tenderness of the Republican Lavallery.—Last Amours of Madame du Barry with Rohan-Rochefort.

THREE journeys to England had not yet restored the possession of her diamonds to Madame du Barry. She was obliged to return for the fourth time to London in the month of October, 1792.[1] In the gravity of the circumstances and under the weight of the suspicions of which she was the object, Madame du Barry took every precaution against letting herself be disturbed, all the guarantees

[1] Note of Madame du Barry on her fourth journey: "Since that time (August 25, 1792) I remained at Luciennes till October 14, 1792, when I set out again for London armed with passports and letters from the Minister of Foreign Affairs. I arrived there on the 22nd, and my case having been finished on February 27th last, the closing day of the sitting of the Court, I hastened back from London on March 3, and arrived on the 5th at Calais, where I was kept till the 18th, awaiting new passports from the executive power, as is proved by my passport from the municipality of Calais and the certificate of my residence there."

251

against the accusation of being an *emigree*. She had obtained a regular passport from Lebrun, but she did not consider it sufficiently explanatory, and addressed to him this letter:

"I have received, Monsieur, the letter which you have done me the honour to write to me, and my passports. I am sensibly touched by the care you have taken to have them authenticated. But as there is no mention in your letter, or in my passport, of my journey to London, where my presence is necessitated by my wretched case, I fear I may experience difficulties in my passage, and, besides, my municipality, not seeing me authorized to travel in foreign countries, may look upon me as being an *emigrce,* and may put the seals on my house. I venture, therefore, to hope, monsieur, from your obliging disposition and the desire you have testified to be useful to me, that you will be kind enough to enlighten me on this subject. I believe that one word from you might remove all difficulties and save me from the unpleasantnesses to which I am liable to be subjected.

"I beg of you, monsieur, to be convinced of the lively gratitude with which I have the honour to be,

"Your very humble and very obedient servant.

"Du Barry.

"Luciennes, this 6th of October." [1]

The minister, Lebrun, seems to have written for her the

[1] Du Barry's "Dossier," National Archives, W[1] 16.

line which she asked him for.[1] Then Madame du Barry informed the municipality of Luciennes that she was not abandoning her country, and in this letter in which the poor woman seeks to humour the terrible Sans-culottes of the locality, she gives her word of honour to return to France:

" Since I have had the honour of living under your eyes, you have been kind enough, messieurs, to recognize that on every occasion I have given pledges of my civism and of my respect for the laws. I flatter myself that, in the same spirit of justice, you will be so good as to accept also the present declaration by which I do not go across to England to abandon my country and my ordinary residence, but that I am compelled to go to London to finish there a case on which depends the recovery of precious articles, which you know have been stolen from me, and which compose the principal part of my fortune, as the only security that my creditors have. I declare at the same time that I give a solemn undertaking to re-enter France as soon as my case

---

[1] A note from Greive, in Madame du Barry's " Dossier," says that in her last journeys Madame du Barry asked for passports from Lebrun, who refused them; that she then made an application to the municipality of Luciennes and the Department of Versailles. Greive either deceived himself or lied. Madame du Barry's letter to Lebrun attests that she had a regular passport from Lebrun, and as for the line mentioning her journey to England, the deliberation of the municipality which took place on the 8th of October appears to acknowledge the receipt of this second letter. It is true, however, that she says in her secret examination: " As for the fourth, I have a passport from the municipality of Luciennes which has been officially authenticated by the administration of Seine-et-Oise."

is finished." [1] This was not enough still. Not at all tranquillised by this declaration, owing to the decree made by the municipality of Luciennes on October 8th, after her appearance before the official authorities the previous day, [2] she addressed the undertaking she had made to the municipality to the President of the Convention:

" Monsieur le President,—A theft which, twenty months ago, carried off my precious effects, and the only security that my creditors have, has occasioned legal proceedings in England, for which I have been obliged to make two very expensive journeys. I see myself forced to make a third on the intimation conveyed to me that the case is bound to be concluded this month, and that under the penalty of being fined for default of appearance and of being at the loss of the heavy sum I have expended in costs, it is absolutely necessary for me to go to London. I have the

---

[1] Du Barry "Dossier," National Archives, W[1] 16.

[2] "This day, October 7, 1792, the Year 1. of the French Republic, there appeared before us, municipal officers of the commune of Luciennes, district of Versailles, department of Seine-et-Oise, Dame Vaubernier du Barry, a resident in the locality, who has declared to us that, being obliged to go to London to be present at the conviction of thieves, who on the night of the 10th or 11th of January, 1791, had stolen her jewels in her chateau of Luciennes, she has made a declaration to us in order that she may not be regarded as an *emigree,* or during her absence be treated as such by any constituted authority, for which declaration she has requested us for a certificate, which we have granted, in view of the letter of M. Lebrun, Minister of Foreign Affairs, dated the 2d inst., which remains annexed at the present minute, and the aforesaid Dame du Barry has signed with us the same day and year as above. Good as a copy compared with the original, October 8, 1792." Madame du Barry, through Le Roi, Versailles, 1858.

honour to assure you, Monsieur le President, that my intention is not at all to abandon my country, where I leave all the property that is left to me, but, on the contrary, I give a solemn undertaking to return to my residence at Luciennes as soon as my case is ended. I have in the same way made this undertaking before my municipality, on the part of whom I am well assured that I have only to wait for attestations which will be favourable to me.

" I am with respect."[1]

Madame du Barry started " by the Calais diligence like a genuine Sans-culotte," accompanied in this last voyage by Labondie, D'Escourt's nephew. She thought her case would be terminated in a few weeks, but the proceedings dragged on for months.[2] During her sojourn abroad, events hurried on in France to a tragic phase; Louis XVI. was executed, and the guillotine threatened all the suspects. Had the journeys of Madame du Barry, this last sojourn in London, a political object, as Greive and Fouquier-Tinville wished to have it believed? Did Madame du Barry give her services to a plan, a party, to political aspirations? The woman's levity scarcely permitted of such an assumption. All her crimes against the Revolution were probably loans to *emigres,* pecuniary services, generous charities, acts of pity similar to those which had so quickly changed the heart of the former Du Barry towards the Queen.

In this journey, the Favourite who had overthrown Choi-

[1] Du Barry " Dossier," National Archives, W[1] 16.
[2] Her case was not completely disposed of till Feb. 28, 1793.

seul found herself once at dinner at the house of the
banker Thelusson, beside the minister's nephew, who had
been anxious, through curiosity, to make her acquaintance.
During this dinner, at which she showed great amiability
towards her neighbour, she talked to him for a long time
about his uncle, deploring the advice which she had followed, making him the avowal with a grace which the Duke
recognized as part of that *real coquetry* which she had, for
a moment, exercised over the minister, but which was
quickly killed by the cold dignity of Madame de Pompadour's former lover. In the high society with which she
mixed, she several times saw Pitt, who gave her the medal
struck in his honour, which was to be so fatal to her. The
English minister urged her to remain in England, not to
attempt at the moment to go back to France, and, when she
spoke to him about her engagements of honour, he predicted for the beautiful and imprudent creature the doom
of Regulus.

In reality Madame du Barry would have easily forgotten
her engagements towards the municipality of Luciennes and
the President of the Convention if she could have taken her
means with her; but she was driven to return to France by
the feeling of a proprietress, by the attachment she naturally
felt for all those riches with which the little palace was
stored. And her return, in those perilous times, was perhaps only brought about by the news of the setting of the
seals on the 16th of February, 1793.[1]

[1] Note of Greive in Madame du Barry's "Dossier":—"She did
not return to France till after the news of the fixing of the seals

Madame Du Barry

On resuming possession of her property, when the seals had been removed from Luciennes,[1] Madame du Barry found around her a terribly menacing state of affairs and an alarming condition of things in the country. There had come into the village an adventurer named Greive, a man half English, half French, describing himself as a man of

[1] "Citizens, Administrators.—The citizeness Jeanne de Vaubernier du Barry is astonished that after all the promises that she has furnished you of showing the reasons which have compelled her to go to England, you have treated her as an *emigree*. Before her departure she communicated to you the declaration that she had made to her municipality; you have it registered in your offices. You know that it is the fourth journey she has been obliged to make for the same motive. She hopes that you will be good enough to remove the seals which have been affixed to her house, contrary to

on her house. An unquestionable fact. Her passport from Lebrun was but for six weeks, and she remained there five months." The verification of the fact alleged by Greive is not possible; Lebrun's passport does not exist in Madame du Barry's "Dossier." Here is the document which led to the attachment of the seals; it was a letter from the Procureur-General Syndic of the district of Versailles, addressed to the administrators of the district and expressed in these terms:—

"The woman Dubarry, proprietress at Luciennes, left France by means of a passport in the beginning of 1792, to prosecute in England the perpetrators of a very considerable theft which took place in her house.

"The doubt inspired as to this prosecution by the lapse of time and by the ignorance as to her effects has necessarily given rise to uncertainty.

"In this state of affairs the administration has thought it right to take conservative measures, as to this woman's property, in order to secure at the same time her rights and those of the nation.

"It authorizes me, in consequence, to invite you to affix the seals on the house of the woman Du Barry at Luciennes, to appoint a

letters, and styling himself "official defender of the brave Sans-culottes of Luciennes, friend of *Franklin* and of *Marat,* a factionist and anarchist of the first order, and disorganizer of despotism in two hemispheres." [1] He had organized a club in this quiet spot, and had already secured by one of his motions, the affixing of the seals on Luciennes.   The re-

---

[1] It is thus that Greive signs his very rare pamphlet bearing the title of "*Equality falsely Contrived,* or Little History of the Protection containing the documents relating to the arrest of the Du Barry, formerly mistress of Louis XV., to serve as an example to Patriots who are too ardent, and wish to save the Republic and to the Moderates who understood marvellously how to destroy it. As it is difficult to do good, . . ." ("Pere Duchesne.")

---

all justice, since the law has never forbidden those who are compelled to go to a foreign country by private and pressing affairs to leave the kingdom. All France has learned about the theft which took place on the night of the 10th or 11th of January; that the thieves have been arrested in London, that legal proceedings followed, which were not ended till February 28 last, the annexed certificate attests."

---

guardian over it, and to address to him the record which will be prepared for the occasion.

"You will be good enough, citizens, to hurry with this operation, and to let me know about it as soon as it is done."

Two days later the members of the directory of the district responded with this resolution:

"Having regard to the letter of the Procureur-General Syndic, the directory of the district has appointed the citizen Brunette, one of its members, to proceed, in the presence of two officers of the commune of Luciennes, to affix the seals on all the furniture, title-deeds and effects of the woman Du Barry, and to procure for the preservation of the said seals one or two solvent keepers. . . . Made at Versailles, October 16, 1793." (Archives of the Seine-et-Oise, document cited by Le Roi in "Madame du Barry.")

MARAT

To face page 258

Madame Du Barry

turn from London of Madame du Barry, upsetting perhaps his plans and his speculations with regard to the gold mine of Luciennes, made him more enraged against the proprietress of the chateau, as to the interior and the occupants of which he had the most minute information through the malignity and the perfidy of the butler, Salenave, and the negro Zamore; for those two servants of the chateau already formed part of the popular club of Luciennes composed of forty of the inhabitants.

Madame du Barry, as soon as she was reinstalled in her own house, turned out of doors Salenave, whom she caught stealing her chinaware. Greive, reinforced by the alliance of the dismissed man-servant, who boldly declared himself the open enemy of his former mistress, and presently sustained by a certain Blache, who, under the mask of a professor of French in England, had played the spy on Madame du Barry in London, and who had been entrusted with a mission of surveillance in the department of Seine-et-Oise,— Greive and these two men, taking advantage of the law passed on the 2nd of June, ordering the authorities through the entire length and breadth of the Republic to have all persons *notoriously suspected of aristocracy and want of civic virtue* seized and arrested, had an address to the administrators drawn up by the club of Luciennes. This address, for the preparation of which Greive had chosen the day of the news of La Fleche having been taken by the Royalist army, marked out the departments of Seine-et-Oise, Mantes, Ruel, Bellevue, Meudon, Saint-Cloud, Suresne,

Bougival, and Marly, as filled with male and female miscreants who held forth their hands towards the insurrection
which overflowed into the department of Eure-et-Loire
after the defeat of the Republicans at Saumur. It showed
a chain of aristocrats of both sexes along the Seine ready
to draw together the Seine and the Loire in a Royalist conspiracy. In this address, dated June 26th, 1793, the good
citizens of Luciennes, with the object of awakening the
paternal interest of the administrators in the perils of the
country and on the best measures to take, asked them to get
the terrible decree passed by the Convention on the 2nd of
June proclaimed.

The deputation, headed by Greive, Blache, and Salenave,
after having obtained from the administrators a correct copy
of the law of the 2nd of June, immediately convoked the
Commune for the purpose of proceeding to the formation of
a list of persons to be arrested; and the name of Madame
du Barry was put forward on the list.

Madame du Barry, having been informed of what had
happened, despatched Morin, her valet, with Labondie, who
had been arrested in her house a fortnight before, to plead
her cause with the members of the head-government.
Greive, and with him the mayor and the municipal officers
whom he had led in his train, were already at the chateau
on the 27th of June, and were on the point of arresting
Madame du Barry when Citizen Boileau, a member of the
district, arrived. Boileau thereupon called for a meeting of
the municipality, reprimanded it for having precipitated the

execution of a law which was to be sent with restrictions and modifications, and reinstalled Madame du Barry in her house.

Greive was not discouraged. He drew up another address and got it filled with signatures; and on the 3rd of July he led the mayor and the municipal councillors to the bar of the Convention to read there this new address, dated the 1st of July, 1793, the year II. of the Republic. " The brave Sans-culottes of Luciennes," Greive said, " felicitated the Convention on the wise, benevolent, and popular decrees passed since the immortal insurrection of the 31st of May. . . . . These decrees had renewed the sacred fire ready to be extinguished under the ice of moderation. The Sans-culottes of Luciennes had just commenced their operations with the arrest of a woman who had been able, in spite of relations notoriously opposed to citizenship, by her riches and her caresses, which she had learned at the court of a weak and dissolute tyrant, to escape from the Declaration of the Rights of Man; of a woman who had made her chateau the centre of liberticidal schemes against Paris, commenced by Brissac, and continued by the aristocrats of every colour with whom she was in perpetual correspondence; of a woman who by her luxury insulted the sufferings of the unhappy women whose husbands, fathers, brothers, and children shed their blood for equality in our armies "—of the Du Barry, in short, whose arrest was indispensable " in order to destroy the vestiges of a false grandeur which fascinated the eyes of the good and simple inhabitants of the country and to put in practice the disregarded principles of equality.[1] The brave Sans-culottes finished by asking for the printing of their adress " in order to give an impetus to the other communes of the department."

Having read his address, Greive, with skilful perfidy, thanked the representative citizens for the decree passed the evening before, a decree which, by prescribing that decrees should be sent directly to the communes, took away from the head-government the means of paralyzing their measures, and put the people into immediate communication with their representatives.

The President of the Convention, Thuriot, replied:

" The National Convention applauds the fresh proofs which the commune of Luciennes has just given of its patriotism, so well recognized since the commencement of the Revolution, and which it manifests at this moment by putting into execution the law of the 2d of June with regard to a woman too long notorious for the misfortune of France. The charges which you have just made against her are too grave; be sure that, if they are proved, her head will fall on the scaffold."[2] Strengthened by the approbation of the Convention, Greive and his friends arrested Madame du Barry, and conducted her to Versailles so that she might be incarcerated in the prison of the department. Goujon, the Procureur-Syndic, inveighed against them,

---

[1] " Equality falsely contrived, or Little History of Protection, containing the Documents relating to the Arrest of the Du Barry."

[2] Ibid.

declared that the arrest was opposed to the wishes of the inhabitants of Luciennes and that the allegations against Madame du Barry were exaggerated and destitute of proof, complained bitterly of the despotism exercised by the club of Luciennes on the neighbouring communes, and ended with threats and with the declaration that he would make them tremble; but all in vain.[1] The Club and Grieve had the best of it; and Madame du Barry, *her niece, Madame de Boissaisson, wife of an emigre, and her servants, notoriously suspected of aristocracy and lack of civic virtue, remained under lock and key.*

Meanwhile, Madame du Barry, having got information as to the charges made against her, got a counter-address drawn up, and soon had it covered with the signatures of all the inhabitants of Luciennes hostile to the club. The petition, presented on the 6th of July, was addressed to the Committee of Public Safety, which, after having deliberated upon it, acceded to the request of Madame du Barry and sent her before the department, which decreed that she should be set at liberty. Madame du Barry was once more saved. In her delight at regaining her liberty, she wrote to a member of the Committee of General Safety:

" I was well persuaded, monsieur, that my cause being in your hands, I should obtain the justice which was due to me. I waited with much impatience for the termination of the

---

[1] It was Goujon who, having been condemned by a military commission on the 20th of May, 1795, stabbed himself while descending the staircase of his prison.

incident to thank you fully. M. de la Bondie has not left
me in ignorance of the zeal with which you have embraced
my defence. I should consider myself very happy if ever
I should find opportunities to testify my gratitude to
you. To-day that you are no longer my judge and that I
have no longer to fear being suspected of having captured
your suffrage, I hope that you will be kind enough to
furnish me with occasions of making your acquaintance and
thanking you by word of mouth. If the place where I live
can excite your curiosity, I shall have real pleasure in receiving you there. I should always find it a genuine boon
to converse with you about my gratitude and the sentiments
with which . . . ."[1] Greive was not a man to let go his
victim. He wrote this pamphlet, which he published on the

[1] Madame du Barry's "Dossier" contains a copy of this letter, at
the head of which we read:

"Letter written, as far as it appears, to some member of the Committee of General Safety of the Convention, after that Committee
had the guilty complaisance to send her back to her friends and
protectors, the administrators of Versailles, after her first arrest by
the Sans-culottes, in the beginning of the month of July. La Bondie
is nephew of the person who was formerly Chevalier D'Escourt,
Equerry of Brissac, and is now imprisoned in La Force. La Bondie,
who was formerly Chevalier, and who is suspected of being an
emigre, is from Cahors, where his goods were seized. He was one
of the frequenters of the chateau and an impudent aristocrat. It
was he who intrigued with the Committee on her behalf. He must be
in prison; if not, he is staying in the Hotel de Suede or the Hotel
du Bouloi." At the back of the letter we read: "This letter was
addressed to Delainville, whose residence she *pretends not to know*.
This Delainville was her official defender with the ex-Committee of
Safety. *It is supposed* that this letter was written to Bazire or to
Alquier, or to Julien of Toulouse." In a note in "L'Égalite Con-

Madame Du Barry

31st of July, 1793. The " disorganizer of despotism in two hemispheres " said in this pamphlet: " If the patriots of Luciennes have appeared to give importance to this woman in the address which they made to the National Convention, this too great celebrity is only due to the intervention, as singular as it is unbecoming, of certain administrators, to the more than ordinary activity with which one of them has flown to the Comtesse, to ward off the blows that menaced her *half-sacred* head. It was in order to make other administrators who would be tempted to intervene between her and the execution of the law feel ashamed that they have thought fit to submit to the entire nation a small number of petty details to prove that the suspicions of aristocracy and lack of civism falling on her, if not known through the misfortune of the administrators of Versailles, are at least of a sufficiently great notoriety in the place where she lives. It is in order to tranquillize the difficult consciences of the adorers of great names that the Sans-culottes of Luciennes are good enough to declare that in the step they have taken they have had no object but the welfare of their country, and that in asking for the decree of the 2d of June from

---

trouvee" Greive says: "This shameless woman has had the audacity to get up an address to the Convention signed by herself and by her official defender, Delainville, where she treats as defamatory libels the facts put forward against her, where she represents herself as a phœnix of patriotism, where she pretends to have broken off her *liaisons* with her old friends since the Revolution. . . . What impudence. . . ."

the department of Seine-et-Oise, far from any personal feeling and from having ill-will against the former distributress
of the graces and favours of the Court, they have regarded
her with the same eye as her chambermaid, with the differ-
ence only that she has an income of fifty thousand crowns,
and that they have exhibited the same firmness against
Gouy, her *concierge*, Pretry, her private councillor, Morin,
her political go-between with the constituted authorities,
and the surgeon Devray." Then followed the reproduction
of the Addresses at the Convention, the President's reply—
a sort of history of the prosecution which he carried on
against Madame du Barry, poisoned with deadly notes, denunciations by persons in her service, conversations re-
ported, words like those which Greive put into the mouth of
the Princesse de Rohan-Rochefort, reproaching Madame du
Barry quite recently with living too well and not sending
her superfluities to the Vendeans.[1]

Madame du Barry soon learned about this pamphlet.
She was astonished at the minute information about her
contained in it, which could only have been given to Greive
by some servants of her household. Instinctively, and with
the first impulse, her suspicions fastened on Zamore, that

[1] On a manuscript note of Greive in the "Dossier" of the Du
Barry we read: "Lastly, the representation made by the woman
Rohan-Rochefort that her table was splendid, that it would have
been better to diminish it in order to furnish succour to the volun-
teers of La Vendee, to which the Du Barry replied, 'Drink, drink!'
with a disdainful air, as if she did not think them worth bothering
about."

negro, of whom the Revolution had made a man and of whom treason was going to make a citizen. She knew the ideas that he had adopted. She remembered that he alone amongst her servants had not been arrested when she was brought to Versailles. It was he, this Zamore, on whom she had heaped favours, who had been held over the baptismal font by Madame du Barry and the Prince de Conti, who sold to Greive the secrets of Luciennes. Madame du Barry dismissed him immediately, she freed her house of a spy; she believed that she had banished an ingrate for ever from her sight. But Zamore was destined to appear once again and for the last time in Madame du Barry's life—at the Revolutionary Tribunal!

The club was becoming more menacing to the chateau, more furious and more declamatory against Madame du Barry. What months were those seven months passed by the proprietress of Luciennes with Greive's club at her door!

Every hour it was necessary to defend herself against imprisonment, against death. Madame du Barry escaped one denunciation only to be exposed some days later to another denunciation. She only left the prisons of Versailles to be menaced by the prisons of Paris. Then, the unhappy woman, as if she were distracted, wrote this letter:

" To the Citizens, Administrators of the Department of Versailles.

" Hitherto, citizens, some agitators have made vain efforts to disturb my tranquillity. I had to oppose to them my conscience and your equity, well convinced that I had in it an assured rampart against their malevolence. They have devised other means of tormenting me. But they will be powerless since my cause is submitted to you.

" When I had only to repel a denunciation, the knowledge of which the law attributes to you, and which it appears cannot go beyond your jurisdiction or have any other issue after your decision, I did not think I ought to have added entreaties to my petition or turn aside your attention from important objects in order to fix itself on a matter which was personal to me. But to-day the denunciation has assumed a character of gravity and of publicity which imposes on me the duty of promptly repelling the calumny. The malignity of my denouncers has reached such a point that I have everything to fear from them. I am, therefore, placed in a position that compels me to solicit from your zeal the promptest execution. I venture to add, citizens, that humanity makes this your duty. . . . I do not want to waste your time by explaining to you all my motives for fear. I shall impart it to the commissary whom you deem fit to appoint, and who will make you understand in his report that I have deserved to have you come to my aid." [1]

The citizen Lavallery was sent to Luciennes, and he persuaded Madame du Barry to withdraw to Versailles under the eyes and under the immediate protection of the department. Madame du Barry confessed to him that all her fortune, consisting of cash, jewels, and plate, was concealed in

[1] Madame du Barry's "Dossier," National Archives, W¹ 16.

different parts of her house, that the members of the club knew it through Salenave, through Zamore, through her chambermaid, the Widow Cottet, who gave information as to everything about the house, and that her departure would expose Luciennes to the avidity of the gang, to the domiciliary visits and the rummagings of all these men, the municipal officers on the one hand, and the National Guards on the other. Nevertheless, on the following day, Madame du Barry changed her mind, and made preparations to go to Versailles ;[1] but on the day after Lavallery's visit, the club of Luciennes held a meeting and decreed that a deputation should be sent to Versailles to denounce Madame du Barry there beforehand to the Revolutionary Committee of the commune.

At the same time, Blache, in his capacity of agent of the Committee of General Safety, was to denounce her anew in Paris to the Committee, whose members had been renewed. The deputation from Luciennes, having reached Versailles, agreed with the Revolutionary Committee of the city that a petition should be made to the Committee of General Safety in order to obtain an extension of powers, which would prevent the department from mixing itself up in the arrest of

[1] One day as she was getting ready to start for Versailles, a woman named Renaut came and asked with screams and vociferations if Madame du Barry was really quitting Luciennes, and, as "La Renaut" heard Madame du Barry asking a chambermaid who was the person who was making so much noise, she flung at the proprietress of the chateau this answer: "It is a woman who was in this country before you, and who will be there after you, do you understand?"

Madame du Barry. It was, moreover, agreed that three members of the department should be denounced, amongst whom was Lavallery, the avowed protector of Madame du Barry.[1]

In the midst of this life of mortal anxieties Madame du Barry continued, however, to love. Like those illustrious prisoners of the Luxembourg prison, who distracted their thoughts from the contemplation of the scaffold by the tender occupations of their hearts, the mistress of Luciennes escaped every moment the menacing present by means of what the age called " instants of happiness." Another succeeded to Brissac, another who idolized this woman of fifty with the passionate tenderness of the defunct old Duke.

[1] In fact Lavallery had become her correspondent, her devoted protector, and in all her difficulties the Comtesse addressed herself to the humanity of the Republican, who was touched by the woman's beauty and grace. Here is a letter addressed to Lavallery, which forms a portion of Madame du Barry's "Dossier": "I have just learned, citizen, that the Minister of Foreign Affairs, in sending on to the administration of the department the translation of the certificates which were delivered to me in London, had drawn attention to the fact that he had not seen without astonishment that in these documents the title of Comtesse had been given to me. I am no less astonished than he, and if I had known of the form in which these certificates were sent to me, I should certainly not have allowed to subsist a title which offends the laws of my country, to which I will remain invariably attached. I have no knowledge of the English language. I had to trust myself to an Englishman to conduct the prosecution on my behalf, and this inadvertence might easily have escaped his attention since he had previously known me under that title; and it was under this title, which was not then prohibited, that he began and continued the legal proceedings which he was employed to conduct on my behalf."

LE DUC D'ANGOULÊME

To face page 270

Madame Du Barry

Truly, we must say it here, there is something inexplicable in the charm which did not cease with age, the fascination of this creature of love, the absolute sway she exercises over the lover, and the tone of respectful and grateful adoration of the letters which at the same time implore and thank the divinity. During this *liaison* between Madame du Barry and the Prince de Rohan-Rochefort, generated perhaps by the tears poured out by them together over the death of Brissac, it happened one day that the happy living one who had taken the place of the dead was called upon to choose a portrait of Madame du Barry amongst those which the Duke had given orders to Madame Lebrun to do of his mistress. And the entire story of this last love of Madame du Barry is given and told us in this letter, so full of attachment toward the woman and her image, in this letter which preceded only by a fortnight the arrest of Louis XV.'s Favourite:

"This Saturday, September 7th, 1793.

"I send you, my dear and tender friend, the picture which you desired to have, sad and fatal present,[1] but which I feel quite as much as you can yourself that you ought to desire to have. In such a situation as ours, with so many subjects for pain and unhappiness, it is some nourishment for our melancholy which we seek and which suits us beyond all else.

---

[1] Doubtless a portrait of Brissac. This letter, which had already been republished with some abridgements by Madame Guenard, has been republished by M. Dauban, as one never before published.

Madame Du Barry

" I have had a search made for the three portraits of you which were *in his possession*. They are here. I have kept one of the little portraits. It is the original of her who wears a chemise or white dressing-gown with a feathered hat on her head.[1] The second is a copy, with the head finished, but the dress only printed in rough outline. Neither of them is framed. The large picture by Madame Lebrun is charming and bears a ravishing likeness to the original; it is a speaking picture with an infinite sweetness of expression; but truly I thought it would be indiscreet to choose it, and the one I am keeping is so agreeable, so life-like and so piquant that I am extremely content with it and transported with happiness at possessing it. The portrait commenced by Letellier is only a pencil-sketch, and the picture is hardly more than a rough draft which might become a good likeness.

" As for your large portrait and the one I am keeping, tell me, my dear friend, whether you wish me to send them or whether I ought to have them brought back to where they were,—in short, what destination you think best for them. I desire nothing more than to have one of them which I can wear about me, and which will never leave me. Come, then, dear love, to spend ten days here. Come and dine at my house with whomsoever you choose. Come and give me some instants of happiness—there is none without you. Reply about everything I have asked you to tell me. Come

[1] Madame Lebrun says it is a portrait which she painted for the' Duc de Brissac.

to see a mortal who loves you beyond everything up to the last moment of his life. I kiss a thousand times the portrait of the most charming woman in the world, whose heart is so good and so noble that it merits an eternal attachment." [1]

[1] Revolutionary Tribunals. The Du Barry's "Dossier," National Archives, W[1] 16.

XVI

Definitive Arrest of Madame du Barry: She is confined in Sainte-Pelagie.—The Anecdote about Madame de Mortemart.—Heron denouncing the Vandenyvers, the ex-Favourite's Bankers.—Greive's Annotations on the Papers seized.—The Preparation of the Heads of the Indictment by Greive.—The List of *Necessary* Witnesses drawn up by Greive.—Transfer of the Accused to the Conciergerie.

A NEW petition had been drawn up by Greive, signed by the members of the Committee of Versailles, and forwarded to the Committee of General Safety, which this time authorized the Committee of Versailles to use for the public welfare powers which had been entrusted to it, and declared that the constituted authorities would be responsible for the obstacles which might be opposed to the execution of these decrees. Then Greive succeeded in procuring a list of the sums paid to the account of Madame du Barry by Beaujon and prepared by Montvallier, Madame du Barry's steward, a list reaching six millions[1] ; and, armed with this document,

[1] List of the sums paid to the account of the Comtesse du Barry by Monsieur Beaujon while she was the Favourite at the Court of France:

JULY 15TH, 1774.
Observation.

Montvallier has drawn attention to the fact that he cannot render the work more complete, considering that he has not the continuation of M. Beaujon's memoranda, and there is even a gap between that of the 15th of February, 1772, and that of the 10th of September following, and that a number of documents without memoranda

Madame Du Barry

and with the decree of the Committee of General Safety, he kept worrying and working upon the members of the Committee of Versailles till he obtained the order to arrest Madame du Barry.

On the 22nd of September, he repaired to Luciennes,

have been delivered up by Madame du Barry for this gap, mounting up together to the sum of 93,200 livres, spent on the following articles, viz.:

FIRST ARTICLE.

From Goldsmiths, Jewellers, and Dealers in Trinkets:

Goldsmiths	313,328*l.*	4*s.*	—*d.*
Jewellers	1,808,635*l.*	9*s.*	—*d.*
Dealers in Trinkets	158,800*l.*	—*s.*	—*d.*
	2,280,763*l.*	13*s.*	—*d.*

ARTICLE II.

From Silk merchants, Lace dealers, and Millinery establishments:

Silk stuffs	369,810*l.*	15*s.*	—*d.*
Linen and Laces	215,988*l.*	6*s.*	—*d.*
Fashionable Articles of Dress	116,818*l.*	6*s.*	—*d.*
Haberdashery	35,443*l.*	14*s.*	—*d.*
	738,061*l.*	1*s.*	3*d.*

From different Perfumers, Furriers, Hatters,
Braziers .... 52,148*l.* 9*s.* —*d.*

ARTICLE III.

For Furniture, Pictures, Vases and other ornaments:

Furniture	24,398*l.*	18*s.*	—*d.*
Pictures, Vases	91,519*l.*	19*s.*	—*d.*
	115,918*l.*	17*s.*	—*d.*

ARTICLE IV.

From Tailors and Embroiderers:

Tailors	60,322*l.*	10*s.*	—*d.*
Embroiderers	471,178*l.*	—*s.*	—*d.*
	531,500*l.*	10*s.*	—*d.*

accompanied by two gendarmes, the Mayor, the Justice of
the Peace, and a number of municipal officers, showed his
order to Madame du Barry, had the seals affixed by the
Justice of the Peace, and forced Madame du Barry to get

ARTICLE V.

For purchases of Carriages and Horses and Forage:

Carriages and keep....................	67,470*l.*	1*s.*	—*d.*
Horses	57,347*l.*	—*s.*	—*d.*
Forage	6,810*l.*	—*s.*	—*d.*
	131,627*l.*	**1*s.***	**—*d.***

ARTICLE VI.

From Painters, Sculptors, etc.:

Gilders	78,026*l.*	—*s.*	—*d.*
Sculptors	95,426*l.*	—*s.*	—*d.*
Gilders	48,785*l.*	12*s.*	6*d.*
Founders	98,000*l.*	—*s.*	—*d.*
Marble-cutters	17,540*l.*	8*s.*	10*d.*
From various working Joiners and Locksmiths	32,240*l.*	8*s.*	—*d.*
Total	**370,018*l.***	**9*s.***	**4*d.***

ARTICLE VII.

For the Old and New Works of Luciennes:

Old Works	111,475*l.*	6*s.*	9*d.*
Gardens	3,739*l.*	19*s.*	—*d.*
New Works	205,638*l.*	16*s.*	8*d.*
Gardens	3,000*l.*	—*s.*	—*d.*
Total	**323,854*l.***	**2*s.***	**5*d.***

ARTICLE VIII.

Sums paid which cannot be applied to different
accounts, the motives or payments not being
known .... 55,619*l.* 2*s.* —*d.*

ARTICLE IX.

For extraordinary expenses, presents, gratuities,
alms .... 47,525*l.* 5*s.* —*d.*

into a public vehicle called a " guinguette," where the gendarmes posted themselves at her side.

It is related that, during the journey, Greive, having found near the engine of Marly the cabriolet of the Chevalier d'Escourt,[1] left the gendarmes in the public vehicle, and stepped into the cabriolet along with the woman whose fate at last he held in his hands. What was it that took place? Did Greive wish to sell life to Madame du Barry?

[1] A note by Greive at the back of the printed heading of an indictment gives us this information: " D'Escourt had already arrived in a cabriolet with a man-servant at the Du Barry's door on the day of her arrest; but, having ascertained what had occurred in her house, he fled at full speed. Our brave Sans-culottes seized him and caught him with some difficulty at the foot of the Bougival mountain." (Revolutionary Tribunals: the Du Barry's " Dossier," National Archives, W¹ 16.)

ARTICLE X.
Sums paid divided into three parts, the first considered as for the account of Madame du Barry and the second for her affairs:

By Madame du Barry directly or on her account to the Comte, Vicomte, and Demoiselles du Barry and others....... 1,081,052*l.* 15*s.* 9*d.*
By her agents and others, including the acquisition of the Pavilion of the Avenue de Versailles..................... 661,623*l.* 16*s.* 9*d.*

ARTICLE XI.
To the account of the construction of the building of the said Pavilion.................. 18,000*l.* —*s.* —*d.*

ARTICLE XII.
Balance payable .... 20,000*l.* —*s.* —*d.*

General total .... 6,521,003*l.* —*s.* —*d.*

Certified to be correct and in accordance with the memoranda mentioned above. At Luciennes, July 14th, 1774.

Signed: MONTVALLIER.

Madame Du Barry

Madame du Barry was provisionally lodged in the prison of Sainte-Pelagie, and her servants were confined in La Force. As she was without anything she required, she was obliged to borrow two hundred and fifty livres from the citizen Montrouy, who sent a bed to her in prison.

In his curious and veracious memoirs,[1] Dutens relates this anecdote. An Irish priest found an opportunity of seeing Madame du Barry in her prison. There he offered to save her, if she could supply him with a certain sum of money to bribe the gaolers and make the journey. Madame du Barry asked him whether he could save two persons. On receiving a negative answer from the priest, she said to him :—" In that case, I will give you certainly an order on my bankers for the payment of the necessary sum, but I prefer to let the Duchesse de Mortemart escape from death rather than myself. She is concealed in a loft in a certain house in Calais. Here is an order on my banker: fly to her aid!" The priest, after having urged her to allow him to save her, seeing that she was determined to sacrifice herself, took the order, drew the money, went to Calais, rescued the Duchesse de Mortemart, dressed her as a common woman, and, taking her under the arm, made her travel on foot with him, saying that he was a good constitutional priest and that he was married to this woman. The people shouted " Bravo! " and let him pass. He thus passed

---

" Memoirs of a Traveller Taking a Rest." Paris: Bossange, 1806. Tome III. He says the Conciergerie; it is more probable that it is Sainte-Pelagie.

through the lines of the French army, and came to Ostend, from which he set out for England with Madame de Mortemart, whom I saw in London. . . . In the case of Madame du Barry, in the case of this woman so much attached to life, so cowardly up to a few days before her death, the heroism of this devotion surprises, astonishes, appears improbable. We hesitate to believe her to be equal to so beautiful and noble an act of self-sacrifice in favour of even the daughter of Brissac, of her whom she had promised to love like a sister, and I would not refer to Dutens's anecdote, if it did not appear from what he says that he heard the story from the lips of the Duchess herself. Now, did Madame du Barry really believe that she would be sentenced to death, and was it not her view that the Revolution would rest satisfied with the confiscation of her property? This is an idea, a hope, which she is shown to have cherished in Sainte-Pelagie,—and it is confirmed by the singular announcement which appeared in several newspapers " that Madame du Barry had been set at liberty and her goods confiscated for the benefit of the nation."

While Madame du Barry was in Sainte-Pelagie, Salenave, that man-servant whom she had dismissed for his disloyalty to her, had become a member of the Revolutionary Committee of Versailles. Greive had an interview with him; and both of them, uniting their efforts, drew on the Revolutionary Committee to take recognizance of the fact that the seals had been affixed to Luciennes by the Justice of the Peace of Marly. They were authorized to cancel these seals,[1] and they had Fournier Pere and Zamore, who had been discharged from Luciennes for his patriotism, appointed keepers with a guard of six patriots.

On the other hand, the inhabitants who were attached to Madame du Barry and who clung to the recollection of her benevolent acts, drew up and signed a second petition to obtain liberty for her. Greive, anxious as to the result of the petition, called upon Heron, the member of the Committee of General Safety, to whom Madame du Barry's "Dossier" had been entrusted. He found in Heron an old enemy of Vandenyver, Madame du Barry's banker, with whom he had formerly come into collision in a banking transaction, and whom he had denounced with the assistance of the pen and the gloomy dreams of Marat in a book entitled:—" Plot to cause a General Bankruptcy of France, of Spain, and, as a result, of Holland and England." The mania of this wretched fear-stricken madman was that he had been continually pursued by these Dutch bankers. He imagined that on the 10th of August he had been shot at five times by Vandenyver. Under the shock of these terrors, under the promptings of his eagerness for revenge, Heron precipitated the indictment against the bankers, who were sure to drag Madame du Barry with them to the scaffold.

At the same time that Heron prepared the materials for his report against Vandenyver, an information was lodged on the evidence of the correspondence seized at Madame du

---

[1] The Du Barry's "Dossier." National Archives.

Madame Du Barry

Barry's house at Luciennes, an information which Heron seems to have entirely given over to Greive..

I have under my eyes all this faded paper,[1] in which are mingled together marked copies of songs with accounts of expenses, those letters written in the security of peaceful years or in the alarms of revolutionary years, these gallant love-letters of courtiers, these *billets-doux* of fine ladies with their framings of blue ribbons or of rosy shells, letters of business, letters in which there is little trace of conspiracy, at the sight of which you are filled with astonishment when you see a cross traced violently in red pencilling on some indifferent lines, and above, fastened by a big pin, a little card containing an accusing commentary. Some of these letters have at the bottom of them a touching, a heartrending entry : — " *Ne varietur.* Sainte-Pelagie, Brumaire, Year II.," which follow the three signatures of *Voulland, Jagot,* and *Du Barry.* But let us give a sample of these cards, of the criminality which the men of the Revolution extracted from the most innocent relations of friendship, from the least reprehensible portions of a correspondence and finally from the regrets of beloved beings who were ever most resigned. On an insignificant letter signed R. R. R. we read :—" Of the old aristocracy the person who was formerly Princesse de Rohan-Rochefort, a woman as

---

[1] Revolutionary Tribunals : " Dossier " of the woman named Jeanne Vaubernier du Barry . . . and of Vandenyver, accused of understandings and counter-revolutionary correspondence with the *emigres.* National Archives, Box W¹ 16.

wicked as foolish, and who enjoyed a certain favour with several administrators of Versailles." On a letter not signed asking Madame du Barry if she was always annoyed by the smell of the river, we read:—" This letter is from the old man who was formerly Prince de Beauvau." On a letter of Louis d'Armaille, which goes back so far as 1786, we read:—" Letter of the former Marquis d'Armaille, arrested the other day by the order of the Commune of Paris." On a letter of Madame Lebrun, dated from Naples, in which she recalls herself to M. de Brissac's recollection as well as to that of the wife of the Portuguese Ambassador and the Marquise de Brunoi, we read: "Letter of the woman Lebrun, painter and mistress of Colonne." On a letter not signed, in which one lady asks another for a loan of her *Greek chemises,* we read: " Marcel thinks this letter is from the woman Bondeville, wife of an ex-President, an enfeoffed aristocrat. These women saw each other always on Fridays at the Opera, a meeting-place of the aristocrats." On a letter of Thelusson, we read:—" He is one of the most important bankers in London, nephew of Thelusson, who was formerly a partner of Necker, and a great enemy of the Revolution." On a letter of Forth, the English police agent whom Madame du Barry employed for the recovery of her diamonds in London, we read: " Proof of her intrigues with emissaries of the Court of London, of Berlin, and with Forth, the celebrated English spy, who has never ceased intriguing against France, and above all since Franklin's time. He and Bethune Charost have been the most active

emissaries of the Court of London, of Berlin, and of The
Hague, and it is this Forth who, it is to be presumed, has
concocted with her at Luciennes the pretended theft of diamonds." On a letter from Lord Hawksbury, paying her
compliments and adding that he would be enchanted to be
of use to her with regard to her case in his country, we read :
" Letter which proves her intrigues with the courtiers of
George III. Lord Hawksbury is the Privy Councillor of
the tyrant who governs Pitt himself, and who has really held
the reins of government for the last twenty years, though
sometimes apparently in disgrace. His son is the great political courier to-day between the Cabinet of London and
the coalition of the Powers in the Low Countries." On a
letter from Rouen, the jeweller whom she had brought to
London,—a letter dated August 27th, 1793, and which con-
gratulates her on having done with the prosecutions, we
read : " Letter of Rouen, the jeweller, who has quite recently intrigued in her favour, with too much success, with
the old Committee." On a letter which speaks of the Abbe
Billardy, we read : " This Abbe Billardy in the next place
has been one of her most constant guests since the Revolution, as well as the Abbe de Fontenille, the ex-Vicar of
Agen, guillotined the other day in Paris. Billardy is dead.
These Abbes were two inseparable friends, and Billardy
was as counter-revolutionary as the other. Here are the Du
Barry's friends ! " On a letter from Cochet de la Croix,
we read : " This bit of a letter is from a man named Cochet
de la Croix, who was formerly chevalier and *attache* to

the former Duc de Croisy. He is an impudent aristocrat, whom I arrested in the month of May, at the moment when he had applied to the Du Barry to be clothed and equipped in order to enter the transport-wagons of the celebrated company of Beaune-Winter, which was starting for La Vendee. He is in the prisons of Versailles."

But it is not enough to make the commonplaces of friendship or business correspondence in letters, some of which were anterior to the Revolution, crimes on the part of Madame du Barry; Greive forces some letters to say what they do not say, attributes to certain passages the blame of events with which they have no connection. He imagines; he supposes; he lies; he finally tortures the phrases and the words, in order to extract an appearance of guilt necessary for his plans, for his hatreds. It is thus that a letter of Rohan-Chabot, with regard to the settlement of 9,000 livres a year on Madame du Barry, in return for a payment of 200,000 livres paid at one time, has this comment: " It is a question of the annexed settlement of 9,000 livres as a yearly income for the Du Barry, in return for 200,000 paid at once,—would not this sum be destined for La Vendee? We shall find another document in which she lends at the same time 200,000 livres to the Bishop of Rouen? Now which bishop, the former or the new? All this is more than suspicious!" A letter of Laneuville, which says that he had lent 200,000 francs in 1787 to Madame du Barry, and which was found in an envelope in the name of Calonne, bears the note: " This letter has been probably given up to the Du Barry during her sojourn in London, where she has always seen Calonne's wife. Laneuville is in La Fource. I arrested him at the Du Barrys' house." An account of the expenditure of Madame du Barry during her sojourn in London in November, 1792, has this comment: "Would this not be money given to the *emigres?* The Du Barry must be asked who are these persons whose names I have underlined—above all this Pauline. We believe she is the Duchesse de Mortemart, daughter of Brissac." And in the last place I will cite a letter—an ordinary letter—of Madame du Barry, dated from La Meilleraie, the 9th of April, 1793, with the comment: "Remark the epoch of this letter; it is that of the treason of Dumouriez." Two of the documents thus annotated are curious in so far as they testify, at Madame du Barry's house on the day of her arrest, to a certain resistance on her part, the petty anger of a woman who kicks up a row and is not afraid to snatch out of the hands of the commissaries the documents which they want to seize. One of these documents, the lower part of which is torn, is a letter from a Sieur Guillemin, soliciting from Madame du Barry a lieutenancy of gendarmerie—a letter on which Greive has written: "Document seized from between the hands of the Du Barry, and which she wanted to snatch out of the hands of a man named Guenon, a brave Sansculotte of Luciennes, on the day of her arrest. She has even succeeded in tearing off the signature from the end of the letter, the sense of which can be understood." The other is

Madame Du Barry

the pamphlet of Bergoeng, a deputy of the department of the Gironde, to his constituents. On this pamphlet, Greive has written: " Document printed by the miscreants who took refuge in Caen, and which I found on her table. She took it out of my hand two or three times."

Out of all these cards, out of all these annotations as headnotes, or at the bottom of letters forming the two bundles of papers, seized at Luciennes, Greive got the materials for an official document which he hurriedly drew up for Fouquier-Tinville and which he styled " Heads of the Accusation against the Du Barry."

He mentions in this official document the silver medal of Pitt, struck in 1789, and found concealed at Luciennes in the apartment of the chambermaid Roussel.

He detailed the books and liberticidal pamphlets, amongst which he cited: " History of the Caricatures of the Revolt of the French, by Boyer of Nismes," etc.

He referred to the bulletin of Madame du Barry's subscription sending to London for twelve copies of the " Last Picture of Paris," by Peltier.

He enumerated the pieces in honour of Marie Antoinette kept and preserved by Madame du Barry: " Portrait of the Queen of France," translated from the English of Burke; " Epitaph of Varicourt, killed at the Queen's door;" manuscript verses on which we read in Greive's handwriting: " We believe these verses are by the Abbe Dellile, the Du Barry's regular poet."

He denounced the anti-revolutionary engravings of Luciennes, amongst which there was a portrait of Charles Philippe of France, Comte d'Artois.

He recalled, with reference to a receipt of the woman Roussel of the 13th of September, 1793, that Madame du Barry had always had herself called "Comtesse." . . . Then Greive came back to the relations of Madame du Barry with the Chevalier de Coigny, with the Portuguese Ambassador's wife (*nee* Canillac), a relative of La Fayette, one of the most deadly enemies of the Revolution, with the former Duchesse de Brancas, the former Marquis de Nesle, the former Marquis de la Vaupaliere, with the former Chevalier de Durfort, with the woman Angiviller, with the woman Vougny, *emigree* to London, whose husband was the friend of Brissac, with Boissaisson, *emigre,* formerly major of Conde's regiment of dragoons, who married Madame du Barry's niece, with Breteuil, with Calonne, with Berthier, with the D'Aiguillons, mother and son, with the Rohan-Rochefort family, with the Polish princess Lubomirska, whose letter contains this passage:

" The Queen is still at the Conciergerie ; it is false that there is a project of bringing them back to the Temple : *be calm.*"[1]

And Greive addressed to Fouquier-Tinville his *counts of the indictment*[2] with this postscript:

---

[1] Bulletin of the Revolutionary Tribunal, Second Part. The Espremenil Case and others.

[2] This is, I think, the nearest English equivalent to " chefs d'accusation."—TRANSLATOR.

Madame Du Barry

"I do not know if the Committee has made you go over a little three hours' work that I did the other day, at the request of Vouland, to aid you in your operation. In any case, here is a copy of it. It is very far from being complete, but if it gives you ever so little assistance, occupied as you are, my end will be attained.   GREIVE.

"*Charged with the Mission to Luciennes.*
"4th Frimaire, Year II. of the Republic." (November 24, 1793.)

These counts in the indictment, to which was soon to be added the list of assassin witnesses which Greive was engaged in drawing up and which he emphatically calls the list of *necessary* witnesses, reveal to us, in this Du Barry affair, all the subterranean homicidal work, all the secret manipulation of a condemnation to death in those days.

Already, five days before, on the 29th Brumaire (November 19th) the Committee of General Safety had made the following decree:

"On the 29th Brumaire, the second year of the French Republic One and Indivisible:

"The Committee of General Safety having taken cognizance of the various documents found in the house of the Du Barry, who has been put under arrest with a view to the general security as a suspected person under the terms of the decree of the 17th of September last, considering that there results from the whole of these documents that the woman Du Barry is accused of being an *emigree* and of having, during her sojourn in London from the month of October, 1792, to the month of March last, furnished to the *emigres* who had taken refuge in London pecuniary aid and maintained with them suspicious correspondence . . . will be transferred to the Revolutionary Tribunal to be there prosecuted and judged with the utmost speed of the public prosecutor."[1]

On the 2nd Frimaire (November 22nd) Madame du Barry, conveyed from the prison called Pelagie, where she had already spent two months, day for day, was interrogated at one o'clock in the afternoon in one of the halls of audience of the Palais by Dumas, Vice-President of the Revolutionary Tribunal in the presence of Fouquier-Tinville.

Madame du Barry declared in this examination that the sums spent by her had been furnished by the private orders given for each payment by Louis XV., and that Beaujon, who had received the order from Bertin, was the only one who had made payments on bonds signed by her.

She did not conceal the fact that she had influenced and determined the King in the appointments he had made. She acknowledged that she had solicited pensions and gratuities for her *proteges*.

She declared that she had no relation with Louis XVI. but the following: As she owed, at the death of Louis XV., a sum of 2,700,000 livres, she had made a request to the King to pay her debt. In 1782, she had petitioned to have agreements for payment of yearly income belonging to her

[1] Du Barry "Dossier": National Archives, W¹ 16.

exchanged for cash to the extent of a million, which, with the product of a part of the jewels, plate, and pictures which she had sold to tne King, had enabled her to pay the greater number of her creditors and reduce her debt to 250,000 livres.

She said she could not fix the value of her moveable property, but would estimate at nearly 150,000 livres the diamonds which had been stolen from her in 1791,—diamonds which were only a part of those which she possessed,—and she admitted that she possessed 90,000 livres as a life-annuity out of the Hotel de Ville, which she owed to the liberality of Louis XV.

She confessed that she had given a room in her house from the month of June to the month of September, 1792, to Laroche-Fontenille, *emigre* priest.

She said she had received only one letter from Madame de Calonne, to which she had not replied.

She gave the dates of her four journeys to England.

She said, in answer to the charge of having emigrated, that she had left on business, and had been fortified with regular passports.

She acknowledged that she saw in London M. de Crussol and his wife, the Prince de Poix, M. and Madame de Calonne, and Frondeville, formerly President of the Parliament of Rouen. She did not deny that she had given Frondeville twenty-two guineas, but added that it was in order to play for her, and that Frondeville had returned them to her in twenty-four hours.

MARIE THÉRÈSE CHARLOTTE, DUCHESSE D'ANGOULÊME

To face page 290

She declared that the money for her journeys to London had been supplied to her by Vandenyver, her banker.

She acknowledged the loan of 200,000 francs to Rohan-Chabot in payment of a settlement for 9,000 livres a year, but she denied the loan to the former Bishop of Rouen, whom she declared she did not know.

She said finally that she had received some letters from *emigres,* but declared that she had never answered them, and had never thought it possible that her journeys to England could bear the character of emigration.

In reply to the question of Dumas whether she had any counsel to defend her, she said she had chosen citizens Delainville and Laflauterie for that purpose.[1]

A few days later, the 7th Frimaire (November 27th), the examination of the Vandenyver father and daughter took place.

The trial was at hand. Greive had, at last, sent his remarkable list of necessary witnesses to Fouquier-Tinville:

" Names of the *necessary* witnesses in the prosecution of the Dubarry:[2]

" Greive, charged with a mission by the Committee of General Safety to arrest the Dubarry . . . He will prove what her intrigues in England were, the expressions she used, and other things.

---

[1] Examination (secret) of Jeanne Vaubernier, Femme du Barry, on the 2nd day of Frimaire, Year the Second of Republic. "Dossier" of the Du Barry: National Archives, W' 16.

[2] Except for some abbreviations, I give this document in accordance with the original and with its underlined words.

Madame Du Barry

" *Gentenot called Marcel*, to prove the conversations she carried on in the commencement of the Revolution on the subject of Paris, as well as the conduct of her servants. Marcel is an excellent patriot, a firm Republican on the grounds of *principle* and *reason*.

" *Salenave*, to prove that she always kept up her relations with the aristocrats, notably with D'Escourt, La Bondie, the Abbe de Billardy, the Abbe de Nesle, named La Roche, formerly Vicar of Agen, who was executed on the Place de la Revolution, a month ago, and who dined at her house on the day of Maussabre's arrest. He will likewise prove some conversations with the former Chevalier de la Bondie on the subject of the scoundrel Morgan, Colonel of the Hussars of Liberty, and of her emigration and her return after the ill-success of Dumouriez. He will likewise prove the protection granted to Gouin, son of her *concierge*, an impudent aristocrat . . . as well as that granted to Chouallet, her Swiss, attached to the army of the North. *Salenave* will also prove to you that the old lady who was formerly Princesse de Rohan-Rochefort proposed to the Dubarry to send some money to La Vendee. Salenave is a man of great character, who has been twenty years in the Dubarry's service. He is a man full of merit, who, born with a Republican soul, could never bow down even under the old *regime*. For a long time, he has secretly communicated to me his fears as to the public interest when he saw the bad dispositions and the bad companionship in which the Dubarry indulged. Sensibility, the inseparable companion of a beautiful and great soul, might have suggested to him the desire to spare a woman whom he sought to believe more weak than wicked, but, summoned by the imperious voice of the country's danger, by his intimate knowledge of the infernal plots whereby it was attempted to destroy it, his warmth has made enemies for him in the house; he has been persecuted; he has, so to speak, been driven out.

" *Zamor* will prove that the Dubarry household was filled with aristocrats, that he has frequently attempted to turn her aside from this patronage which could only end in her loss. He will prove that he was sent away for his patriotism at the same period as Salenave. *Nota.* Zamor is an Indian transported from the heart of Bengal by the slaves of Louis XV., himself a slave of the Dubarry, for whom this wretched child was snatched away at the age of four from the arms of his parents who were unknown, and delivered up to this vile courtesan like an ape or a parrot. But what wonders does not education produce!

" Jean-Jacques Rousseau, that is to say, his works, having fallen into the child's hands, he became a man, and, in spite of the corrupting influences of the Court, he has always shown himself the most zealous friend of the Revolution and always equal to the circumstances of the hour. Well, this unhappy child, to whom she owes protection and *maternity*, she has treated since the manifestation of these principles with atrocity, and has ended by sending him out of doors under the most aggravating circumstances. He threw himself on my bosom, abandoned as he was by all the universe.

"*Froment,* her ex-gardener, was dismissed for the same cause.

"*Devrey,* a surgeon without a *certificate of citizenship,* and formerly a young lad in a hairdresser's shop, was arrested for aristocracy on the 2nd of July, the period of the Dubarry's first arrest. He will prove to you that the Dubarry spent the night in burning papers on the anniversary of the death of Brissac. If he does not care to do so, Marcel, Montier, and Cave, notables of the commune of Luciennes, will prove to you that he said it.

"*Xavier Audoin,* assistant in the War Office, will prove to you that on the occasion of the visit of the Marseillais and of the Battalion of the Petit-Augustins, in August, 1792, the Dubarry said that nobody was concealed in her house, that the room in which Maussabre slept was a condemned room.

"*Masson* and *Pierre Laporte,* National Guards, will prove to you that she said, when speaking to Masson: "Good! he is a fine young fellow, a good Royalist."

"*Fournier,* Justice of the Peace of the Canton of Marly, will prove to you that Morin, her man of affairs, who will be also brought before your tribunal, has avowed to him that the woman Dubarry was sure of protection from the administrators of Versailles through the agency of Lavelerie, a villainous administrator who committed suicide the other day to avoid the guillotine.

"*Cochet de la Croix,* formerly chevalier and creature of

Madame Du Barry

Coigny, *will be obliged* to prove to you or in his default *I will prove* that the Dubarry has supplied sums of money several times since the flight and emigration of Coigny. This La Croix is a villain, whom I arrested with my own hands in the month of May, at the moment when he was begging for money to go to *La Vendee* in the transport-wagons of the infamous *Beaune-Winter.* This wretch ought to be in the prisons of Versailles.

" *The widow Cotte,* relict of the late Cotte, upholsterer to the Dubarry. It is from her, the aristocrat Devrey said, that he ascertained the fact of the burning of Brissac's letters. N. B.—This impudent Devrey, though married, is the ' good friend ' of the widow Cotte.

" *Blache, called Dumas,* commissary of the Committee of General Safety with the 48 sections, . . . will prove to you all her aristocratic intrigues in London, the protection she enjoyed from the Court and the courtiers as well as the confession that she made to him, Blache, at Luciennes, of her *innocent* correspondence with the Mortemart and other *emigrees* in violation of the law, and we judge of this innocent correspondence by the expressions of the letter of Mortemart,[1] written on the 11th of August, 1793, *on the subject of Marie-Antoinette,* in which she amuses herself at the expense of the Convention, seeking to tranquillize (knowing the cause) the good Citizeness Dubarry in order to show the villainy of several members of the old Committee of Public Safety.

[1] Greive here refers to the Duchesse de Mortemart· as " Mortemart."—TRANSLATOR.

"*Boileau,* a member of the district of Versailles, a corrupt man who came to Luciennes to threaten the municipality, to defy the laws, and to protect Dubarry.

"*The Abbe Rotrue, Devaize, Chaillou, Gazon,* members of the department and the district of Versailles, guilty of the most infamous protection of the Dubarry.

"*Olivon,* municipal officer of Luciennes, respectable patriot, who will testify as to the infamous conduct of these administrators and the persecution of the patriots.

"*Renaud L'Aine,* a virile and patriotic man, formerly Vicar of Luciennes, as to the fact of the persecution of the patriots.

"*Ledoux,* ex-Mayor, as to the same fact.

"*L'Heureux,* tutor, firm patriot, as to the same fact.

"*Cheton,* commandant of the National Guard of Luciennes, as to the same fact.

"*Moutier* and *Cave,* notables, who will testify, as well as the other inhabitants, as to the persecution and menaces that I have endured for having sustained the cause of the Sansculottes.

"*Blache,* who *is urgent to see,* will furnish you with the witness named La Touche, the witness named Beda, the man-servant of an *emigre* in London whose name I have forgotten, and other very interesting witnesses of the uncitizen-like conduct of the Dubarry in London. The witnesses are brave French patriots driven out of London by the miscreant Pitt.

"I likewise send you the receipt of the representatives Jagot and Vouland, to whom I have delivered 26 important documents relating to the Dubarry and on which they have based the examination to which they have subjected this woman. . . .

" You will find, amongst other documents, an account of the infamous prosecution of the unfortunate tailor *Favier*, whom this woman has caused to be confined for twenty years and a half in the prisons of Senlis for having been a witness of the filthy loves of the crapulous tyrant, the Sardanapalus of the French. He has been released by the Constituent Assembly. You shall find amongst the documents the petition of Xavier and of his son and daughter, and his attorney. Would it not be good to have them made public? . . . Moreover, it is for you to decide whether it would be necessary for us to have a conference before the opening of the trial. . . . You should see Blache as soon as possible. It will be well also to produce the *Augustin*, her postilion, imprisoned with her men-servants in La Force, but *without giving him any previous notice of it, for* fear of his being *indoctrinated* by his comrades, in addition to the fact that he is an aristocrat himself. It is he who was the daily courier between her and Brissac at Orleans."

Blache, who under the cloak of a Professor of French, played the spy on behalf of the Committee of Public Safety, in London—Blache, who is *urgent to see*—Blache, whose deposition Greive asks for three times in his list of *necessary* witnesses, made a deposition in the following terms some days afterwards :[1]

[1] Extracts from the Deposition of the Citizen Blache. Revolutionary Tribunals: Du Barry " Dossier," W[1] 16.

Madame Du Barry

First fact.—Deposes to having seen the Dubarry on the occasion of her journey, the day after her arrival, get into a carriage with the woman Calonne, the man named Forth, an English spy, who at the time of the American war, came to Paris with my Lady Barimore to prostitute her to the former Comte d'Artois, with the sole object of causing, through this channel, a variance between France and America; that in this first voyage, the Dubarry took lodgings in the house of a man named Grenier, that this Grenier had been cook of Orleans in Paris, that this Grenier was in London, since his establishment, the agent, the steward of Orleans.

Second fact.—The second journey of the Dubarry to London takes place a short time after her return to France; she went to lodge in Margaret street, Oxford, that there she received all the *emigres* of the upper class and continued her relations with the woman Calonne.

Third fact.—The Dubarry came back to France . . . about October, 1792. Saint Phar, putative brother of the Duke of Orleans, had taken furnished lodgings in Bolton

street Berkeley Square, for Bouille. As the
latter did not arrive, the lodgings were given
up by Saint Phar to the Dubarry, who occupied this house with (1) Saint Phar, (2) La
d'Henin, (3) La Mortemart, (4) Bertrand de
Molleville, (5) Breteuil, and that at this period the Dubarry made the young daughter of
D'Aiguillon emigrate, passing her off as one
of her chambermaids.

In accordance with the fact.

Fourth fact.—In the month of January, the
Dubarry, after the death of Capet, wore
mourning with the greatest English pomp.
She was at all the services which were celebrated in the chapels of the powers hostile to
the Republic.

In accordance with the fact.

*   *   *   *   *   *   *

Sixth fact.—That the witness, forced to quit
England by arbitrary order of the King, was
entrusted by the Committee of General Safety
with several important operations, which necessitated several journeys to Luciennes. Invited by the Dubarry to stay at her house,
he accepted her invitation. Chatting with the
Dubarry, he talked to her about journeys
which she, Dubarry, had made to London
and the association which she had made with
the persons before mentioned, that he re-

proached her with holding correspondence with La Calonne, La d'Henin, La Mortemart, Bertrand de Molleville, and Breteuil, that the Du Barry replied to him: "*Yes, it is true; but these were only commonplace things that we wrote to each other about; I only keep up by this correspondence some friendly connections, nothing more.*" That the deponent placed under her eyes the law of March, the law which punishes with death every individual who has correspondence direct or indirect with the enemies of the Republic. That the next day a lunch was served up to the municipal officers of Luciennes, to which he was invited to come; that there the Dubarry, with Morin, having strongly urged these officers to declare why they had arrested La Bondie, and these having declared that they did not know, invited them to put this declaration into a letter which led to the liberation of La Bondie from prison that same evening, but that Salenave having said that he was a "ci-devant," whose parents had been *emigres,* assuming it to be an act of deliberate wrong-doing, retired from the Dubarry's house.

Seventh fact.—In another interview with the Dubarry, Blache relates that, as she asso-

Had not been
said by the
witness at the
time of his
deposition.

ciated with the Rohans and La Laporte . . . and as all this section of society described themselves as Prince, Princesse, Comtesse, he was protesting against these titles when the Dubarry replied: "Why, that was only a joke we made together."

On the 13th Frimaire (December) the indictment[1] against Jeanne VAUBERNIER, "Femme" DUBARRY, Jean-Baptiste VANDENYVER, Edmé-Jean-Baptiste VANDENYVER, and Antoine-Augustin VANDENYVER, Dutch bankers, was read and adopted in the council chamber, then printed, then distributed at the meeting of the Jacobin Club, and after that sent to the affiliated clubs. The witnesses received subpœnas to appear on the 16th and 17th Frimaire. The indictment directed that Jeanne Vaubernier, "Femme" DUBARRY, should be removed under good and sure guard of the prison of Sainte-Pelagie in order to be transferred to the house called the Conciergerie, in the jail book of which her name would be entered to remain there as in a place of legal confinement. Madame du Barry occupied Marie-Antoinette's room in the Conciergerie, as if it had been her fate to usurp even in the face of death the bed of a Queen.

The attentions of the woman Richard could not arouse Madame Du Barry out of her deep dejection. She had learned through a lady whose statement could be relied on

[1] "L'acte d'accusation."

Madame Du Barry

that Zamore, that man-servant driven by her from her house, was to-day master of Luciennes. She knew that her cellar had been pillaged, that her most valuable card-boxes of lace were disappearing every day, that, in short, her pretty pavilion was searched, rummaged, and gradually broken up. Then, under the blow of the mortal accusation, to all those violent deaths which had, so to speak, brushed past her—the death of Brissac, the death of Maussabre, and other deaths (sad and terrible omens!)—came to be added in these last days the death of that Republican who with his life paid for the amorous sentiment he appeared to have felt towards Madame du Barry,—of that Lavallery who threw himself into the Seine from the wharf at Marly.[1]

[1] Here is the closing part of a letter from this Lavallery; from this member of the district of Versailles to Madame du Barry, published by M. le Roi: "Citizeness, be assured that if opportunities arise in which I can make my efforts valuable, you have the right to create them. Your sex gives you the right to desire tranquillity and so does your amiability. A thousand pardons, citizeness; a Republican and a stranger should only speak the language of business. Accept the assurance of my respect and of all the interest which you have the right to inspire." *Lavallery,* Versailles, May 17th (Year II. of the Republic).

XVII.

On the 16th Frimaire of the Year II. of the Republic (December 6th, 1793), at nine o'clock in the morning, the sitting of the Revolutionary Criminal Tribunal was opened.

The Tribunal was composed of the Citizens Rene-François Dumas, Vice-President acting for the President François-Joseph Denisot, Alexandre-Edme David, Charles Bravet, Judges; Antoine-Quentin Fouquier, Public Prosecutor,[1] and Robert Wolf, Registrar. On the jurymen's bench sat the Citizens Trinchard, Prieur, Billion, Mercier, Klispis, Meyer, Martin, Topino Lebrun, Lohier, Sambat, Vilatte, Payan.

The Tribunal and the jury having taken their places, the woman Du Barry and the Vandenyvers, father and sons,

---

[1] Literally, "Public Accuser," but the dignity of a trial seems to justify the use of the word "Prosecutor" instead.—TRANSLATOR.

were led into court, and also the citizens Chauveau and La-
fleutrie, men of law, advocates and official counsel for the
defence.

Dumas, Vice-President, to the Accused Woman.

Question. You, accused woman, who are seated in the
armchair, what are your names, your age, your profession,
birth-place, and residence?

*Answer. Jeanne Vaubernier, aged forty-two, born at
Vaucouleurs, living on my income, usually residing at Luciennes.*

Q. Are you not the wife of the man who was formerly
Comte du Barry?[1]

A. *We are legally separated.*

Vandenyver, that old man of sixty-six years, and his two
sons, gave their names, their professions, and their residences.

Then after the President had called upon the accused to
pay attention, the Registrar read the indictment.[2]

Antoine Quentin Fouquier, Public Prosecutor of the Ex-

---

[1] Hardy says in his "Manuscript Journal," dated June 3d, 1772:
"We have been informed that on the previous Monday the irre-
movables of the new Parliament had pronounced a judicial separation between the Comte du Barry and his wife, and it is alleged
that several noblemen of the Court had given evidence against the
Comte in order to favour and support his wife's claims. It is astonishing that she did not get her marriage annulled and set aside
sooner. The suit of the heirs informs us that by the contradictory
sentence of the Chatelet of Paris of the 1st of April, 1772, she was
separated from the domicile of her husband, Guillaume du Barry, on
whom she settled 5,000 livres a year."

[2] "L'acte d'accusation."

FOUQUIER-TINVILLE

To face page 304

Madame Du Barry

traordinary and Revolutionary Criminal Tribunal, established in Paris by decree of the National Convention of the
10th of March, 1793, the second year of the Republic, without any recourse to the Tribunal for Reversal of Judgments,
explained that, by a resolution of the Committee of General
Safety and of Surveillance of the National Convention of the
19th day of the last Brumaire, Jeanne Vaubernier, wife of
Du Barry, Jean-Baptiste Vandenyver and Antoine Augustin
Vandenyver had been transferred to the Revolutionary Tribunal; that the said Vaubernier, wife of Du Barry, had been
confined as a prisoner in Sainte-Pelagie, and that the Vandenyvers, father and sons, bankers, had been confined as
prisoners in the prison of La Force, that the evidence to be
produced against the accused had been brought to the Public Prosecutor on the 30th day of Brumaire, and that the accused had been interrogated on the 2nd, 4th, and 7th Frimaire following by one of the judges of the tribunal. After
this preliminary statement and a history of the Du Barry's
life at the Court of Louis XV., he said that, on an examination " the Aspasia of the French Sardanapalus "[1] had been,
after the memorable victory of the French people, the instrument and the accomplice of the *emigres,* the support and
the asylum of the former great ones left in France; and he
mentioned by name Laroche, formerly a noble, Vicar of
Agen, condemned by the Revolutionary Tribunal, as hav-

---

[1] This rhetorical flourish on the part of Fouquier-Tinville shows
that worthy's ignorance of classical history.—TRANSLATOR.

ing found a refuge in her house. He said that in the desire to be useful to the *emigres*, she had counterfeited a theft of diamonds[1] on the night of the 10th or 11th of January, 1791; that this pretended theft had been a pretext and a comedy concocted with Forth, an English agent, in order to bring herself into relationship with all the agents of the counter-revolution existing in London; that, in order to prosecute the authors of this pretended theft, she had the talent to manage to get different passports as well from the Minister of Foreign Affairs as from the municipality of Luciennes and from the department of Seine-et-Oise, of which many members protected her openly, and especially the man named Lavallerie, who had since taken his own life; that, during her four sojourns in London, she had lived only with the *emigres*, with the lords who were hostile to the Revolution, " with the infamous Pitt, that implacable enemy of the human race, a medal of whom she had brought back containing an effigy of the monster." He said that her treasures were open to the enemies of the home country; that she had paid a sum of 200,000 livres in settlement of an annuity to Rohan-Chabot, possessor of considerable estates in Ven-

---

[1] When Fouquier, in his indictment ("acte d'accusation") spoke of a counterfeit theft, he knowingly lied in this statement in the indictment, having in his possession all the proofs of this theft, and notably Blache's manuscript deposition, in which it was acknowledged that " he had seen at the office of the Lord Mayor of London diamonds which he was told had been stolen in France at the house of the accused woman "—a deposition which the witness repeated in his examination.

dee, " where had been formed," remarked Fouquier, " the nucleus of the rebels ; " that through the interposition of the Chevalier d'Escourt she had lent a like sum of 200,000 livres to La Rochefoucauld, a former Bishop of Rouen; that, in short, this same D'Escourt, the before-mentioned La Bondie, his nephew, and the person who was formerly the Vicomte de Jumilhac, an *emigre,* had received from her considerable sums. He said that she had brought about assemblies in her pavilion of Luciennes, " of which she wanted to make a little stronghold, a fact sufficiently proved by the eight guns out of which her good friend the villain D'Angremont cheated the municipality of Paris for her benefit." He spoke of all the treasures hidden by her, and, as a proof of her faith in the counter-revolution, he mentioned the rare collection of documents and engravings of a counter-revolutionary character found in her house. He referred to the mourning worn by her publicly in London, on the occasion of the death of the tyrant. He spoke about her perpetual correspondence with the most cruel enemies of the Republic, the Crussols, the De Poix, Calonne, D'Aiguillon, Beauvau, Chavigny, Mortemart, Brissac, Frondeville, Coigny, Brancas, De Nesle, Maussabré, Breteuil, Boissaisson, and Narbonne.

Passing to the Vandenyvers, Fouquier-Tinville painted them as the intermediaries between the *emigres* and the Du Barry. He accused them of having transmitted diamonds belonging to the Du Barry into Holland. He accused them of having supplied her in the space of two years with a letter of credit for 6,000 livres sterling, another of 2,000, another of 50,000, another for an unlimited sum, of having supplied her with the 200,000 livres for La Rochefoucauld, and of having supplied all these sums for the *emigres,* and subsequent to the law against *emigres* which entitled them to regard the Du Barry as an *emigree.* He also accused the Vandenyvers of having at all times been enemies of France, of having been in 1792 accomplices in a plot between the tyrant and the King of Spain to bring about a bankruptcy of the two nations, to swallow up the public wealth, and to perpetuate the slavery of the French. Then, coming back to the Revolution, he ended by accusing them of having been amongst the number of knights of the dagger and of having co-operated " for the massacre of the people."

Then begins the taking of evidence.

George Greive, aged forty-five, man of letters, born at Newcastle, in England :

" Deposes that it is within his knowledge that the accused woman Du Barry had prevented the recruiting at Luciennes; that he found on the night of the 22nd of September last, the day of her arrest, a considerable quantity of plate in a place used for keeping the gardener's tools, and, near a high-road, the celebrated service of gold, and in another place buried louis and pieces worth six livres, more bronzes, a bust of Louis XV.; that there had been found, within a recent period, in a heap of dung near the high-road, a great quantity of precious stones, gold and silver, and, a few days since, the portraits of the Regent and of Anne of Austria, and furthermore, in the room of the woman Roussel, the medal of Pitt concealed in a drum, besides a great number of pieces which had been announced as stolen, notably a pencil-case and a gold opera-glass. Take note," continues the deponent, " that Fournier, the Justice of the Peace of the district, has drawn up a statement as to the effects which have been discovered. There was a packet of 134 rubies; but he could not say whether they formed a part of those carried in the list of which he had spoken.

" In the gardens he found a tassel used for a watch-chain, a gold pencil-case. . . . We found in the papers of the accused a letter showing the signature of Forth erased, as well as that of Betmaschuson, who was closely allied with him. I have seen the accused woman, who had many domiciles in Paris, visited by emigrants or their partisans.[1] With regard to the diamonds of 1791, the general opinion in Luciennes was that the theft was a pretended one. I notice that, on the return of the accused woman on the occasion of the first journey to London, there was shown me an English certificate signed by the Duc Guicusbert, a great enemy of the French Revolution. It is in accordance with this cer-

---

[1] This information must have come from Salenave, who, in a letter to Madame du Barry, exculpates himself as to her denunciation, and declares that it was not he who said she had three residences in Paris in the month of September last, and that it was not he who said she had been secretly at the house of M. Nevernois.

tificate that she applied for all her passports to the department and the Minister of Foreign Affairs."

Dumas, Vice-President, to the Accused Woman.

Q. Whose portrait is that of the woman which was found in the garden buried in the dunghill with that of Louis XV., dressed as a Carmelite?

A. *I don't know.*

Q. Have you received Forth at your house?

A. *Yes.*

Q. You stated in your first examination that, on your return in March, 1793, your case was finished; now I ask you why the certificates import that it was necessary for you to return to England?[1]

A. *It was to get my diamonds and pay the costs.*

Greive continued his statement, and added that the accused had imposed on the Convention, in order to obtain permission to go to England by pretending that her jewels, said by her to be stolen, were her creditors' only security, while she possessed immense wealth—150,000 livres a year out of the Hotel de Ville of Paris; 186 shares in the Discount Bank of the value of 700,000 to 800,000 livres, diamonds and precious stones, gold and silver coins in a consid-

[1] On a card of Greive we read: "After her forced return from London in the month of March, she did everything possible to get a new passport, under the pretext that her presence was necessary in London for the 17th of April. I have had between my hands certificates for that purpose signed by the Duke of Queensberry and and by a certain Whitshed Kesne, two of the meanest of George III.'s lackeys, most bitter enemies of the Revolution, a fact to which I have alluded in my pamphlet."

erable quantity, an immense amount of worked gold and silver plate, an enormous wardrobe of stuffs and of the richest merchandises; considerable landed property, a fortune, in fact, in moveables and immoveables, which might be estimated at from ten to twelve millions, and that she kept at the same time a house of the most ostentatious description, with nearly forty servants.

Another witness is called.

Xavier Audouin, aged thirty-nine, clerk in the Ministry of War, deposes that a few days after the 10th of August, 1792, passing with an armed force through the neighbourhood of Saint Germain-en-Laye, he was warned that the chateau of Luciennes was filled with persons who had formerly been noblemen of the Court. Making his way thither, the accused woman ordered refreshments for them, and said there was nobody in the house; that, having asked her what was in an apartment the door of which was closed, she answered that it was soiled linen, and that she did not know where the key was. Her prevarications appearing to him suspicious, he had the door of the said room opened, and in it was found a young man named Maussabre lying down; that the accused woman took a great interest in this man: seeing that they were determined to bring him on to Paris, she offered her carriage to convey him there. She even appeared moved when this Maussabre began saying that *if they sent him to Paris he would be massacred.* Since then there appeared many times at her house, as he deposes, a certain Chevalier d'Escourt, in order to obtain the liberty of the said Maussabre, a request with which he did not wish to comply, seeing that this individual, when he was arrested at the house of the accused woman, was not found armed with any documents to indicate that he was a patriot.

Another witness is called.

Jean-Baptiste Blache, aged forty-one, commissary of the Committee of General Safety of the National Convention, residing in No. 109 Rue du Temple, Paris, repeats in almost identical terms the written deposition cited above.

Dumas, Vice-President, to the Accused Woman.

Q. *What answer have you to give to the witness's deposition?*

A. *The answer I have to give* is that I have seen Mesdames de Calonne and Mortemart as a matter of fact in London, but all our relations were confined to mere friendship.

Q. Have you worn mourning for Capet in London?

A. *I wore a black dress because I had not brought a dress of any other colour with me.*[1]

Q. Have you petitioned for Labondie's liberation?

A. *I have done so, because he had been arrested at my house as a suspect.*

Another witness is called.

Louis-Marguerite-Bernard Escourt, aged sixty-eight

---

[1] The Tribunal had a deposition of the chambermaid Roussel, who stated that Madame du Barry had brought with her black and some white dresses.

years, ex-captain of cavalry, usually residing in the Rue de Grenelle, Paris, and actually confined in La Force, deposes that he knows the accused woman Du Barry, as well as Vandenyver Senior and the elder of his two sons. It is about two years since he made the acquaintance of the accused woman, but he has rarely been at her house. She wrote to him from London to assist her in getting a power of attorney, and to go and ask for 200,000 livres from the Vandenyvers, who lent them to Rohan-Chabot when he was staying at the Hotel de la Rochefoucauld in the Rue de Seine.

After three or four questions put by Dumas to the witness with regard to the negotiation of this loan, the public prosecutor rises up.

"Seeing that the Sieur d'Escourt in his declaration has not ceased to be manifestly in contradiction with himself, from which contradictions it results that it is evident the declarations of the said D'Escourt are false, that these shufflings have for their object to hide the complicity existing between him and other accomplices in a criminal correspondence, the public prosecutor requires and orders that a *proces-verbal* will be drawn up by the President of the contradictions, depositions, tergiversations, and falsities put forward by the said witness in his declaration, and that the said D'Escourt may be arrested, and conducted to the prison of the Conciergerie in place of that of La Force, with a view to his being prosecuted as one accused of forgery and complicity in a criminal and counter-revolutionary correspondence."[1]

Dumas, Vice-President, to the Accused Woman.

Q. How did you happen to make the witness's acquaintance?

A. *I made his acquaintance at the house of M. de Brissac, to whom he was aide-de-camp.*

Then commenced the deposition of the witnesses recommended, patronized by Greive. The latter—for it was necessary that every baseness, down to the baseness of the antechamber, should be embraced by the Terror and wait upon the guillotine—the latter were servants dismissed for theft or for patriotism, sent from the service to the Committee of Surveillance of the district, avenging themselves by turning informers and bringing to the conduct of the case grudges so vile that only the justice of the Revolution could gather them together without being soiled.

François Salenave, aged thirty-eight, born at . . . department of Basses-Pyrenees, formerly in the employment of the accused woman, at present employed by the Committee of Surveillance at Versailles, deposes that he has seen the accused woman visited by Levaupaliere, Brissac, Labondie, D'Escourt, the former Marquis Donissant, the ex-

[1] On the 21st Frimaire, Year II. (December 11th, 1792), on the depositions of Madame du Barry's chambermaids, on the deposition of François-Denis Nee, engraver, who declared that he had heard the "assignats" decried to please the King and the Royal family, Bernard Escourt was condemned to death and executed the same day.

Madame Du Barry

Vicomte de Pons, the former Marquise de Brunoi, the former Duchesse de Brancas, with whom she made the journey to London, and who remained there since then, and the former Chevalier de Maussabre; adds that in his character of patriot he incurred the ill-will of the other servants of the house, who were aristocrats, and who prejudiced against him the mind of the accused, who dismissed him from her service.

The Accused Woman: I have to say to this deposition that the Dame de Brancas is not an emigree. On the contrary, she even returned to France sooner than myself. As for the witness, I did not turn him out of doors for his opinions, nor through the advice of anybody whomsoever, but for his dishonesty with respect to chinaware, which disappeared every day from the house.

Louis-Benoit Zamor, aged thirty-one, born in Bengal, in India, employed by the Committee of Safety in Versailles, residing there in the Rue de la Loi, declares that he was brought up by the accused woman since the age of ten; that he was brought into France by a sea-captain; that seeing that the patriotic newspapers often spoke of her rather freely, he had advised her to sacrifice a part of her fortune towards the nation in order to retain the other part; that the accused woman, very far from taking his wise advice into consideration, continued to receive aristocrats into her house, as he assumed they were, on seeing them applaud the checks experienced by the armies of the Republic; that he renewed his appeals to the accused woman on this sub-

ject, but she did not condescend even to appear to pay
attention to him. " On the contrary, having learned that
I kept company with an old friend of Franklin, and Marat
(Greive), and that I was on very intimate terms with the
patriots Blache, Salenave, Fremont, and a great number of
others, she took the liberty of saying to me in an imperious
tone that she would give me three days to leave the
house." [1]

*The Accused Woman: It is false that I received aristo-
crats at my house. As for the advice which the witness says
he gave me, I have received none from him. With regard
to his expulsion, it was in connection with keeping company
with the persons he mentioned.*

Jean Thenot, aged twenty-five, tutor at Luciennes, deposes to having served five years in the capacity of a man-
servant (he had left Madame du Barry three years since),
and to having heard it said by her in 1789, the time of the
death of Foulon and of Berthier, that the people were a pack
of wretches, of villains.

The Accused Woman, interrupting the witness: *In what
place have you heard me making such a remark?*

The Witness. It was while going to your melon-bed.

---

[1] The work done by Zamore as an informer did not secure him
from persecution by the Sans-culottes, who did not forgive him for
his past. M. Dauban has dug up out of the National Archives, in one
of the registers consecrated to the correspondence of the police,
the following notice dated the 9th Nivose, Year II. (December 29,
1793) : " Arrest by the Commune of Sever, department of Seine-et-
Oise, of a man named Zamor, a pupil of the Du Barry."

The Accused. This is a false statement; it is an atrocious perfidy.

Then came the chambermaid's turn.

Henriette Picard, wife of Couture, aged twenty-three, in the service of the accused woman, deposes to having accompanied her in her journeys to London with Pretry, the valet, Marechal, a man-servant, the woman Roussel, and the former Chevalier d'Escourt; has seen French *emigres* visit the accused during her stay in London.

Marianne Labitte, Widow Cottet, aged forty-seven, upholsterer in Luciennes, deposes that to her knowledge at the time of Brissac's arrest the accused woman spent the night burning papers.

The Accused Woman. I did not burn any papers.

On the 17th Frimaire (December 7th) the same tribunal, the same judges, and the same jury, resumed their sitting.

The same prisoners were brought in, and witnesses were called who seemed the witnesses of the previous day.

Devrey, surgeon, declares that he cannot indicate the time when, shortly after Brissac's arrest, the Widow Cottet told him that the accused associated with the *emigres*.

So great was the Terror that except D'Escourt, none of the witnesses, even when well-known for their sympathy and pity for the accused, dared to seek to speak up even slightly for the innocence of the wretched woman. There is to be found amongst the witnesses, who knew that at the first word they risked in favour of the proprietress of Luciennes they would be accused, two curious testimonies of their cowardly terror. To the summons served on that Boileau who was opposed to the arrest in the month of June is annexed a certificate from the officers of health of the Versailles Infirmary, attesting that " Paul Boileau is kept ill in bed by a humoral fever accompanied by a violent headache, that in consequence he is unable to leave his bed or to attend to any business." To the summons served on Chaillou, another patron of Madame du Barry, is also found a certificate annexed from the administrators of Versailles attesting that their colleague is ill in his bed for the past three days, that his condition makes it impossible for him to get to Paris to answer the summons served him by the public prosecutor.[1]

Nicolas Fournier, aged thirty-three years, measurer of buildings, formerly Justice of the Peace for the District of Marly and residing there, gives evidence from personal knowledge of the precious objects found in the various places connected with the residence of the accused woman. The house where the goods were is situated on the high road, and is occupied only by the gardener. Part of the stuffs were cut, but the greater number were in parcels. Witness observes that amongst the jewels which have been found, he has recognized a watch-chain, an opera-glass, a pencil-case, forming part of the articles alleged to have been stolen, and contained in the stamped list according to the verification made by the commissaries of the National Convention.

[1] Du Barry "Dossier": National Archives, W¹ 16.

Madame Du Barry

*The Accused. I draw the attention of the Tribunal to
the fact that the three objects of which the witness speaks
were sent to M. de Brissac, who gave a louis to the porter
and that they were then brought back to me.*

Marie-Joseph Lamonte, wife of Roussel, aged fifty-four,
chambermaid of the accused woman, residing at Luciennes,
deposes the same facts as Couture.

Vandenyver Senior, in answer to Dumas, said he had
charge of the affairs of the accused woman for about four
years past; that the current expenses of her house were
1,200 livres a month; that he had supplied her with a first
letter of 6,000 livres sterling, a second of 2,000 livres sterling; that he had written in the month of.December, 1792,
a letter to a London banker, by which he was ordered to
supply the accused woman with the little sums of which she
might have need; . . . that he had signed the two letters of credit.

Whereupon Vandenyver Junior said: " I point out to
the Tribunal that we have furnished letters of credit to
Madame du Barry, because she had established the fact and
satisfied us as to her having passports, and not being judges
of their validity, we.thought there was nothing improper in
supplying her with the sums she demanded."

La Fleuterie pleaded on behalf of Madame du Barry, and
Chauveau on behalf of Vandenyvers Senior and his sons.

The Vice-President Dumas delivered a *resume* of the case,
in which he referred to " the courtesan of the predecessor of
Louis XVI.," the instrument of Pitt, the accomplice in the

war with foreign countries, the rising of Calvados, the insurrection of Vendee, and the troubles in the South. . . .
After which, he put the questions to the jury.

The death of Madame du Barry cost a quarter of an hour more to the conscience of the Terror than the death of Marie Antoinette. At the end of five quarters of an hour, the jury re-entered court, the accused were brought back, and heard their sentence:

" The Tribunal, according to the declaration of the jury, giving judgment unanimously to the effect: that it is proved machinations have been carried on and understandings held with the enemies of the State and their agents in order to induce them to commit hostilities, to point out to them and favour the means of undertaking and directing them against France, notably in making different journeys abroad to concoct hostile plans with our enemies by supplying them and their agents with assistance in money:

" That Jeanne Vaubernier, wife of Du Barry, residing at Luciennes, formerly courtesan, is found guilty of being one of the agents or accomplices of these machinations and understandings:

" That Jean-Baptiste Vandenyver, Dutch banker, domiciled in Paris, Edme-Jean-Baptiste Vandenyver, banker in Paris, and Antoine-Augustine Vandenyver, banker in Paris, are found guilty of being accomplices in these machinations and understandings:

" The public prosecutor having been heard in his conclusions on the application of the law:

Madame Du Barry

" The said Jeanne Vaubernier, wife of Du Barry, the said Jean-Baptiste Vandenyver, Edmé-Jean-Baptiste Vandenyver, and Antoine-Augustine Vandenyver, banker in Paris, are condemned to the penalty of death, in conformity with the first article of the first section of the first title of the second part of the Penal Code:

" The goods of the said woman Du Barry, Jean-Baptiste, Edme-Jean-Baptiste and Antoine-Augustine Vandenyver are declared forfeit to the Republic, conformably to the article II. of title II. of the law of that 10th of March, 1793.

" And it is ordered that with the utmost speed of the public prosecutor the present judgment be executed in twenty-four hours on the Place de la Revolution of this city, printed and affixed throughout the entire Republic." [1]

At the reading of this sentence, prostrated, overwhelmed by stupor and horror, Madame du Barry suddenly lost the coolness and the remnant of dignity which she had exhibited in her answers. When she saw that all was over, that she was about to be led away, and that the witnesses who had been present during the scene rubbed their hands and enjoyed her agony shamelessly, she was stricken with such feebleness that the gendarmes were obliged to support her on

[1] Proces-verbal of the sitting of the Revolutionary Criminal Tribunal established by the law of the 10th of March, 1793, and in virtue of the law of the 3rd of April of the same year, sitting in Paris in the Palais de Justice, the 16th and 17th Frimaire, Year II. of the Republic. The case of Madame du Barry does not figure in Clement's *Bulletin of the Revolutionary Tribunal*, the gap between the third and fourth part ranging from the 8th Frimaire to the 1st Germinal of the Year II.

their arms, and that the public was afraid that she would not
have the strength to live up to the time when she should die.

The trouble, the fright, the utter helplessness, the prostra-
tion of the woman in the presence of death, and of such a
death, were so great that she, who all her life had thought
only of living, in one moment forgot everything, affection,
gratitude, debts of love, sacred engagements, the secrets and
the devotions of those who had compromised themselves for
her. Hoping to save her life by selling the lives of others,
believing that she could buy pardon or at least a reprieve by
giving up what remained of hidden treasure, we find her
on the day of her execution, the day of her death, at ten
o'clock in the morning, quite pale after a night of terror,
trembling and supplicating between the two wickets of the
Conciergerie, flinging towards the advancing executioner,
towards the hour of doom so nigh, towards the guillotine
looming above her, the precipitate and breathless confession
of everything that she had buried, concealed, kept back
from the scent of the Republic, from the cupidities of the
country of the Year II.![1] To Justice Denisot, to Claude
Roger, substitute of the public prosecutor, Madame du
Barry gives details as to the precious objects buried in the

---

[1] See in the Appendix: *Declaration of Madame du Barry, made
between two wickets of the Conciergerie after the Judgment which
condemned her to death.* This document, which has to-day disappeared from the "Dossier" of Madame du Barry, is given by Favrolles in his "Historic Memoirs of Jeanne Gomart de Vaubernier,"
in which he has reproduced the greater part of the documents forming part of the National Archives.

MADAME ELISABETH

To face page 322

garden of Luciennes, buried in the thickets, concealed in
the corridors, in the cellar, in the garden of her valet, that
faithful Morin, who will pay afterwards with his head for
his mistress's disclosure, concealed in the house of the
woman Deliant, concealed on the premises of Citizen
Montrouy. Under the stroke of terror, she remembers, she
finds everything again, bit by bit, louis by louis, down to a
plate, down to a spoon, for it is her life she is going to recover. In her zeal, in her anguish, fearing that all this
treasure would not suffice still to pay for her pardon, she
undertakes to write to London, if it is the good pleasure of
the Tribunal, to get back all the articles in the theft of
1791, deposited with Morland, with Moncelet, and Ram-
son . . . Unhappy being! She forgot that the Revolution would be her heir!

It was a time when courage had no sex. Condemned
like men, women died like men. One might have said they
were jealous of the privilege of dying. Some of them
ascended the scaffold as if to a sacrifice; others as if to a
rostrum. Some appeared to march towards posterity,
others towards a fatherland. Each was worthy of all. The
women of the middle class died like Romans; the great
ladies died like grand seigneurs; the Queen died as a
King should die. But all had the strength of an idea, of
a principle, of a faith, of a duty, of a right, of a passion, of
an illusion, of something which in the end sustains the soul
and endures death's agony. But Madame du Barry had
none of these things to assist her in dying; and if this is a

scandal in her history which we ought to forgive, it is the scandal of a death which even moved the Terror to pity.[1] As she stepped up into the cart, Madame du Barry, to whom that morning when she made her declaration between two wickets the Justice Denisot had vaguely promised her pardon, and who, when her hair had been already cut, did not believe she would die,—Madame du Barry turned pale as the robe she wore. The crowd, the Sunday crowd, was waiting for the unfortunate woman. And in that crowd in the foreground the condemned one could perceive Greive, who that evening said:—"I never laughed so much as

[1] The Comte Jean du Barry was guillotined almost at the same time in Toulouse. In a petition addressed to the Corps Legislatif, Anne-Marie-Therese Rabaudy, widow of Jean Baptiste du Barry, asked permission to re-enter into the possession of a house in Toulouse of 20,000 livres, of a house in Levignac of 8,000 livres, of a demesne in the same commune called the demesne of Ceres, the whole of a value of 78,000 livres, which had been assured to her by a will of April 20th, 1779. Almost the entire of the Comte Jean's fortune consisted of an annuity of 80,000 livres which was extinguished by his death. The Widow du Barry terminates her petition in these words: "If you deign to consult the members of the Haute-Garonne, they will tell you the sacrifices that my husband made for the Revolution, the enormous expense he undertook on its behalf. They will not leave you ignorant of the fact that almost an entire legion at Toulouse of which he was for years colonel was dressed, armed and equipped at his cost. They will inform you of the resistance he made to the disorganizer Chalot during his sojourn in Toulouse without a mission—a resistance which was the sole cause of his punishment." The Comte Guillaume, the husband of the Du Barry, escaped the guillotine, and, after marrying a second time Jeanne Madeleine Lemoine, died at Toulouse on the 2d of August, 1811, at the age of 79 years.

to-day, when I saw the grimaces that beauty made—at dying."

The horses began to walk at a slow pace.

The people pressed forward to look at the *courtesan of the former tyrant.*

She whom they were staring at saw nothing, heard nothing. She did nothing but moan, sob, suffocate. Her companions on the journey, who were to be her companions at the end of it, the Vandenyvers, sought to sustain her with some cheering words; the conventional Christmastide was urged as a ground for taking courage. She only replied to them with lifeless words, movements of inert lips.

Suddenly, near the Palais Royal, at the Sergeant's Barrier, raising her eyes, she saw the balcony of a millinery establishment at which the work-girls had planted themselves in a row in order to get one last look at her who had been Madame du Barry passing along. This was the very establishment where she had been a working milliner's apprentice. . . . Perhaps at that moment, in one of those flashes of agony, in one of those lucidities of the final hour which memory and the images of an entire life precipitate, Madame du Barry revived her whole past, her youth, then Versailles, then Luciennes. Dream of a second, from which she started, breaking out into shrieks, piercing shrieks, which reached from one end to the other of the Rue Saint-Honoré.

The executioner and his two assistants had difficulty in supporting the condemned woman, in holding back on the cart this frenzied body which the convulsions of fear urged her to cast on the ground.

To violent movements, to shrieks, succeeded entreaties mingled with tears; and the woman, her forehead and her eyes swept by her short hair, leaned over towards those who stood by curiously awaiting her death to say to them:—" My friends! save me! . . . I have never done harm to any-one! In Heaven's name, save me! "

The crowd was stunned. People had became so accus-tomed to see others dying, to see them dying *with a show of bravado,* that this woman seemed for the first time a woman whom they were going to kill. She, in the meantime, still weeping, repeated:

"Life! Life! Let them leave me life. . . . I give all my goods to the nation."

" Your goods! But you cannot give the nation what al-ready belongs to it. . . ."

A coal-heaver, standing in front of the insulter, turned round, and, without saying a word, gave him a blow in the face.[1] It rose up in the silent, stupefied crowd—that first emotion which amongst the populace is like the shock of pity.[2]

The officer had the horses drawing the cart moved for-ward with a lash of the whip and hurried the spectacle to a close.

[1] Narrative of Madame du Barry's death extracted from the jour-nal, "La Nouvelle Minerve." This narrative, given by M. le Roi in his pamphlet, should be consulted with the distrust due to an ocular witness who saw black hair on Madame du Barry.

[2] "The Revolutions of Paris" (No. 219) attempt to deny this

Madame Du Barry

The cart arrived at the Place de la Revolution at half-past four in the afternoon.[1] Madame du Barry was the first to descend. She was heard on the stairs of the scaffold, dismayed, hopeless, wild with anguish and terror, struggling, imploring, asking for mercy from the executioner, asking "One minute more, Monsieur le Bourreau!"[2] then, under the knife, shrieking, "Help! Help!" like a woman assassinated by thieves.

[1] *Proces-verbal* of *death:* "The second year of the French Republic, on the 18th Brumaire, at the request of the citizen acting as Public Prosecutor, the Extraordinary and Revolutionary Criminal Tribunal established in Paris by the law of the 10th of March, 1793, without any recourse to the Tribunal for Reversing Judgments, which refers to the record of the said Tribunal sitting in Paris, we . . . Crier of the said Tribunal, remaining in Paris as undersigned, are transported into the House of Justice of the said Tribunal for the execution of a Judgment given by the Tribunal of to-day's date against the woman named *Jeanne Vaubernier Femme Dubarry,* who has been condemned to the penalty of death for the causes stated in that Judgment, and have delivered her up in consequence to the executioner of Criminal Judgments and to the gendarmerie who have conducted her to the *Place de la Revolution of this city,* where, on a scaffold on the said Place, the said Vaubernier F. Dubarry has in our presence undergone the penalty of death at *half-past four in the afternoon,* and of all that has taken place above have made and drawn up the present *proces-verbal,* so as to serve and be valid as justification for this legal act.   DEGUAIGUE."

Registered gratis at Paris, the 22nd Frimaire, II. of the French Republic One and Indivisible.

[2] "Mr. Executioner."—There is something childlike, pathetic, and peculiarly characteristic of Madame du Barry in this appeal.—TRANSLATOR.

---

sentiment, attested by all the different witnesses: "On the route, she did not inspire the slightest pity. Moreover, her physiognomy would have repelled it. She carried still on her face the imprints of vice."

APPENDIX.

I come back to the bust *all in plaster* of Caffieri in the Library of Versailles,—a bust which is to me the only one that gives an idea of the beauty of the Du Barry, and of the character of her beauty. Pajou's bust—the official image in marble of the Favourite with the " Bourbonnien " nose, the eyes level with the head, the entire effect of the sheep-like face—betrays nothing of the perfection and of the sprightly daintiness which is brought home to us by the admiration of her contemporaries. I will say more: the nose which Pajou gives her in his statue is not the nose of her portrait by Drouais, the nose of her portrait by Cosway; and the graceful impudence of her face is only explained by the nose which she has in Caffieri's bust, a nose slightly hooked, a nose like Roxalana's with a gentle and almost imperceptible aquiline curve. It was only thus that she appeared with the rebelliousness of a young nymph, not a trace of which exists in Pajou's bust. I am aware that some persons, confused by the lack of close resemblance between Caffieri's bust and Pajou's bust, are not disposed to see in this plaster cast the portrait of the Favourite. It must, however, be mentioned that the donor, M. Ferrand, the painter, gave him, according to tradition, something like a portrait of Madame du Barry, that, on the other hand, the *Revue des Documents historiques* has published a receipt which attests in the most positive manner the execution of a bust of the Comtesse by Caffieri;[1] that finally the date—*J. J. Caffieri*, 1770, the moment when the great favour of the mistress had been declared,

[1] Here is the receipt republished by Guiffrey in his book entitled " Les Caffieri," Morgand and Fatout, 1877 :—" I acknowledge having received from M. Humbert the sum of a thousand livres for having finished the bust in marble of Louis XV. belonging to the Comtesse du Barry, without prejudice to the fact that the Comtesse du Barry ought to have had her portrait taken by me. Given at Paris this 5th of November, 1779, Caffieri."

renders very acceptable the theory of the modelling of the Du Barry this year. As for me, I repeat it, until a positive proof comes to demonstrate that it is the portrait of another woman, I persist in being convinced that it is the portrait of the Du Barry just as it evolves itself from the memoirs and the poetic ideas of the time; and I ask that proofs in plaster may be taken from this unknown bust, proofs destined to avenge the beauty of the Favourite on Pajou's calumny.

"I have called at your house, Monsieur le Duc, in order to thank you for the lively interest you have taken in the favour which the King has granted to my brother. I believe he owes you, Monsieur le Duc, the advantage of having been able to retain his company of dragoons,—a favour which my brother prizes infinitely, just as I do, since it enables him to continue as before to show his zeal for the King's service.

"I am, Monsieur le Duc, with sentiments of the utmost respect and gratitude.

"Your very humble and very obedient servant,

"DUBARY.

"Compiegne, the 10th."[1]

"I thank you, Monsieur le Duc, for the courteous reception you have given to the Sieur Nalet. You have known for a long time all the interest I take in him; I will be enchanted to see him re-established in the post which he filled for many years. I believe the moment is favourable for the purpose, and I will be infinitely obliged if you put him in such a position that he may profit by it. I have the honour to be, with extreme consideration,

"Your very humble and very obedient servant,

"THE COMTESSE DUBARRY.

"From the Chateau of Versailles, this 30th of June."

[1] The handwriting of this letter is very curious. The characters are big and badly-formed, like those of a child beginning to write—characters which in no way resemble the little feminine hand which makes us at once recognize the Favourite's letters, when she has learned to write properly. The four letters which we give here, written by Madame du Barry, in the early days of her career as the Favourite, to the minister Choiseul, have been communicated by the Duc de Choiseul, nephew of the Minister, to the *Revue de Paris* (November, 1836), in an article in which he refuted the false memoirs published by Lamothe-Langon under the name of the Comtesse du Barry.

Madame Du Barry

"You are deceived by those around you, Monsieur le Duc, otherwise it would have been impossible that you would have written to me, six months ago, saying that as the interests of the King required the supplies of Corsica to be looked after, you would give the post to the Sieur Nalet, for the services with which you were pleased, as soon as the Sieur de Lisle had arrived. It appears that this administrator has plans different from yours, since he is so slow in complying with your orders. You must realize better than I do how little necessary is his presence here for the execution of your will. Whether he arrives or not, you can give the contract to the Sieur Nalet if you continue to believe that he is capable of fulfilling his duties. Let us speak no more about it, Monsieur le Duc. If you have changed your opinion, I shall not remain less convinced that you intend to do something which is agreeable to me. I have the honour to be, with extreme consideration, Monsieur le Duc,

"Your very humble and very obedient servant,

"THE COMTESSE DUBARRY.

"VERSAILLES, December 16th, 1769."

"I take, Monsieur le Duc, all the interest possible in M. d'Arambal. You know better than anybody how good a servant he is to the King, and I desire that my recommendation may be added to a claim which is so precious to you. I shall see with the utmost satisfaction all the benefit that you can obtain for him. I am, Monsieur le Duc, with extreme consideration,

"Your very humble and very obedient servant,

"THE COMTESSE DUBARRY.

"VERSAILLES, July 5th, 1770."

The close examination of the catalogues of autograph letters scarcely show anything more than signatures at the end of receipts and orders for payments. I do not find a single letter of any interest except one love-letter to Lord Seymour, given by Barrier to Janin, who sold it, and that other letter dated July 15th, 1780, in which, when asking to have indispensable repairs made in the chateau of Luciennes, she says:—"The existing degradations cast a dishonour on the buildings that wounds my *amour-propre*."

Madame Du Barry

ORIGINAL CONVERSATION

And which may serve as a History of the Eighteenth Century.[1]

The Comte du Barry had an order for 17,000 livres on the Royal Exchequer. Although he did not dare to hope for immediate payment, he had nevertheless applied for it to M. Turgot, and M. de Vaines. His claim having appeared indisputable, it was immediately paid. The gratitude of the Comte du Barry, or perhaps his astonishment, induced him to call upon M. de Vaines in order to convey his thanks to that gentleman. The latter was only too delighted to have such a fine opportunity of making him chatter. Here is their conversation and the way the Comte started it with his Languedocian accent.

"Monsieur, I come to return thanks to you for having *squared* my claim.[2] Never would that rascal of an Abbe Terray have done so much for me."

"That is very astonishing, Monsieur, with all the credit that you have."

"I, credit! No. Once I put this hussy on the throne, she turned her back on me."

"What! she has done nothing for you?"

"Excuse me—the worst she could."

"And what did you do then?"

"Ah! I am going to tell you. I got her valet and her chambermaid to sell themselves to me—I paid well, and they kept me well posted in what was going on. One day amongst others, I learned soon after the occurrence that this creature had the ingratitude to say to that scoundrel of an abbe in the King's presence: ' I forbid you, abbe, to give anything to the Comte du Barry: not

[1] This unpublished fragment, which paints in a rather lifelike manner that immoral Gascon, the Comte Jean, was communicated to me by M. Maurice Tourneux, the learned editor of *Grimm's Correspondence,* published by the Garniers. The three stars placed at the head of it indicate that it is an article communicated by Madame d'Epinay to Meister, who arranged the " Correspondence " in the place of Grimm. This conversation was written in December, 1775.

[2] This is the nearest approach I can find in English for the Comte Jean du Barry's slang.—TRANSLATOR.

one sou, I don't take any interest in him, and I don't want anyone belonging to me to be a burden on the country.' . . . Do you know, Monsieur, what I did? I came back to Paris like a shot; I called on the abbe at his own house, and as soon as he came home, 'Well,' said I, 'has that hussy over there played her part nicely? Has she displayed much disinterestedness before the King? Was it a proper thing for her to declare that she did not want you to do anything for me?' The abbe was gulled by this, and I managed to get out of him this time a few 'thou'—not much —a trifle. I was only once able to drag nearly 40,000 livres out of him—faith, I believe that was all."

"However, you are rich?"

"Rich? No. I have a yearly income of 75,000 livres for life, and I have had to give it up for four years to my creditors, and I kept for myself 2,000 livres a month which the King pays me out of the Exchequer. As I like the Republic and fish, I mean to spend these four years in Marseilles."[1]

"Madame du Barry must have some brains anyhow?"

"Brains? Not at all; but in her case there is a close relationship between mind and body. In the morning, when she gets up, she is lovely, pretty, fresh as a rose—it must be admitted she is ravishing. About eleven o'clock, her jaws fall; her complexion fades; yellow spots come under her eyes—she is no longer anything but a sapless rose, a mere rag. When the candles are lighted, though, she picks up again, and becomes just as beautiful as ever. Well, 'tis just the same way with her mind; she has some flashes of wit, a good memory, and enough of skill to make good use of what she hears—sometimes charmingly clever things drop from her lips as if out of Heaven. And then I have got up a regular little academic college composed of the Abbe Arnaud, Marin, Turpin, La Morliere and other clever people, who have kept her well versed in current literature, and who have taught her how to have a fling at philosophy. She has got some good out of it more or less."

"Have you not lost your wife?"

---

[1] Marseilles is a large seaport, and was then also a hotbed of Republicanism. It was the men of Marseilles who, after the outbreak of the Revolution, marched to Paris singing the " Marseillaise."—TRANSLATOR.

Madame Du Barry

"You see me in mourning for her. I have taken off the 'weepers,' because I have given up weeping over her. A decent woman, handsome and well-deserving, though she hadn't a sou. She used to pray to God every day as an atonement for my unfortunate life. I had the greatest respect for her; but I didn't love her. She was a relation of Malesherbes—I mean soon to let him hear of this bereavement. The fact is, we're not a lucky family. 'Tis only that beggar who disowns his own family's name that makes his fortune. He has married La Fumel, who will give him more than 200,000 crowns. I did a foolish stroke of business about my son's match. I'm saddled with that Tournon girl; she had nothing, but she was related to Soubise. She was a beauty, and the King gave her a dowry. I had cherished some hopes; all these are dashed."

"And what, Monsieur, has become of Madame de Muralt?"

"Ah! charming creature! she is relegated to some third floor, I suppose. I have a great regard for her—she has character. Just fancy! while I was wasting gold and jewellery on her, she said to me:—'I hate you with the most deadly hatred; I detest you; I execrate you. There's not a penny-boy hanging round the street-corners that I wouldn't prefer to you!' Oh! I must do her that much justice—she has character, that woman. Well, she is dying of hunger in some hole or other."

They had got to this point when in came M. d'Harvelay.

The Comte rushed over to him.

"Ah! good day, Monsieur d'Harvelay. I'm the person—am I not?—that you made the Court's banker?"

"I don't think so, Monsieur. M. de Vergennes, when he got into the Ministry, thought fit to confide some details to me."

"Then apparently I've muddled it up. Well, good-bye, messieurs. I'm off to see Malesherbes."

When he reached M. de Malesherbes' house, the Comte du Barry communicated the fact of his wife's death to that gentleman on the ground that she was related to him and the Chancellor Maupeou.

"How is that?" said M. de Malesherbes to him.

M. du Barry entered into an account of his wife's genealogy.

"Well, really," returned M. de Malesherbes, "she is much more

Madame Du Barry

of a relative of mine than she is of M. de Maupeou."

"Well," said Du Barry, in response to this remark, "I accept the exchange."

FURNISHED TO THE COMTESSE DUBARRY BY BUFFAULT, MERCHANT, PARIS.[1]

For her use.

September, 1769.—Delivered to Madame Sigly[2] 14 ells ¼ gross of Tours, grey foundation plated with silver, broche silk and striped silver netting-silk, at 60 livres .... 855*l.*

September, 1769.—Delivered to Madame Sigly 14 ells ¼ white fluted persienne striped, white satin, broche rosette, plated with gold and cherry-coloured chenille, at 48 livres .... 684*l.*

September, 1769.—16 ells of white ottoman silk striped, with a satiny sheen, rose-coloured, at 15 livres .... 225*l.*

September, 1769.—Delivered to Madame Sigly 20 ells white satin foundation with medallions, broche, chenille, double foundations, lilac and white, at 34 livres .... 680*l.*

September, 1769.—17 ells jonquil foundation, fluted, striped, with a white satiny gloss, spangled with shaded variegated bouquets, at 24 livres .... 408*l.*

November, 1769.—Delivered to Madame Sigley, for a robe on the large pannier, 15 ells, white satin foundation streaked with gold, broche, bouquets of mother-of-pearl, chenille, and little wreath of citron-coloured silk, at 54 livres .... 810*l.*

June, 1771.—For six rosewood parasols, taffeta of different colours, trimmed with white silk and silver, at 39 livres each.. 234*l.*

[1] I give here some fragments of the accounts of Madame du Barry from the manuscripts in the National Library (French Supplement, 8157, 8158). These accounts are not only interesting in connection with the history of the Favourite: they give information as to the value of the beautiful articles of the period, and give us the exact prices of the most luxurious, the most showy specimens of the artistic industry of the eighteenth century. I begin with the orders for dress. Madame du Barry's silk-merchants were Buffault, Lenormand, Barbier, Pourjot, Assorty. Her fringe-maker was Fremont; her lace-maker was Lejeune; her button-maker was Kiriel.

Madame Sigly was the dressmaker who usually did most work for Madame du Barry.

Madame Du Barry

FURNISHED TO THE COMTESSE DUBARRY BY LE NORMAND, PROSPER LE DUC ET CIE., PARIS.

For her use.

Fourth of October, 1772.

FULL-DRESS COSTUMES.

A full-dress costume with large satin-body white foundation, embroidered with knots of rose-coloured spangles and gold and silver spanglets, with the hemming of the end of the dress and of the skirt-petticoat ································· 5600*l*. ⎞
Laid out on additional embroidery in gold spangles 240*l*. ⎠ 5 40 .

A beautiful robe on a foundation of white satin striped, plated, with gold folds, forming waves, wreaths of small and large spangles, bouquets of spangles enamelled with rubies, the whole very rich.
2400*l*.

ROBES ON THE PANNIER.

13 ells, foundation of plated silver striped with a large blade, doubly embroidered, frieze of gold, wreaths of rosebuds and pinks, little ribbon, shaded gold spangles, very rich, at 96 livres. **1248*l*.**

Satin foundation Marly white and silver, pea-roses, garland of roses, rich shading ································· 708*l*. 15s.

Satin broche, white foundation, a thousand flowers, little garland of lilacs, marigold and rose shade, at 39 livres ········ 526*l*. 10s.

Egyptian satin on a green foundation, spangled with a thousand flowers, variegated shade, reduced to 24 livres ·············· 312*l*.

White satin with patches of rose-coloured striped chenille, Egyptian white ································· 324*l*.

ROBES SUITABLE TO RANK.[1]

16 ells satin foundation, white, striped, silver wreath, strewn with blue bouquets and bouquets of chenille lilac and rich green, at 51 livres ································· 828*l*. 15s.

[1] "Consideration Robes."

Madame Du Barry

ROBES DE TOILETTE.

Satin mixed flesh colour and white ermine, at 8 livres .. 148*l.*
Satin flesh-coloured, polished rose-coloured, and little rose-coloured point-lace, at 8*l.* 10*s.* .... 157*l.* 5*s.*
Indian silk, sky blue, at 14 livres .... 196*l.*
October, 1773.—A full-dress suit of white velvet, with the body embroidered over with spangles large and small, shaded and enamelled in addition to a beautiful border for the skirt and the tail of the robe, the whole matched very richly .... 12,000*l.*
October, 1773.—A full-dress costume satin, rose-coloured and silver, with the large body embroidered in silver, embroidered over with spangles, enamelled rose-colour with wreaths, very rich edging[1] .... 7600*l.*

FURNISHED FOR THE COMTESSE DU BARRY BY LE NORMAND, PROSPER LE DUC ET CIE.

For the Use of the King.

Fourth of July, 1773.

11th *September*, 1773.—A white Indian silk morning-gown, with embroidered edges, spangles, shades with the cushion and the slippers, the entire matched and very rich .... 2,400*l.*

FURNISHED TO THE COMTESSE DU BARRY BY PAGELLE'S MILLINERY ESTABLISHMENT, *The Pink of Fashion.*[2]

November, 1773.—For having trimmed a full-dress costume of white satin in variegated silver, embroidered with green and rose-

---

[1] In the goods supplied by Le Normand, there are a certain number of articles intended to be given as presents. We find there waistcoats for seigneurs of the Court, dresses for the Duchesse d'Aiguillon, for Mlle. Emilie, etc. In October, 1772, mention is made of a dress of white Ottoman silk for the little gardeneress of the Trianon.

[2] "Aux traits galants." The name of M. Pagelle's establishment is untranslatable. "The Pink of Fashion" conveys the idea.—TRANSLATOR.

Madame du Barry was not afraid to keep her trades-people waiting. In a memorandum of Pagelle, of July, 1771, we read 'Journey to the Meuse, having waited from 2 to 7 o'clock in a hackney-coach."

22

coloured spangles, wreaths of roses and marten, a wreath of marten and roses in the lowest flounce, a wreath entwined at the top, a wreath of roses and myrtle, with a net overhead to sustain the wreath, the tail of the skirt puffed out, cut by some rows of wreaths in branches, at the edge a wreath doubly entwined for the body, the bracelets, the fur-tipped, the court tassels, the wreath for the head, the topknot .... 10,500*l.*

Carriage of the costume to Versailles .... 10,512*l.*

November, 1773.—For having trimmed a full-dress costume of white satin in gold and silver blond with shells, puffed out above and below, the columns festooned with bouquets of roses in the hollows of the festoons, the tail of the dress matched with the trimming of the body, tassels to set off the tail of the dress and bracelets .... 1245*l.*

March, 1774.—For having trimmed a robe with a silver foundation in blond lace with fine silver and jasmine, the robe fully trimmed with a chicory-coloured border, heightened and picked out with jasmine and borders of puffs, bouquets in the openings with little knots, and for having edged the robe with silver ...... 573*l.*

For having trimmed a silver robe with silver blond lace and white plumes, the robe fastened, the flounces puffed out with a festoon lower down, great plumes at the top of each shell, puffs in the hollows of the sleeves, the knots, the plumes, the necklace, the sleeve-knots and that of the chignon .... 450*l.*

FURNISHED TO THE COMTESSE DU BARRY BY BERTIN, MILLINER TO THE
QUEEN.

August, 1784.—A cloak of Italian gauze bordered with a white "comet" and trimmed with hemmed gauze .... 44*l.*

August, 1784.—The trimming of a "Pierrot" corsage[1] of rose-coloured taffeta, the petticoat trimmed with a gauze flounce with an edging underneath of a beautiful black lace of great depth, English foundation, a very fine chicory-coloured tulle lining. The "Pierrot" trimmed all around with beautiful black lace. A double "chicoree," the same as the petticoat at the top. The upper collar

---

[1] The "Pierrot" corsage had two little raised lappets at the end the back. It was, no doubt, originally suggested by a clown's dress.—TRANSLATOR.

Madame Du Barry

bordered with very fine imitation lace, ruff of lace like the " Pierrot," the sleeves trimmed in raised fashion with imitation lace like the upper collar .... 380*l.*

September, 1784.—A jockey cap, of yellow straw, tied round with a white ribbon; a large ribbon striped brown and white around the shape; a knot on one side, and behind the same ribbon, a tuft sideways of five white feathers and a heron's feather .... 120*l.*

November, 1784.—A white taffeta pelisse lined and wadded, trimmed with very deep blond lace, a tulle foundation with shells. 300*l.*

January, 1785.—A crepe mourning-cap, the " papillon " with large borders, the pinners the same, a gauze headdress of black wool. 36*l.*

March, 1785.—A piece of ribbon cross of St. Louis .... 58*l.*

Two sword-knots of ribbon, at 15 livres .... 30*l.*

July, 1785.—A pair of little ruffles in two rows edged with pretty blond lace .... 58*l.*

6 fichus of English gauze of one ell, at 12 livres............ 72*l.*

August, 1785.—A " Quakeress " hat of sarcenet-taffeta of English deep-blue trimmed with a large rose-coloured and white ribbon, striped and satiny .... 58*l.*

A band-box .... 3*l.*

December, 1785.—The trimming of a Turkish robe of real English violet satin, the facings trimmed with drapery in white satin and lilac, a twisted piece of blond lace, foundations of point d'Alençon, very rich, with folds on the reverse side; the under-petticoat of white taffeta covered with beautiful broche gauze, hemmed with the same blond lace as the robe, the same drapery as on the top of the robe .... 300*l.*

January, 1786.—A girdle worn like a scarf of very large English green ribbon broche and white .... 34*l.*

May, 1786.—A puff edged with a ribbon with white feathers with the upper part blond; a plume of three violet feathers, a knot below of beautiful blond lace and a fichu of gauze behind .... 144*l.*

September, 1787.—A cloak of beautiful black broche gauze, edged and trimmed with black lace, of unusual length, the foundation of Alençon with pea-coloured dots, rich border, the back trimmed with a very beautiful crimpled tulle .... 400*l.*

March, 1789.—A hat *a la Provençale* of gauze with a thousand stripes, trimmed with many ribbons grey and white .... 54*l.*

Madame Du Barry

February, 1791.—A hat-bonnet of grey satin, edged with a high black lace, on a background of Alençon with stars and a ribbon of rose-coloured satin tied in a garland .... 120*l.*

FURNISHED TO THE COMTESSE DU BARRY BY VANOT, MERCHANT TO THE KING, RUE SAINT DENIS, *a la Picarde.*[1]

October, 1770.—A very beautiful toilette of point d'Argentan and her surtout .... 9,000*l.*

December, 1770.—Two headdresses, with a background of exceedingly fine point, three rows of ruffles in full made expressly; 1 ell '/₁₂ of point at the two sides for the fichu, and ²/₃ of the frill for two in front of the "turret," the whole amounting to ...... 4000*l.*

November, 1771.—A mantle of superfine point and 6 ells of point lace at the two sides as trimming .... 2400*l.*

March, 1772.—Two gathered bodies on a foundation of point lace, 6 rows of ruffles in full, '/₃ frill for two in front of the "turret," and two ells on two sides for the fichu .... 6000*l.*

June, 1772.—Two gathered bodies and foundation of superfine English lace. Six rows of ruffles complete, two well supplied with ribbon and two well supplied with frilling, the whole........ 6500*l.*

July, 1772.—41 ells ³/₁₆ of real Valenciennes, of great depth, at 90 livres .... 3706*l.* 17*s.*

October, 1773.—A gorgeous English morning-wrapper composed of two rows of ruffles in full, fringed with silk and silver on both sides, height four fingers, 1 ell '/₁₂ lace made expressly, fringed on the two sides, '/₃ frill for the front of the "turret," 2 ells ¹/₄ of a foot to trim the slopings; the whole of superfine English material.
4500*l.*

Same month.—Another gorgeous morning-wrapper, the whole in English material .... 7000*l.*

The account which begins in October, 1770, and which stops at the end of April, 1774, reaches the sum of 91,107*l.* 10*s.* on which she had only paid an instalment of 54,000 livres.

---

[1] Madame du Barry's lace and cloth-merchants were Gruel, Gabriel Dumoustier and others. We find an account of Gruel for laces commencing July 1st, 1768, mounting up to 67,999 livres, on foot of which Madame du Barry remained in debt to him 35,000 livres.

Madame Du Barry

FURNISHED TO THE COMTESSE DU BARRY BY BERTIN, OF THE *Great Mogul.*

October, 1779.—A large shaped hat of white straw, raised at both white and blue-fluted ribbon spotted with black, a large tuft of black and white feathers which the Comtesse has furnished. 24*l.*

February, 1780.—A large crepe apron striped with bands of white satin cut up and sewn on the flat; a beautiful piece of blond lace, of great length, with stars switched all round and a flat band of satin on the seam .... 96*l.*

August, 1780.—A large-shaped hat of blue English straw lined with taffeta; a "turret" and two knots of large *satine* ribbon...... 24*l.*

December, 1783.—A fichu edged at the bottom with a "comet" of white satin and a beautiful blond background of Alençon lace with straight edging, the frill trimmed with two rows of the same blond and with white satin ribbon at the back .... 120*l.*

January, 1784.—A chemise trimmed with crepe, the facings edged with black velvet, the sleeves trimmed with flat folds, an armlet in the middle of rose-coloured satin edged with black velvet, and a steel buckle, a piece of crepe with two rows of steel buttons running over it at each side, an under-petticoat of crepe trimmed in the lower part with a flounce edged above and below with black velvet, a skirt of Italian taffeta edged with black velvet[1]...... 144*l.*

May, 1784.—The trimming of a robe *a l'Anglaise* of white stuff with yellow stars, the facings trimmed with large chicory-coloured Italian gauze cut in strips, with two cords of the same chicory material in the under-petticoat[2] .... 90*l.*

With the arms of France, CHARDON, MERCHANT HATTER. *The only one in Paris who keeps the real English beavers for the ladies wearing their natural plumes, shaggy or not shaggy, Amazon's hats, hats for balls, for horseback, and for hunting,* HAS FURNISHED TO THE COMTESSE DU BARRY :—

September, 1779.—A superfine shaggy beaver............. 30*l.*

[1] This fancy of Madame du Barry reminds us of the fact that "good Queen Bess" wore a black velvet night-gown.—TRANSLATOR.

[2] A quantity of articles are sent by Le Normand, Pagelle, Mlle. Bertin, and Bertin of the "Great Mogul," to Madame Sigly, Madame du Barry's dressmaker.

Madame Du Barry

A trimming of large English ribbon, a bouquet of beautiful white and fine feathers and a puce "follette".................... 103*l.*

MEMORANDUM FOR MADAME DU BARRY OF THE WORKS AND VALUABLE ARTICLES MADE BY CARLIER, MASTER-TAILOR IN PARIS.[1]

March, 1774.—For the courier, made a fashionable polonaise of sky-blue cloth edged with silver lace, waistcoat and breeches of chamois-coloured net silk .... 15*l.*

Furnished one ell and a half of sky blue cloth, at 22 livres an ell .... 33*l.*

3½ ells of twilled chamois for the lining of polonaise, at 6*l.* 10*s.* an ell .... 22*l.* 15*s.*

11 additional ells of silver lace to the ell which trims the polonaise and waistcoat, weighing 7 ounces 2 grains, at 7*l.* 10*s* .... 541*l.* 7*s.* 6*d.*

Furnished 6 silver puffs trimmed with cord.......... 19*l.* 2*s.* 6*d.*

Two pieces of chamois silk network for the waistcoat and the breeches, at 24 livres each............................... 48*l.*

12 big silver buttons for the polonaise................. 6*l.* 10*s.*

3 dozen and a half little ones similar to the waistcoat, breeches, and sleeves of the polonaise...................... 11*l.* 7*s.* 10*d.*

1 pair of silver garters matched with the buttons..... 12*l.*

March, 1774.—For Zemord (*sic*), made a polonaise, and supplied two camlet breeches.. 12*l.*

Furnished 5 yards of iron-grey baracan for the polonaise and 2 pairs of breeches, at 6 livres............................. 30*l.*

9 ells of flat silk braid for the trimming of the polonaise and the waistcoat, at 12 livres for the one, etc .... 58*l.*

November, 1774.—For Zemord. For having made a frock-coat and waistcoat of English broadcloth, lined with braid to suit, the button-holes made of the same and the breeches in like fashion .... 12*l.*

April, 1775.—For Zemord. For having made a complete dress-coat, lined with gold lace, in the English fashion and two pairs of breeches .... 15*l.*

---

[1] In this account there are particulars of a suit of clothes supplied to M. Desontaines, the Comtesse du Barry's secretary.

Madame Du Barry

Furnished 3 yards of green Saxony for the dress-coat, waist-coat, and breeches, at 26 livres each........................ 78*l.*

8 ells of gold lace for lining the dress-coat and waistcoat, weighing 3 ounces 7 gross, at 11 livres.................... 42*l.* 12*s.* 6*d.*

In Carlier's other accounts, preserved in the library of the City of Versailles, M. le Roi has again turned out for Zamore:

A hussar's costume, white, with silver lace, coat, breeches, cap and stout silk buskins, silver buttons, belt, and little sabre.

A plume on the cap, with tufts and spangles.

A hussar's costume of cherry velvet with silver lace, the belt and the scabbard of the little sabre in velvet of the same colour.

Another costume, flesh-coloured, plume and tuft on the cap of the same colour.

Another of rose-coloured ribbed material trimmed with silver.

Another of stuff of silver and rose-colour.

Another of white taffeta trimmed with silver.

A sailor's costume of Silesian dimity, cap and breeches of dimity, the whole trimmed with silver braid, rose-coloured silk ribbons in the cap, belt of taffeta with silver fringes.

This tailor's accounts, these accounts of Carlier, are, in reality, full of historic revelations. Thus we see how the priest Gomard de Vaubernier, who had held out his brother as the father of "La Lange," and who was about to have the forged birth-certificate fabricated for the marriage, was dressed at the Favourite's expense in order that he might take the necessary steps for this purpose in proper attire. In the month of March, 1768, Carlier got an order for a complete suit of black cloth and two pairs of breeches[1] for the Abbe, and in the month of August, still for the Abbe, a frock-coat of maroon-coloured barracan with gold buttons, a coat, waistcoat, and breeches of Lille camlet, a short cassock of cloth and a cloak of Saint Maur nap—frock coat, coat, cassock, and cloak having been certainly all worn by Gomard de Vaubernier at the ceremony of the marriage of "La Lange" with Guillaume du Barry, which took place in the parish-church of Saint Laurent on the 1st of September, 1768.

---

[1] "Bulletin of the Library of the City of Versailles." (Article of M. le Roi.) No. 111, 1872.

343

Madame Du Barry

These accounts of Carlier present to our view all the Favourite's staff of servants in their full-dress and their undress livery.

Madame du Barry had eight valets—Degle, Pellier, Fremont, Bellecour, Bourguignon, Augustin, Luxembourg, and Paris. She had eight footmen—Noel, Morin, Desmoulins, François, Raclot, Deflandre, La France, and Étienne.

The full-dress livery consisted of a coat of scarlet cloth with gold lace and lined with white Neapolitan stuff on the skirts, the front of the coat and the sleeves adorned with braid and puffed out with fringes, breeches and scarlet waistcoat with gold buttons, garters of gold braid, the ends and the buckles of the breeches trimmed with gold.

For the undress livery, the coat was of chamois cloth with gold lace, waistcoat and breeches of chamois silk with silver buttons. The garters under the breeches, as well as the ends and the buckles, were of silver.

In bad weather, the lackeys wore over their livery a great-coat of grey cloth.

There were two coachmen—Comtois and Mazieres. Their livery was of sky-blue cloth with chamois waistcoats and silver buttons.

The outriders who went in front of her carriage were Delorme, Tavernier, and Morlot. Their uniform was of blue cloth slashed with silver at all the seams and with silver-laced buttonholes.

The postilions—Madame du Barry always driving with four horses—were named Lajeunesse, Durand, and Mathurin. They wore blue cloth waistcoats with silver lace like the button-holes.

Two chair-bearers, then required when taking an outing in the Park or paying visits, wore a livery of scarlet cloth with silver lace.

Five grooms, and two assistant grooms, in blue livery with gold lace, completed the equipage.

Besides these, a steward, a butler, two wardrobe attendants, a Swiss and two gardeners, all wearing blue livery with silver lace, formed the male portion of the servants of the King's mistress.[1]

[1] "Bulletins of the Library of the City of Versailles." (M. le Roi's Article), No. III, 1872.

Madame Du Barry

Twelve large armchairs of yellow Indian silk, embroidered with edgings of silk flowers, shaded naturally according to the picture, in the midst of which edging there is for each a medallion on a white ground, representing different landscapes and figures also in accordance with the picture, embroidered in shaded and sheeny silk, which medallion is held up by a beautiful knot of striped ribbon; the arms of the said armchairs embroidered also with edgings and medallions, at 60 livres .... 7,200*l*.

Ottoman embroidered in the same way with six large medallions representing "The Reapers" .... 2,400*l*.

Firescreen in the same style .... 450*l*.

MADAME DU BARRY'S BILL FOR WORK DONE AND DELIVERED BY ME, DAVAUX, EMBROIDERER, RUE SAINT-DENIS.

January, 1770.—Delivered a full-dress robe and the petticoat and corset and the stomacher of silver tissue, embroidered with gold and silver spangles and gold network, and patches of colour and shaded silk with all kind of nosegays. Price arranged with the Comtesse .... 10,600*l*.

October, 1770.—Delivered an armchair on a white background with a garland of roses embroidered in shaded silk for .... 432*l*.

Besides, for having paid to M. de Saint-Aubin for the same armchair .... 60*l*.

Besides, for having paid to M. de Saint-Aubin for the design of the full-dress robe .... 200*l*.

April, 1774.—Delivered a pair of stockings, the four corners embroidered in gold and silver, small and large spangles of bright colour .... 48*l*.

AMOUNT DUE FOR ARTICLES SUPPLIED AND FOR THE REPAIR OF MADAME DU BARRY'S WATCH BY THE SAID SIEUR LEPAUTE.

For the price of a watch adorned with diamonds, sold by the said Sieur to the said Lady, the sum of five thousand four hundred livres .... 5,400*l*.

Madame Du Barry

And for repairs to the watch of enamelled gold belonging to the same lady, according to the memorandum of said Sieur of June 7th, 1774 .... 96*l.*

LIST OF GOODS WHICH FONTAINES, DEALER IN FOREIGN STUFFS AT *The King's Laurel,* HAS HAD THE HONOUR OF FURNISHING FOR THE SERVICE OF MADAME DU BARRY.

December 6th, 1769.—1,500 flowers of Indian silk, embroidered and shaded at the rate of 20 sous each, great and small indiscriminately .... 1,500*l.*
A snuff box garnished with "burgos" of an oval shape.... 576*l.*
A pin case of arborized agate, garnished with gold......... 240*l.*
A ring of arborized agate, surrounded with brilliants....... 480*l.*
January 2nd.—15 coffee-napkins of Indian dimity, at the rate of 15 livres each.................................... 225*l.* ⎱
For the cylinder .... 6*l.* ⎰ 231*l.*

MEMORANDUM OF BINDINGS MADE FOR THE COMTESSE DU BARRY BY VENTE, BOOKBINDER, PARIS.

March 31st, 1774.—Bound six quarto volumes in red morocco with strings and edgings in gold, with the arms of the Comtesse, which volumes contained the portraits and an extract from the lives of celebrated men of every sort, at 15 livres the volume......... 90*l.*

Manufactory of Stores.

Delivered to the Comtesse du Barry by the Manufactory of porcelain to the King during the years 1771, '72, '73 and '74.

Viz.:

January 15th and *January* 30th, 1771.—25 children in biscuit fashion, at 30*l.* each.. 750*l.*
8 horns of plenty at 15 livres........................... 120*l.*
1 vase with garlands .... 48*l.*
1 basket .... 36*l.*

NOTE.—*All the articles of sculpture and of biscuit-work have been ordered by the Sieur Bonneval, Madame du Barry's chef, who approved of them and had them placed on the table at dessert.*

August 29th, 1771.—A complete service with *little roses and garlands,* composed of 145 plates at 42 livres, 8 salad-bowls at 96 **livres,**

Madame Du Barry

4 lozenged baskets at 216 livres, 2 sugar-bowls at 120 livres, 2 butter-coolers at 96 livres, 2 mustard-pots at 78 livres, 2 cheese-bowls at 120 livres, 12 salt-cellars in three parts at 48 livres, 4 olio-pots and earthen jars at 600 livres, 1 punch-bowl and cover at 600 livres, 4 saucers at 54 livres, 36 pails for glasses at 60 livres, 4 pails for liqueurs at 120 livres, 2 oval pails for liqueurs at 168 livres, 4 pails for half-bottles at 156 livres, 8 pails for bottles at 216 livres, 4 crenelated pails at 240 livres, and 2 pails for ice at 252 livres, amounting to... 21,438*l.*

NOTE:—*This must be the service which the Comtesse was in the habit of using at her large suppers. It had, so it was said, served to replace the one which had been previously supplied to her by the manufactory and which she had sold to the Sieur Bufau for England.*

October 7th, 1771.—1 dejeuner service of lapis............ 160*l.*
December, 1771.—6 biscuit-work services, one of which was for the Dauphiness, at 144 livres .... 864*l.*
1 water-jug and basin.................................... 126*l.*
1 tobacco-jar .... 27*l.*
2 pomatum-pots .... 20*l.*
1 chamber-pot .... 42*l.*

Year 1772.

February 20th.—1 stewed fruit-dish of sky-blue colour with flowers .... 54*l.*
March 30th.—1 goblet and saucer....................... 60*l.*
May 13th.—2 busts of Madame du Barry at 144 livres.... 288*l.*
October 5th.—1 pannier, green and gold................. 120*l.*
1 goblet and saucer, purple and gold.................... 60*l.*
December.—1 olio-pot and ornamental tray.............. 600!*l.*
1 mosaic dejeuner-service .... 144*l.*
1 jug without basin.................................... 42*l.*
1 milk jug... 30*l.*
1 "love-grinder"[1]..................................... 96*l.*

[1] "*Amour remouleur.*" Possibly some cosmetic or hygienic face appliance.—TRANSLATOR.

Madame Du Barry

Year 1773.

January 26th.—2 very beautiful basins of stony material at 360
livres .... 720*l.*

February 22.—2 Verdun basins with garlands of flowers at 240
livres .... 480*l.*

1 Courteille basin with birds............................... 240*l.*

NOTE:—*These basins for putting in flowers were ordered by the
Comtesse from designs chosen by her; and she is not ignorant of the
number of them which perished in the fire before succeeding with
those which have been delivered her.*

1 eye-sponge with gold fillets .... 4*l.*

March 2nd.—Delivered to M. Lebanc, on behalf of the Comtesse,[1]
1 bust after Lemoine .... 144*l.*

April 28th.—Brought to Luciennes a Brie cheese tray, white in
colour .... 24*l.*

June 17th.—Group representing the scene of the "Spanish Conversation" .... 432*l.*

2 groups at the sides..................................... 384*l.*

4 accessory figures....................................... 288*l.*

July 6th.—2 defective chestnut-dishes at 96 livres .... 192*l.*

July 7th.—1 Courteille dejeuner of Chinese design........ 600*l.*

NOTE:—*This article ordered, tray and Chinese figures, by the
Comtesse, and delivered to herself, is of the most exquisite workmanship. It cost two months and a half of work to the best
painter of the manufactory.*

[1] Baron Ch. Davillier informs us, in his pamphlet "Madame du
Barry's Sevres Porcelains," that the denominations of Verdun and
of Courteille came from the names of a shareholder and an administrator of Versailles, who, as much as the artists, gave a name
to a new form or a new decoration. There are the Duplessis vases,
the Bachelier vases, the Falconet, the Boizot, etc. M. Davillier also
points out the existence in the Museum of Sevres of a plate executed for Madame du Barry in 1788. The edge is adorned with
ten loves holding garlands of flowers and tambourines on which
may be read the initials D. B. In the centre is represented Folly
shaking her bells.

Madame Du Barry

August 29th.—A group of Boizot: *Zephyr and Flora*..... 360*l.*
Love and Friendship.................................... 360*l.*
August 31st.—Chinese service composed of 10 plates with figures
from pictures and Chinese miniatures, 4 shell stewed fruit-dishes,
1 sugar-bowl, 1 triangular tray, three cups for ices, 2 pails for
half-bottles, 2 pails for bottles, 1 oval basket, amounting to.. 3,804*l.*

NOTE:—*This service was delivered at Luciennes the day the King
supped there. The pictures are as precious, and by the same painter,
as the Chinese dejeuner above-mentioned.*

December.—1 chocolate-goblet and garland............... 84*l.*
1 goblet with a portrait on a gold background and saucer.. 96*l.*

NOTE.—*Presents made at Versailles by Madame to various persons as in preceding years.*

December.—1 service of roses and foliage composed of 36 plates,
11 stewed fruit dishes, 4 salad-bowls, 2 pails for bottles, etc., with
a supplement of 12 plates etc. delivered on March 14th, the whole
amounting to .... 4,856*l.*

NOTE.—*The Comtesse du Barry made a present of this service to
the Marquis du Barry at the time of the Porcelain Exhibition at
Versailles.*

Year 1774.

January 21st.—1 goblet and saucer with medallion of the
King .... 144*l.*
April 13th.—Brought to Bellevue 1 large teapot, ribbons, verses,
and hatchings of gold and carmine....................... 66*l.*

The accounts rise in 1771 to 27,732 livres; in 1772 to 2,760 livres;
in 1773 to 15,426 livres; in 1774 to 3,101 livres; total, 49,019 livres,
on which sum had been paid 22,000 livres.

Madame Du Barry

LIST OF FOUR PIECES OF TAPESTRY DEALING WITH THE SUBJECT OF THE
LOVES OF THE GODS FROM THE PICTURES OF MM. VANLOO, BOUCHER,
PIERRE AND VIEN, MADE IN THE MOST EXCELLENT STYLE OF WEAVING
IN THE GOBELINS MANUFACTORY FOR THE COMTESSE DU BARRY FROM
MEASURES GIVEN BY M. LE DOUX, ARCHITECT, WHICH PIECES WERE TO
BE EXECUTED BY THE SIEURS COZETTE AND AUDRAN. (IST OF NOVEM-
BER, 1772.)

Carl Vanloo: *Neptune and Amimonna*, 2 ells, 11 sticks, 8
tenths .... 3,554*l*. 14*s*. 5*d*.
P·erre: *The Abduction of Europa*............. 3,554*l*. 14*s*. 5*d*.
Boucher: *Venus and Vulcan*................... 3,554*l*. 14*s*. 5*d*.
Vien: *Pluto and Proserpine*.................. 3,554*l*. 14*s*. 5*d*.

May 29th, 1774.

MEMORANDUM OF THE THREE PIECES OF TAPESTRY MADE BY THE SIEUR
COZETTE, CONTRACTOR OF THE ROYAL MANUFACTORY OF GOBELINS, AT
448*l*. 5*s*. THE ELL SQUARED THE ONE IN THE OTHER ON ACCOUNT OF
THE PIECE REPRESENTING VENUS, WHICH IS EXCEEDINGLY LADEN WITH
FIGURES AND DIFFICULT WORKS, SO AS TO RENDER THE DISBURSEMENT
FOR THE WORKMAN AND THE SILK MATERIALS, OWING TO THE
VARIETY OF TONES, VERY DEAR; FOR THE THREE SAID PIECES THE
SUM OF .... 12,496*l*.

By order of the Comtesse given to the workman who worked on
the said pieces.. 72*l*.

The Sieur Cozette has the honour to represent that for similar
pieces the late *Madame de Pompadour* gave him in 1752 *as a
reward and honorarium for each piece* 50 *louis,* which makes for
the three .... 3,600*l*.

The 10th of June, 1775.

Venus and Vulcan. Girard, Worker in Tapestry, 87 weeks at 24*l*.;
3 additional workers, 9 livres.

Pluto and Proserpine. Ostende, 50 weeks at 18 livres; 2 workers
at 12 livres.

The Abduction of Europa. Roby, 33 weeks, with two young
workmen under him; 36 livres for the three; next 48 weeks for two.

Given for drink to the workmen the last time Madame du Barry
came to the Gobelins.. 72*l*.

Madame Du Barry

MEMORANDUM OF THE WORKS IN THE GILDING OF FURNITURE DONE FOR
THE COMTESSE DU BARRY, BY CAGNY, AS WELL IN HER APARTMENTS AT
VERSAILLES AS IN HER HOUSE OF LUCIENNES, THE SAID WORKS DONE
BY HER ORDERS IN THE COURSE OF THE YEARS 1769, 1770 AND 1771 BY
CAGNY, MERCHANT PAINTER AND GILDER IN PARIS, WHERE HE RESIDES
IN THE RUE DES MENETRIERS.

For Versailles.

The Salon.—Twelve large oval armchairs with frames, gilt with
burnished gold. The back with wand cut with an ornament in the
shape of a diamond with laurel leaves and berries; another wand ornamented with ribbons in a screw with three pearls threaded through
a very rich bouquet in the middle of the back, with many flowers tied with a ribbon. Acanthus-leaves with their berries. Branches
of olive-leaves, enwreathings and flowerets. Seven garlands of flowers, very rich, with their falls as much in front as on both sides;
four feet fluted each with a dozen flutings, with sunleaves crowning the said flutings, and a piece of rosework turning in each case.
The said armchair prepared, softened with water, repaired with care,
with constraint and precaution to revive the sculpture and enhance
its value afterwards when gilt with strong burnished gold, the most
beautiful gold, estimated with respect to the time of the restorers,
gilders, expenditure and double supply of gold, having regard to
the great richness and delicacy of the ornaments, and the entire
perfection of the articles the sum of...................... 340*l.*

The eleven other armchairs, similar in every respect, together cost-
ing the sum of.. 3,740*l.*

A large sofa with six feet, on the same plan as the armchair.. 1,250*l.*

Twelve oval chairs and a large chair for the King at 150*l.* 1,800*l.*

A large oval fire-screen............................... 775*l.*

Dining-room.—Thirty chairs for table and a large chair for the
King at 80*l.*.. 2,400*l.*

The Bed-room.—A large gilt bed with four sides, the pillars in sheaths
adorned with squares forming volutes, with a semi-circular cutting
of folded ribbons surrounding ornaments threaded together, flower-
border, and wand cut in pearls, a gorge, square, and semi-circular
cutting of olive-leaves with their berries, a rosework shaped like a
shamrock on the volute with acanthus-leaves in the lower part, a

decoration of rolled flowers and leaves, then another piece of rosework revolving in its case, a very rich garland of flowers bearing
volutes enveloping the said pillars, and drooping flowers on each side,
the pillars already mentioned even to the canopy fluted with a
dozen flutings adorned with flower-work interwoven with flower-
like water-jets, branches of leaves emerging from these floral ornaments and laurels, winding around the mouldings. Four strong feet
in their sheaths, fluting-work with a screw, laurel-leaves, ovolos,
and square cases with suns in the centre on the two front sides.
The two backs on an eminence, an arched eminence, carved on the
two surfaces, enriched with similar mouldings to the pillars and the
ornaments on the central portions of the bed, very rich intertwin-
ing flowers sustaining two pecking birds, with branches of myrtle
on one side and of olive on the other, together with their berries,
piastres threaded together, ribbons, a wand cut in pearls, ribbons,
and strings. Four very rich cross-beams, each adorned with three
wands, the one in the middle threaded with pearls, split leaves
winding round the surface of the said wand, a square, a flower-
border, another wand in the foreground adorned with pearls; in
the middle of the cross-beams, trophies of love and country life
very rich and with different variations, such as quivers, head-
bands, crowns of olive-leaves, a bow, and branches decked with
all kinds of little flowers.

The top of the bed with a very rich crown ornamented with
mouldings, cut with darts and ovolos, doucine in heart-rays, a great
gorge adorned with twinings of sunlight and flowers in the midst
of the two huge cross-beams, a medallion representing a vase sup-
ported by a trophy of love, garlands of flowers clinging to the
medallion with their drooping; two laurel branches in the shape
of chains and ribbons, four corner-pieces forming chests-of-draw-
ers, branches of poppies green and budding, enriched with mouldings of balusters and flower-work all very rich. Within the canopy,
two ovals one over the other adorned with mouldings of archi-
tecture, sustained by four curves in the shape of consoles, with
three faces; adorned with volutes in "collicornes" (*sic*), acanthus-leaves, and shapes of hearts on the mouldings and little
threaded flowerings, cleft-leaves and leaves formed of water on the
doucine, the wand ornamented with pearls and with filleted wedges,
a cord with its greenery and ends in osier entwined over the wand,

a tail-piece in the midst of the said summit adorned with a double piece of flower-work, garnished with berries and water-flowers, estimated, having regard to its grandeur, richness, and the delicacy of the ornaments and the carvings, the concentration and the considerable time lost by the gilders and restorers, the large expenditure for gold, false cutting, and double staff of persons employed, at the sum of .... 5,945*l.*

The seats of the same sort............................ 260*l.*

Six oval cabriolets for the little library. Two branches of myrtle tied by a ribbon to the middle of the back, two birds overhead, each at.. 290*l.*

The Little Gallery.—Eighteen gilt chairs and a large one for the King. The back, trophied with such attributes as War, Music, Science, Hunting, Love, Fishing, each at................... 142*l.*

Two canopies trophied with love, torches of love, vases, crowns, branches of roses, each at................................. 426*l.*

For Luciennes.

The Salon.—Twenty-five chairs, six of which are gilt. Bands of flowers, garlands of flowers, cut pearls, fir-cones, on the corners, acanthus-leaves, arranged in flower-work, the chairs gilt at.. 298*l.*

The others at.. 237*l.*

Two large armchairs, each at........................... 180*l.*

A large table-claw with four consoles in a case, a medallion in the middle, knotted with a ribbon, with a trophy in bas-relief 1,090*l.*

The Gallery.—Three big table-claws. The medallions in the centre ornamented with women's heads wearing Roman head-dresses, each ......:... 995*l.*

Twelve large armchairs; in the middle of the centre, a rich trophy, some of the group representing Music, others Country Life and the attributes of the Chase, each at..................... 490*l.*

Thirty-one chairs gilt, at .... 84*l.*

Four large sofas with subjects of children and ornaments analogous to the sciences, each at........................... 450*l.*

A firescreen. Four women's figures holding up the firescreen .... 550*l.*

The Dining-room.—Twenty-five chairs, vinestocks and clusters of grapes, all kinds of fruit, each at........................ 115*l*

Madame Du Barry

A large gilt frame for the portrait of the Comtesse.[1] Two children holding a crown of flowers and with horns of plenty, with garlands of flowers and olive-branches, two turtle-doves and branches of roses...................................... 2,250*l.*

Another frame for the portrait of Madame. Two figures at the base lifting drapery, with a cartel adorned with Madame's cipher .... 1,575*l.*

A gilt frame for the portrait of Zamor .... 135*l.*

The entire bill mounts up to 90,759 livres.

ARTICLES SUPPLIED TO THE COMTESSE DU BARRY BY ROETTIERS FATHER
AND SON, GOLDSMITHS IN ORDINARY TO THE KING.

The 23rd of September, 1769.—Two little chandeliers for the toilette table, adorned with pearls....................... 236*l.* 18*s.*

The 20th of January, 1770.—Furnished with plate utensils adorned with pearls and cut into a bend.

10 dozen of plates.

8 oval dishes.

In addition 12 flambeaux with their covers.............. 30,174*l.*

The 8th of January, 1771.—Furnished 4 flambeaux for chandeliers, very rich and on new models, representing the four elements enriched with portions of rams' bodies and laurel-wreaths.. 11,837*l.*

The 4th of May, 1771.—Furnished a milk-pot adorned with gold, surrounded with garlands of flowers on the circumference, with the entire coffeepot, the spout adorned with ornamental flutings and hollow flutings in which are growths of myrtle-leaves, the cover with projecting godroons is terminated by rods adorned with par-

---

[1] This is the celebrated frame of the large portrait of the Comtesse as a Muse, which, having been exhibited at the Salon in 1771 before the picture was placed there, excited the admiration of connoisseurs. It is a masterpiece, the " Secret Memoirs "say, of carving and gilding, the richness and the elegance of which we admire at the same time. The top is shaded by foliage arranged with great delicacy, in the midst of which are found two Cupids, one of whom bends his bow, while the other, who springs forward in front of him, holds a crown suspended and seems to be awaiting the goddess who must have placed him there. At the bottom and, as it were, at his feet are two doves who peck in the most voluptuous fashion. The frame was selected under No. 40 by the Committee of Arts charged to make a trio amongst the marvels of Luciennes.

sley-leaves which are intertwined. On the upper portion is a group of roses; the hinge is also much ornamented, as well as the handle, which sustains the haft and the knob.

Fashioned with the utmost finish and carried to the highest degree of polish .... 2,687*l.*

The 13th *of August,* 1771.—Furnished two olio-pots, trays and spoons for two services, trays and forks of the richest kind being adorned with children holding garlands, the four covers surmounted by paintings on four different subjects. The arms in bas-relief, the feet adorned with rams' heads, with trophies of flowers and quivers, the whole finished with the greatest care............. 24,000*l.*

Fashionable plate utensils in new models, adorned with laurel-leaves and with clasps in all the surface, at 24 livres the half-pound, being chased and finished with the greatest care.......... 20,259*l.*

On the 4th *of March,* 1773.—For having paid a journeyman gold-smith during three months, which are December, January and February, 1773, who worked every day till midnight and on to two o'clock in the morning,—that is to say, for four months and a half of days at 5 livres.................................. 675*l.*

On the 5th *of March,* 1773.—Two sugar-spoons of gold very rich, adorned with a Love holding garlands of roses, droopings of gar-lands of roses, rosettes and a garland of vine-leaves, the entire exe-cuted with the greatest care and polish................... 2,054*l.*

On the 1st *of July,* 1773.—A mustard-pot, its stand with a double ground, and a gold spoon, adorned with bas-relief and the arms also in relief .... 5,184*l.*

On the 4th *of April,* 1774.—For the knob of a walking-stick for Madame du Barry's courier .... 546*l.* 10*s.*

From the 23rd of September, 1769, to the 20th of January, 1770, the first bill of Roettiers Father and Son amounts to...... 34,735*l.*

The second from the 30th of November to the 13th of August, 1771, amounts to...................................... 156,028*l.*

The third from the 7th of September to the 29th of May, 1772, amounts to... 55,657*l.*

The fourth, from the 12th of June, 1772, to the 3rd of November, 1773, amounts to...................................... 93,606*l.*

Madame Du Barry

DIFFERENT MODELS AND EXECUTIONS OF WORKS IN BRONZE, CHAS-
ING, AND GILDING BY THE ORDERS AND FOR THE SERVICE OF THE
COMTESSE DU BARRY BY GOUTHIERE, CHASER AND GILDER FOR THE
KING'S PRIVY PURSE IN PARIS, QUAI PELLETIER, *at the Golden
Buckle.*

*Memorandum for Models and Execution of works in bronze, chas-
ing and gilding done by Gouthiere*[1]

OVAL DRAWING-ROOM.

Sketches and Models of Arms of Roses.

For the first sketch made with three branches, modelled in wax,
composed of branches of roses and myrtle, fastened with a knot of
ribbons, estimated at the sum of......................... 170*l.*

For another model in wax with two branches, which model has
been destroyed.. 150*l.*

For all the different models of roses and rose-buds of different
sizes and varieties, with their leaves and branches, as many roses
as myrtle and knots of ribbon, all of which models have been made
in wax and each finished separately with the greatest skill, estimated together to the sum of.......................... 300*l.*

For having moulded in plaster all the said models, having melted

---

[1] M. de Roi did not discover the important memorandum of
Gouthiere for the works executed at Luciennes. I was not more
fortunate than he in the examination of the "Accounts of Madame
du Barry," preserved in the National Library. This account I have
at last found in the Library of the City of Versailles, in the papers
carried off from the archives of Seine-et-Oise and delivered up to
Madame du Barry's heirs, perhaps, which were restored to it a
few years ago. This memorandum, so interesting with regard to
the works of this great art-craftsman, shows a degree of refinement, skill and luxuriousness in the decoration of Luciennes, which
was never carried to such a pitch in the details of the house-orna-
mentation. We shall find there window-knobs, handles of sash-
fastenings, bolts for which there had been models, mouldings in
plaster, meltings in copper and tin, castings, *finishings with the
greatest exercise of craftsmanship,* gildings and over-gildings. Of
this memorandum, which deserves to be published one day entire
in a "History of the Decorative Arts of the Eighteenth Century,"
I give only a few extracts, so that the public may have an idea
of what an artistic jewel Luciennes was. (Library of the City of
Versailles. Papers of the Du Barry. Tome I.)

thick wax, restored and fixed each piece on moulds of plaster so as afterwards to mould them in sand for that purpose........ 96*l*.

For having moulded them in sand, having melted them in tin and chased them, each arm valued at the sum of 1,000 livres, making for the eight arms the sum of...................... 8,000*l*.

For the moulding and finishing of the solderings made with the greatest craftsmanship, each arm valued at 300 livres, which makes for the eight arms the sum of .... 2,400*l*.

For having gilded and double-gilded them with ormolu and having them put into dead colouring; the gilding of each arm reaching the sum of 1,200 livres, makes for the eight the sum......... 9,600*l*.

Models of the Chimney-piece.

For the models of the mounting of the space above the tablet, having carried on this moulding in wood from two feet in length, on which we have modelled in wax ornamental leaves of water, the entire estimated at the sum of............................ 60*l*.

For having brought together with the claws two ends of the same moulding .... 30*l*.

For having moulded the said mouldings in sand.......... 150*l*.

For having got a model of twining for the cross-beam cut in wood .... 72*l*.

For the wax models of the twinings of rose-branches...... 200*l*.

For having moulded the twinings in plaster, having melted them in tin and chased them................................. 320*l*.

For the wax modelling of two rose-branches entwined for the little panel of the cross-beam........................... 40*l*.

For moulding the wax in plaster, melting it in tin and chasing .... 60*l*.

For the modelling in wood of the frame which surrounds the rose-branches .... 6*l*.

For one end of doucine moulding in wood on which we have modelled heart-rays in wax .... 24*l*.

For moulding in sand, melting in wax, and chasing and scooping out of the heart-rays.................................... 72*l*.

For the model of a tripod decorated with two goats' heads, a garland of vine, two bouquets of drooping flowers, a fillet with hearts entwined, a vase isolated in the tripod, the said vase decorated with a flame and a moulding, the said moulding cut in heart-rays and berries....................................... 500*l*.

Madame Du Barry

For a second moulding on the gorge cut in ovolos and darts, a vine-branch winding in the gorge of the vase, an end-piece in water-leaves and ornamental shell from which issues a stem bearing a flower, a bud with berries from which issues a thyrsus, a fir-cone and in the middle a serpent. All the large models and mouldings estimated in their entirety at the sum of............. 500*l.*

For the model of a ploughshare in which the tripod rests.. 30*l.*

For moulding laurel-leaves in wax on a wreathing of wood 24*l.*

For moulding in sand, melting in copper and chasing...... 55*l.*

Execution of Bronzes for the Chimney-piece.

For 5 feet 5 inches of doucine moulding fixed on the tablet: this moulding decorated with ornamented leaves and leaves of water .... 325*l.*

For having cast a steel blade of the same length as the moulding, for having filed it and polished it brightly.................... 60*l.*

For the panel underneath the moulding for which I have made a frieze in double interlacing of rose-branches, the entire well-chased and fastened with a folded screw so that no screw is visible .... 1,500*l.*

For two ornaments of rose-branches of the little cross-beam, the said branches well-chased............................ 300*l.*

For having gilded in ormolu and dead gold colour....... 1,600*l.*

For the two frames which surround the said ornaments.. 40*l.*

For having gilded these two frames in ormolu........... 48*l.*

For four goats' heads for the two tripods................ 240*l.*

For six posts for the said tripods decorated with ornamental work all through and on the faces, and with a gorge behind........ 600*l.*

For the chasing of two fir-cones and two buds with berries.. 40*l.*

For two serpents on which the scales have been put on in bits .... 160*l.*

For two circles at the foot of a turret and for having fixed in the piece entwined hearts with small ornamental leaves, chased and with openings.. 144*l.*

For four other circles, with flower-borders introduced into them .... 96*l.*

For two circles decorated with ovolos, darts, and flower-borders .... 144*l.*

Madame Du Barry

For two garlands of vine with round embossments and four bouquets of drooping flowers........................... 360*l*.

For the vase, two end-pieces, with water-leaf and stalks of flowers; also a little branch of vine winding around the neck of the vase... 300*l*.

For the two circles above the neck decorated with leaves, berries, and a string .... 120*l*.

For two flames on the said vase........................... 60*l*.

For the flower-borders and two fillets of ornamental leaves 246*l*.

For bodies of vases in steel............................... 300*l*.

For having mounted the said tripods, without any screw being visible .... 384*l*.

For the gilding of all the bronzes of the said tripods...... 1,000*l*.

For the marble pedestal for which I have made two laurel-wreaths .... 96*l*.

For thirty-five stems of laurel to put into the twisted flutings .... 87*l*. 10*s*.

For two smooth bands above the flutings............... 72*l*.

For having gilded with ormolu the entire garniture of two pedestals .... 250*l*.

For the frame of the winding door-case, a frame decorated with a doucine on which I have made heart-rays .... 264*l*.

For having cast eleven feet of steel bands, having filed them, and polished them well.................................... 132*l*.

For having gilded and double-gilded the entire with ormolu 264*l*.

For having moulded in sand and melted in copper all the pieces of bronze .... 286*l*. 15*s*. 6*d*.

For having mounted all the bronzes on marble with screws, the said mounting made with much skill....................... 300*l*.

Also for having touched up all the steels with violet....... 48*l*.

Model of the Knob of the Window Shutting on the Lower Portion.

For having made a wooden knob modelled in wax, a crown of roses, adorned with Madame's cipher, with a chaplet and a sunflower which serves as a rosette for the button, a plate and berries on which the sun's rays rest, the entire estimated at the sum of 48*l*.

Model of the Sash-Fastening.

For a wooden handle scooped out in an open fashion in the form of a lyre, on which we have put at either side the heads of a chr,

Madame Du Barry

let. For another model in wood for the knob of the said handle, for having modelled in this knob a branch of roses winding all round the upper part, which knob is decorated with Madame's cipher in the middle. Again, for having modelled a branch of *fleur-de-lys* for the centre of the said handle. For two rosettes, one of which serves to keep the knob on the handle, and the other on the sash-fastening. All of which models, in wood as well as in wax, are estimated together at[1]............................ 150*l*.

In the large salon, for which Gouthiere gives the estimate of a second chimney-piece, there are all the details of door-locks, of which he has made models as well as of bolts. It is an arabesque decorated with Madame's cipher, an arabesque opening to the light.

The doors have also bronze decorations of which all the ornamentation is found in this long memorandum.

There is a further interest attached to Gouthiere's memorandum, as he mentions in the most minute detail all the decoration in bronze of the little palace, a fire for the salon with the bakehouse adjoining, which is valued, including the bronzes and chasing, framing and gilding in unpolished colour, at 5,000 livres.

The memorandum mounts up to 134,218*l*. 8*s*. 4*d*.

On this memorandum Gouthiere acknowledged having received from Madame du Barry the sum of 99,218 livres, with which has been adjusted the present memorandum of MM. Roettiers, goldsmiths to the King, of the 31st of December, 1773.

MEMORANDUM OF THE ADVANCES MADE BY THE SIEUR ALLEGRAIN, SCULPTOR TO THE KING, FOR THE ERECTION OF A STATUE OF DIANA, ORDERED BY THE COMTESSE DU BARRY AND FROM THE ACCOUNTS HE HAS RECEIVED.

Viz.:

For the preparations of the Model...................... 150*l*.
For the models of women............................ 1,300*l*.
For the expense of the mould........................ 500*l*.
For the models of women which have served to restore a plaster-cast of the said figure in order to have it seen by the Comtesse .... 300*l*.

---

[1] The execution of the bronzes of the sash-fastenings reached the sum of 2,782*l*. 11*s*. 3*d*.

Madame Du Barry

For the transport of the block of marble from the Port Saint-Nicolas to the Porte Saint-Martin, for having got it placed in the work-yard and having a rough sketch made of it... 5,000*l*.

Total............... 7,250*l*.

NOTE.—The Sieur Allegrain observes *that he has been occupied an entire year, without distraction, in making the model in clay; that he has spent three months in restoring the figure in plaster in order that it might be in a condition to be seen by the Comtesse and the ladies who came with her.* The Sieur Allegrain cannot bring this undertaking to a close[1] till he has been assured on the part of the Comtesse that he will be paid on foot of the 18,000 livres, including in this sum the 7,250 livres which he has expended in advance and the 2,000 livres of gratuities agreed upon according to the assurance of the Sieur Ledoux, architect of the Comtesse.

And of foot of these 18,000 livres the Sieur Allegrain acknowledges having received from the Comtesse the sum of 4,000 livres in two payments.

LIST OF WORKS OF SCULPTURE DONE FOR THE COMTESSE DU BARRY BY LE COMTE, SCULPTOR-IN-ORDINARY TO THE KING, ACCORDING TO HIS ORDERS, GIVEN BY M. LE DOUX, ARCHITECT TO THE KING, COMMENCED IN 1771.

A figure of four feet and a half in proportion in marble to serve for a candelabrum in the dining-room of the pavilion of Luciennes, for the model as well as for having moulded it, dissolved the plaster, and having it executed in marble................. 10,000*l*.

For a little model of a girandole composed of ten female figures, eighteen inches in proportion, bearing branches of flowers, to receive the wax-candles, as much for the model as for having restored some talcs, eight hundred livres.... 800*l*.

For her dwelling at Versailles the pediment above the entrance door composed of her arms, support, accessories,

[1] The statue of Madame du Barry as "Diana at the Moment of Entering the Bath" was not finished and brought to Lucienne till July, 1780. (Secret Correspondence, Political and Literary, Tome X.)

and two allegorical figures of six feet in proportion, executed on the spot in firestone, as well for the modelling, moulding, execution, journeys, etc., seven thousand four hundred livres .... 7,400*l.*

Idem.—In the corners two centaurs nine feet high; bas-relief executed in stone of Conflon, as well for the modellings and execution, ravels, etc., two thousand six hundred livres .... 2,600*l.*

Idem.—For the niche of the horsepond, a figure of seven feet in proportion, which is to be executed in lead as agreed upon, according to the sketch, representing Hercules fighting the Hydra, destined to serve as a fountain to fill and renew the water of the horsepond. The model and the hollow made ready to be cast for that object, finished, and put in its place, four thousand eight hundred livres........ 4,800*l.*

Total................ 25,600*l.*

Let us point out at the end of this memorandum of Le Comte a receipt for 960 livres published by M. Paul Mantz, in the "Archives of French Art," 1852, for the bas-relief forming the pediment of the Pavilion of Luciennes; a Bacchanalian group of children, 22 feet long and 4 feet high, *moulded and cast in talc.*

MEMORANDUM OF THE WORKS OF STATUARY WHICH THE SIEUR PAJOU, PROFESSOR OF THE ROYAL ACADEMY AND PENSIONER OF HIS MAJESTY, HAS MADE FOR THE COMTESSE DU BARRY DURING THE COURSE OF THE YEARS 1770, 1771, 1772, 1773, AND THE COMMENCEMENT OF THE PRESENT YEAR 1774.[1]

ARTICLE I.

The portrait in clay of the Comtesse, of natural size, made at Versailles at Easter, 1770, and exhibited in the Salon of the Louvre on the 25th of August of the same year (this bust is in my possession and I am prepared to deliver it up) ; for this........ 1,200*l.*

[1] The memoranda of Pajou and Drouais have been published by M. Pichon in the "Melanges," published by the Society of Bibliophiles, 1856.

Madame Du Barry

ARTICLE II.

Another bust of the Comtesse, half the size of the preceding one, ordered to be executed in porcelain in the Sevres manufactory, which has been furnished and executed for the 1st of January, 1771; for this .... 600*l.*

ARTICLE III.

Another bust of Madame, of the same proportions, ordered and furnished at the manufactory of Sevres, arranged and with the hair done differently from the preceding one, and executed in porcelain; for this........................ 600*l.*

ARTICLE IV.

Another bust of Madame which she asked to have with the hair dressed in the style of the Falconet's " Begneuse," which, after having been made and occupied my time, and compelled me to take many journeys to Versailles and to other Royal houses, has not had the advantage of pleasing and has been suppressed; for this....................... 600*l.*

ARTICLE V.

Another bust of Madame, of natural height, different from the others in attitude and arrangements, which is executed in white marble of the same size by the orders of the Comtesse, and has been exhibited in the Salon of the Louvre, the 25th of August of the year 1773, and delivered to the Comtesse while at Versailles (paid), including the material and the stand which is of marble of the colour of Aleppo notch (a kind of wood) .... 6,000*l.*

ARTICLE VI.

A medallion of Madame's portrait which was made for the pavilion of Luciennes and placed over the door.......... 96*l.*

ARTICLE VII.

A white marble figure, of four feet two inches in proportion, representing a young girl holding a horn of plenty, which was intended to carry lights and to decorate a room of the house at Luciennes (the dining-room). It has been transported two days before the illness of the late King. The price of this figure is the sum of.................... 10,000*l*.

If Madame finds this price too high, I ask to take back my figure, for I believe my demand is fair. I shall have no difficulty in getting purchasers at this price.

ARTICLE VIII.

A plaster bust[1] restored carefully and supplied to a manufactory of porcelain established in the Faubourg du Temple, to be executed of the same material, of natural size, which has been made and presented to the Comtesse, which she has received, and of which she has made a present to Mademoiselle du Barry.. 96*l*.

Total.............. 19,192*l*.

MEMORANDUM OF THE PAINTINGS ORDERED BY THE COMTESSE DU BARRY FROM DROUAIS, PAINTER TO THE KING, FIRST PAINTER TO MONSIEUR AND TO HIS WIFE, COMMENCING IN DECEMBER, 1768.

In the first place, in 1768 the portrait of the Comtesse du Barry as Flora on an oval canvas of twenty, without hands, sent from Toulouse .... 1,200*l*.

1769. The second portrait of the Comtesse in hunting-dress on an oval canvas of twenty, without hands, sent to England .... 1,200*l*.

A copy of the portrait of the Comtesse as Flora, on an oval canvas of twenty, without hands, sent to England..... 360*l*.

A picture of a little boy holding an apple................ 720*l*.

[1] A note by M. Pichon informs us that this bust was the one executed and delivered in November, 1773, by the Sieur Loire, contractor for the manufactory of German porcelain established in the Rue Fontaine-le-Roi. The products are marked with two arrows. He ventured to ask 12,000 livres for the execution in porcelain of this bust. Madame du Barry wrote on his memorandum:—" M. de Montvallier (her steward) has made inquiries of the man of the German manufactory; he has supplied only a bust. They are sold at Sevres for six louis, and he asks 12,000 livr . . . For the sake of accommodation Madame du Barry will give ten louis."

Madame Du Barry

1770. On Sunday, June 24th, delivered to the Comtesse four pieces over the door for the old pavilion of Luciennes, one representing the Graces, the second Love embracing the Universe, the third Venus and Cupid, and the remaining piece Night. These four above the doors painted by Fragonard, painter to the King. They have been bought by the Comtesse from the Sieur Drouais, to whom they belong.... 1,200*l.*

According to the order of the Comtesse for having put on canvas three of the pieces mentioned above the doors, for having enlarged, made the enlargements correct in proportion, money disbursed.................................... 420*l.*

The third portrait representing the Comtesse in her first youth on an oval canvas, of twenty, with hands........... 1,200*l.*

A copy of the portrait of the Comtesse, whose head has been made twice, at different times and in different manners, and whose costume as Flora, with the hands, has been entirely made according to nature by M. Baujon........... 1,200*l.*

On Friday, the 30th of August, delivered two of the designs over the door for the old pavilion of Luciennes, one representing the portrait of Mademoiselle Betzi, the other a child holding a bird's nest............................. 2,400*l.*

On Saturday, the 8th of September, delivered the portrait of Mirza .... 300*l.*

On Sunday, the 9th of September, delivered the portrait of Mademoiselle Luxembourg crowning Mirza.............. 720*l.*

1771. On the 1st of January delivered to the Comtesse her miniature portrait in oval form........................ 600*l.*

On Saturday the 2d of February, delivered to the Comtesse the portrait of Mademoiselle Betzi[1] playing with a cat 720*l.*

On Monday, the 7th of October, delivered to the Comtesse a copy of a miniature of the King in oval form...... 288*l.*

A copy of a portrait of the Comtesse for the King of Sweden. The attire of this portrait, consisting of a Court robe, has been entirely made according to nature on an oval, a canvas of twenty....................................... 672*l.*

1772. On the 1st of August delivered to the Comtesse four

---

[1] Portrait presumed to be that of a daughter of Madame Quantiny.

pieces above the door for the new pavilion of Luciennes, one representing Madame Betzi playing a triangle, the second a little boy flying away with grapes, the third Mademoiselle Laroque offering roses, and the fourth a little boy playing a tambourine .... 2,880*l.*

When some of the first works were executed by the Sieur Drouais for the Comtesse, he was promised that he would be supplied with the carriages necessary for the different journeys and transports required from him, but temporary difficulties have determined the Comtesse to ask the Sieur Drouais to take at his own expense the carriages which he would require, and to keep a note of the expenses so that he would be reimbursed. According to the exact estimate that he has made, from the 13th of December, 1768, down to September, 1772, these expenses amount to................. 1,758*l.*

The fourth portrait of the Comtesse, full length, representing a Muse on a canvas of six and a half feet high by four feet five inches wide.

The artist entreats to have it taken into consideration that this picture was at first entirely finished in a style of costume accepted by the Comtesse through all the gradations of the first rough draft to the finished work, and that in order to satisfy the desire of the Comtesse, who wished to have the costume entirely changed, he has substituted the present details, which have compelled him to have recourse to a double expenditure of time and infinite trouble...... 15,000*l.*

1773. The fifth portrait of the Comtesse as Flora, on a canvas of twenty, with the hands....................... 1,200*l.*

A copy of the portrait of the Comtesse as Flora, retouched from nature for the Marechal de Soubise.

It is to be noted that the Comtesse has fixed cn all the copies to be made for her from this picture, and to be retouched according to nature, at 600 livres each............. 600*l.*

For the frame of the said picture, money disbursed...... 60*l.*

1774. A copy of the portrait of the Comtesse as Flora, retouched from nature for the Duc d'Aiguillon.......... 600*l.*

For the frame of the said picture, money disbursed...... 120*l.*

On Tuesday, the 8th of February, delivered to the Comtesse a copy in miniature of the portrait of the Duc d'Aiguil-

Madame Du Barry

lon, ordered by the Comtesse, in order to make a present of it to the Duchesse d'Aiguillon........................... 288*l.*

The portrait of the Vicomtesse du Barry, on an oval, with the hands, ordered by the Comtesse..................... 720*l.*

For the frame of the said picture, money disbursed...... 60*l.*

A copy of the portrait of the Comtesse as Flora, retouched from nature for Mademoiselle du Barry................ 600*l.*

For the frame of the said picture, money disbursed ..... 60*l.*

A copy of the portrait of the Comtesse as Flora, retouched from nature for the Prince des Deux-Ponts................ 600*l.*

For the frame of the said picture, money disbursed...... 60*l.*

A copy of the portrait of the Comtesse as Flora, retouched from nature for Madame de Montrapt (Montrab)[1]........ 600*l.*

For the frame of the said picture, money disbursed ..... 60*l.*

A copy of the full-length portrait of Madame du Barry representing a Muse, on a canvas six feet and a half high and four feet five inches wide, the price of this copy, which has been made for the landgrave of Hesse-Cassel, has been fixed by the Comtesse at..................................... 1,000*l.*

For the expenses of the journey and transports made since the 27th of September, 1772, to this day, according to the exact list of disbursements which has been made out.... 894*l.*

Total .... 40,360*l.*

On which there has been received on account:

June 2nd, 1770........................ 6,000*l.*

During July, 1771..................... 3,000*l.*

September 17th........................ 3,000*l.*

and

March 10th, 1774..................... 3,000*l.*

Total of the amount received........ 15,000*l.*

The artist would not be sorry to have notice taken of the fact that in the employment of the time required for these sittings he has lost, while waiting, the benefit of four entire months of his time, and that the Comtesse, perceiving the very great disturbance which this has caused to him, had promised to indemnify him for it.

[1] The lady whose name was thus misspelled was the mother of Madame du Barry.—TRANSLATOR.

Madame Du Barry

Madame du Barry wrote on a copy of this memorandum which M. Pichon possesses:

To be deducted for the journeys not paid for .... 1,758*l.*
In addition 894l. for the same object .... 894*l.*

Total .... 2,652*l.*
I owed formerly on the account above set out .... 33,268*l.*
2,652*l.*

Total .... 30,616*l.*
I owe to Drois .... 30,616*l.*
He has received on account .... 15,000*l.*
There remains due to him .... 15,616*l.*
Reduce this sum to .... 15,000*l.*

To pay him 5,000 in cash[1] and bind myself to pay the remaining 10,000 at the end of next year; Drois will be satisfied with this arrangement. The portrait of Zamor will be a bust, and Drois will forward all my pictures to Luciennes.

LA COMTESSE DU BARRY.

ACCOUNT OF LEDOUX, ARCHITECT.

Pavilion of Luciennes, of which I have made the designs, looked after the workmen, settled the Bills, and made the necessary Journeys.

For the bronzes of M. Goutier, of which I have made the designs on a large scale, superintended the modelling and execution; the bills prepared by M. Roettiers.

Abstract of the various articles which are included in his bill:

The dining-room .... 1,704*l.*
The vestibule .... 698*l.*
The square drawing-room.............................. 19,706*l.*
The oval drawing-room................................ 31,272*l.*
The drawing-room adjoining the bake-house............. 6,660*l.*
Ante-chamber and wardrobe............................ 1,109*l.*
The pedestals, a capital, the whole not determined, estimated at....................................... 20,000*l.*

Total .... 81,239*l.*

[1] Madame du Barry spells the word "comptant" (ready money), "contant." She even misspells the painter's name.—TRANSLATOR.

Madame Du Barry

Minot, sculptor .... 8,000*l*.

Feuillet and Motivier, sculptors, for works at Luciennes.. 37,676*l*.

Rostenne, musician of the Chapel...................... 1,512*l*.

Vien, painter .... 16,000*l*.

Vernet, painter, for the remainder of a picture[1]............ 4,000*l*.

Caffieri, sculptor, for his disbursements................. 3,000*l*.

Guichard, sculptor .... 6,409*l*.

Musson, painter .... 6,120*l*.

Duvivier, contractor to the Soap Manufactory........... 9,087*l*.

Pajou, sculptor .... 18,902*l*.

La Vallee, painter of equipages........................ 10,960*l*.

Boileau, picture-dealer, for commissions and disbursements .... 651*l*.

Forty, painter .... 288*l*.

Greize, painter .... 2,800*l*.

On the 2nd of September, 1774, while Madame du Barry was in
Point-aux-Dames, and while we find her having permission only
to see her jeweller, she made up her mind to sell a fashionable
piece of finery, which she had got made for extraordinary recep-
tions, and which the jeweller thus describes: A body with two
cuttings in front and two behind, two epaulets, with a knot behind
called a "crupper."[2] The body itself adorned with 1013 diamond
brilliants; the cuttings behind had 1054 brilliants, and in the cuttings in front and the epaulets there were 1413 brilliants. Madame
du Barry had in addition ordered a diamond rose of exceptional
brilliancy to be attached to the belt, and, not caring to have this
toilet spoiled by ordinary pins she had ordered 22 pins, all of diamonds, the heads of which were composed of brilliants mounted con-

---

[1] The "Anecdotes" relate that one day Madame du Barry chanced
to call in at Vernet's studio at the moment when two pictures were
being packed up to be sent abroad. She became suddenly seized
with a rage to get possession of them. And, when Vernet told her
that the pictures no longer belonged to him, that it would be quite
impossible to let her have them, the Favourite had them taken
away by force, flinging him a slip of paper on which she had just
written an order for 50,000 livres on Beaujon, banker to the Court.

[2] Literally: "Tuck-up tail."—TRANSLATOR.

spicuously and which cost 10,471 livres. So it was this article of
attire that the Favourite gave the Sieur Aubert to sell. Here is
the authority contained in the papers of the Du Barry preserved
in the Library of Versailles:[1]

"I, the undersigned, consent and authorize the Sieur Aubert, to
whom I have given power to do so, by these presents, to conclude
the sale of my dress with large body mounted in diamonds, composed of the body, the epaulets, four divisions and the knot called
the crupper, and that for the sum of 450,000 livres payable at the rate
of 50,000 livres every six months.

"Furthermore, I authorize him and give him the same power
aforesaid to conclude the sale of my dress adorned with rubies and
diamonds, composed of a collar with a knot and jewels and buttons
at the side, with a pair of earrings with knots and jewels, with four
topknots and a garland for the head, the said dress for the sum of
150,000 livres, for which I consent to sell the articles on condition that
this sum will be paid me in the space of three months, counting
from the day of the sale, of which the Sieur Aubert will give me
all immediately, reserving to myself, as of right, to make of the
amount of the one sum or the other such use as I please as belong
to me, not doubting that the Sieur Aubert will do everything in his
power, to take care of my interests and to procure for me the utmost advantage in the matter which I have entrusted to him.

"Signed, *the Comtesse* DU BARRY.

"Made at Pont-aux-Dames, September 22d, 1774."

According to a note which accompanies this authority, the large
dress appears to have been sold for 390,000 livres and the other for
188,000 livres to the Comtesse d'Artois. This note is followed by
the acceptance of these sums under the hand of Madame du Barry.

TWO THOUSAND LOUIS TO GAIN.[2]

DIAMONDS AND JEWELS LOST.

"There were stolen from the house of Madame du Barry, the
chateau of Luciennes, near Marly, on the night of the 10th or 11th

[1] Published by M. le Roi in the "Bulletin of the Library of
Versailles."

[2] This is the advertisement of the theft committed in Madame du
Barry's house one night in January, 1791. This exceedingly rare

of January, 1791, the diamonds and jewels below-mentioned: A ring of white brilliants with a large diamond, weighing about 50 grains, mounted in a cage-shaped case, a ditto of brilliants weighing about 50 grains, a ditto of brilliants from 26 to 28 grains, a ditto of sapphire with a large square stone with a Cupid engraved upon it and two brilliants showing in front; a ring-box with a green rosette containing from 20 to 25 rings, one of them being a large emerald ring; jewelled watch without a case, weighing about 36 grains, of a beautiful colour but very common, having the works very large; an onyx ring representing the portrait of Louis XIII., of which the hair and the moustaches are in sardonyx; one of a Cæsar of two colours, surrounded with brilliants; one of an emerald of large, square form, weighing about 20 grains; one of a dark puce colour, weighing from 14 to 16 grains; one of an antique Bacchus, engraved in relief on a burnt cornelian; one of yellow sardonyx engraved by Barrier, representing Louis XIV. with paltry Dutch roses twined around his person; one a large heart-shaped sapphire, well mounted and with diamonds encircling the stone and half of the ring; the heart-shaped sapphire of Louis XIII. and the square emerald are mounted in the same way and garnished with diamonds, roses, and brilliants. There is, moreover, in this ring-case an antique "bonus eventus" engraved on an onyx over the tissue paper; a white brilliant weighing 29 grains; a ditto weighing 25 grains; a ditto of pendant-form weighing 28 grains; a round ditto weighing 23 grains; a ditto *idem* weighing 24 grains; a ditto of inferior quality, large and square, weighing 23 grains; three dittos *idem*, each weighing 28½ grains; a pin-shaped brilliant, of long shape, weighing 30 grains; a lozenge-shaped brilliant weighing 35 grains; two very beautiful brilliants formed into ear-drops, each weighing 50 grains; two bracelets weighing together 24 grains, one of them weighing from 15 to 16 grains; a rose finely mounted with 258 white brilliants, of which one large stone in the centre of crystal weighs about 24 grains; a necklace of 24 beautiful brilliants finely mounted in open bevil, 15 to 20 grains each; eight pieces of ribbon in puffs, each with 21 brilliants, distinctly visible, and each brilliant weighing from 4 to 8 grains; a pair of shoe-buckles of 84 brilliants,

---

placard is to be found in the National Archives, in the "Dossier," W⁻ 300.

weighing 77 carats for a fourth part; a cross with 16 brilliants, weighing from 8 to 10 grains each; 64 bezils, weighing from 6 to 10 grains; a beautiful pair of chandeliers with large brilliants of the value of 120,000 livres; a silver purse in blue silk, with its slides, its tassels, and their fringes, the whole in little brilliants finely mounted; a double row of pearls with its fall worn by slaves, the whole of about 200 pearls, weighing 4 or 5 grains each; a large brilliant in the upper part of the fall, weighing 25 to 26 grains, and below a tassel with fringes and its knot, the whole in brilliants conspicuously mounted; a pair of bracelets with six rows of pearls, weighing from 4 to 5 grains each. The ground of the bracelet is an emerald surmounted by a cipher in diamonds, giving two L's for the one, and a D and B for the other, and two padlocks of four brilliants weighing from 8 to 10 grains; a row of 104 stringed pearls, weighing from 4 to 5 grains each; a portrait of Louis XV. painted by Masse, surrounded by a gold frame with laurel leaves, the said portrait from 5 to 6 inches high; another portrait of Louis XV., painted by the same, smaller, in a gold medallion; a simple Romilly gold watch; a gold case with an enamelled tooth in green, with a very large brilliant at the end, weighing about 12 grains, attached to the whole by a screw; a pair of sleeve-buttons formed of an emerald, a sapphire, a yellow diamond, and a ruby, the whole surrounded with rose-coloured brilliants, weighing from 36 to 40 grains, mounted in neck buttons; two strings of watch-guards composed of sixteen links with three stones, one being a large emerald and two brilliants of three or four grains on each side, and three other little cords of two links each like to those above described. A cap with a very big brilliant, large and square, weighing about 60 grains, with three large emeralds underneath, weighing from 8 to 10 grains, with two brilliants, one at each side, weighing one grain each, mounted conspicuously: it must be observed that this cap is not of elegant pattern; a ring with a brilliant of about 26 grains, well mounted, with some brilliants on the body of the ring; two golden chandeliers forming flambeaux mounted on two shafts of a column of gold, enamelled in lapis-lazuli, surmounted by two silver turtle doves; quivers and arrows made by Durand; a gold case enamelled in green, at the end of which is a little watch made by Romilly, surrounded by four diamond hoops, and at the other side armorial bearings; two other gold cases, one enamelled with blue ribbons and the other in enamels of colour and landscapes; seventeen diamonds entirely out of shape, weighing each from 25 to 30 grains, one of them being a pendant mounted weighing 36 grains; two other enclosures of bracelets detached equally from four diamonds each, weighing the same on the other hand; sixty-four bevils in a single thread, forming a necklace weighing 8, 9 and 10 grains each, in diamonds set prominently; two earrings of pearl-shells with portrait of Louis XIV. by Petitot; another portrait of the late Monsieur, both in enamel, as well as a portrait of a woman likewise by Petitot; an inkhorn of superb old lacquer adorned with gold and forming a workbox, all the utensils in gold. Two souvenirs, one in red lacquer work, and the other in lacquer with a gold background and figures, the one mounted in gold and the other mounted in gold enamel; two little silver candlesticks for a dressing-room, adorned with pearls and armorial bearings, a box of rock crystal covered a double box in open work; Portuguese gold coins; Spanish guineas and half-guineas; 1 ditto of Noailles, of Louis XV., struck nearly in this shape; in every corner of this piece are fleur-de-lis, one of M. de Bignon, of M. de la Michandiere, of M. Canmartin, with the arms of the city; one of the Regency; in addition 40 diamonds, weighing one carat each; two opera-glasses, one enamelled in blue, the other in red with the portrait of the late King, both mounted in gold; a souvenir in blue enamel with pictures in grey, representing on one side an offering and on the other side a flower-stand with a little dog with long ears; a reliquary of about an inch of very pure gold enamelled in black and white; a little cross mounted above, rather in the Gothic style, and a fine pearl of the size of a pea below, and many other jewels of very good value.

"Address to the house of Madame du Barry, Luciennes, near Marly; and in Paris to the office of Maitre Rouen, notary, in the Rue des Petits Champs, to M. Rouen, merchant, goldsmith, jeweller, Rue Saint Louis, at the Palace, and to the Clerk of Works, Rue des Orfeves. Reward fair and in proportion to the value of the objects which will be brought back."

Madame Du Barry

DECLARATION OF MADAME DU BARRY, MADE BETWEEN TWO WICKETS OF THE CONCIERGERIE, AFTER THE JUDGMENT WHICH CONDEMNED HER TO THE PENALTY OF DEATH.[1]

To-day, the 18th Frimaire, the second year of the French Republic, One and Indivisible (December 8th, 1793), 10 o'clock in the morning, on the announcement being made to us that Jeanne Vaubernier "Femme du Barry" had some important declarations to make:

We, François Joseph Denisot, Judge of the Revolutionary Tribunal, assisted by Claude Royer, substitute for the Public Prosecutor at the said Tribunal, and Jean-Baptiste Tavernier, Clerk and Registrar, repaired to the Prison of the Conciergerie, where we found the Citizen Dange, Administrator of Police, and the said Jeanne Vaubernier, "Femme du Barry," who said to us:—

(1) That in the place where the gardening implements are shut up, opposite her ice-house at Luciennes, there is buried a gold dressing-case containing a porcelain tray mounted in gold, a tea-pot in gold, a kettle, a chafing-dish with spirits of wine, a milk jug, a large chocolate-pot, a small coffee-pot, a bowl without a cover and its plate, three small spoons, a little strainer for the tea-pot, a hundred counters with her arms and the initials D. B., the entire in gold and of very precious workmanship, attention being drawn to the fact that the handles of the said articles are in blood-red jasper and mounted in gold.

(2) In a box or basket, buried in the same place, 1531 gold louis of twenty-four livres each; a chain of diamonds with its two tassels and the key mounted in an open style; two ear-chains, each composed of nine or ten stones, those in front very large; three rings, one of white diamonds, one of rubies and white diamonds, one in emerald and white diamonds; a very beautiful engraved stone, mounted with chains of gold for a necklace; two coral necklaces, one of which is mounted in gold; a necklace of five pearls; a collar of pearls set in gold, and two or three gold chains for the neck; a portrait of Louis XV., surrounded with a gold frame.

[1] This declaration no longer exists in the National Archives in the two "Dossiers" W¹16 and W⁶300, consecrated to Madame du Barry. I give it from the copy which Madame Guenard must have taken of it at the time, and which she has printed in her "Historic Memoirs of Jeanne Gomart de Vaubernier Dubarry." Lerouge, 1803.

Madame Du Barry

(3) In a little deal box, sent to the wife of a man named Deliant, floor-cleaner, residing at Luciennes, a repeater adorned with diamonds; a little packet of fourteen or sixteen diamonds of from 5 to 6 grains each; a packet of small rubies; two small flat diamonds to mount in rings; another portrait of Louis XV. in a worked frame mounted and plated in gold, a little child in the form of a "tirelire" in gold with blue enamel; sixteen new half-guineas and two guineas wrapped up in paper; a pair of gold spurs with ciphers, belonging to the late M. de Brissac; a little cardboard box shut up in the box aforesaid, in which is a chain of emeralds, and diamonds, one large stone weighing 50 grains, the tassels of which chain are in the box referred to in the second article; attention being drawn to the fact that in the second or third article will be found a gold pencil adorned with diamonds; a box likewise sent to the woman Deliant, containing a gold mustard-pot, a little tray, and two gold goblets, and many other objects which do not come back to her memory; two liqueur-cases filled with flagons of rock-crystal, one of which belongs to her and the other to the late Brissac; a little vermilion bowl with its tray.

(4) A chest covered with blue velvet, furnished with gilt silver, placed under a staircase in an apartment forming a wardrobe, at the side of that which she occupied, in which chest there are a dozen gold covers with armorial bearings, four sugar-spoons, two olive-spoons, a punch-ladle, the entire in gold; a case containing twelve gold tea-spoons; several portraits of women; two gold seals, one an office-seal, and a small one; three medals, one representing the Bridge of Neuilly, the second the School of Surgery, and the third the Mint; the two other medals representing the marriage of the former princes, also in gold; a very large gold medal belonging to the late Brissac, and some other articles which she cannot designate; in addition, two Turkish daggers mounted in rubies and other stones.

(5) In the apartment at the side of the bed-room used as a passage, in the chest-of-drawers, a pair of gold buckles, adorned with pearls, a little box of smooth gold; a box of blond shell, mounted in gold, with the portrait of a nun; a stopper of a gold flagon in blue enamel, with a large diamond.

(6) In a chest of drawers, in the bed-room, a water-jug and its basin of rock crystal, garnished with gold, two cups cf blood-red jasper mounted in gold; an antique bracelet mounted in gold, com-

posed of different stones; a goblet of rock-crystal and two carafes and the tray, all mounted in gold; twenty-one or twenty-two rings of different engraved stones mounted in gold; a box mounted in a gold case, with the portrait of Brissac's wife; a portrait of the daughter of the latter, mounted in gold; a portrait of the son of the same, also mounted in gold; another of his brother; a blond shell box mounted in gold, with a very beautiful engraved white stone, in which is a portrait of Brissac and of the woman making this declaration; a jasper box mounted in gold, enamelled; another box of mother-of-pearl, adorned with pearls and mounted in gold; a portrait in enamel of Brissac's grandmother, two gold cups with coral handles, and some other articles belonging to Brissac.

(7) In the cellar for ordinary use, under the stairs, a large pail, nine dozen and seven plates, eighteen flambeaux, three of them with two branches; a dozen saucepans; a large and a small porridge-pot, all of silver; nineteen large silver dish-covers; sixty-four dishes also of silver, and other articles of plate, the list of which is in her house.

(8) Several figures in bronze of different kinds. One portion of them must be in one of the thickets near the pavilion, another above the pavilion, the whole lightly covered with earth.

(9) In the garden of Morin, valet, are hidden eleven sacks of 1,240 double louis, brought from London on her last journey; a shell box mounted in gold, on which is the portrait of Marie-Antoinette, painted by Sauvage, and in which will be found a gold medal and some other objects which are within the knowledge of Morin, who has been charged by her to conceal all the said objects comprised in the present article.

(10) Attention is drawn to the fact that she deposited with Morlan, A. Moncelet, and Ranison and Company, bankers, at Palmer, in London, all the articles relating to the thefts, except those underlined in the margin and brought into the printed notice of the reward promised for the discovery of the theft in general, which has been initiated by her and by us, as well as by the Citizen Dange.

(11) That she has confided to the Citizen Montrouy a silver syringe and three tubes, also of silver; a little flexible half-ell of gold; a ring with the name of "atriodes;" a portrait of Brissac; two gold-bladed knives for removing powder, with two little hoops of diamonds, and black handles; another gold knife enamelled; a gold watch, and a little gold seal with an emerald; attention being

drawn to the fact that she has received from the said Montrouy two hundred and fifty or three hundred livres by way of loan, as well as the bed of which she has made use during her detention down to this day.

The above declaration having been read to her, she says that it contains the truth, and that she has nothing else to declare; adding that if it is the good pleasure of the Tribunal, she will write to London, and that without difficulty she will recover the objects concerning the theft, paying at the same time the expenses which the case has occasioned, and has signed this along with us—Denisot, Judge; Royer, Substitute for the Public Prosecuter; Jeanne Vaubernier du Barry; Dange, Administrator of Police; Tavernier, Clerk and Registrar.

SEARCHES MADE BY THE ORDER OF THE REVOLUTIONARY TRIBUNAL IN THE CHATEAU AND PAVILION OF LUCIENNES, FOR THE PURPOSE OF CARRYING AWAY JEWELS, GOLD AND SILVER, WHICH WERE CONCEALED THERE, AND SUMMONSES SERVED ON MORIN, MADAME DU BARRY'S VALET, TO DECLARE WHERE THEY ARE.

" The 24th Frimaire, the Second Year of the Republic One and Indivisible.[1]

"According to the invitation made by us to the Citizen Public Prosecutor to the Revolutionary Tribunal in Paris, there appeared before us, Commissioners, Justice of the Peace, and Mayor named in the *proces-verbal* of the other parts, at 10 o'clock in the morning Denis Morin, valet of the Dubarry, accompanied by Maximilien Brassan, Pierre Ducolet, gendarmes of the 1st division attached to the tribunals, and by Jean Audray, Summoning Officer of the Tribunal, which Auvray has produced to us the powers of which he was the bearer, as much on his own behalf as on that of the above-named gendarmes.

"We pointed out to the above named Morin, in the presence of the aforesaid witnesses, that he is not ignorant of what has happened to his mistress, the critical position in which he is himself, having always been recognized as her confidant, that he must not, moreover, be ignorant of the fatal end of the former Chevalier d'Escourt; that the best thing he, the person appearing before us, could do, would be to

[1] The original of Morin's two examinations exists in the National Archives.

Madame Du Barry

answer the questions which would be put to him, with that truth, that frankness, which inspire interest under all circumstances; that, besides, all dissimulation would only serve to render him culpable, the more so as we have information through the documents placed in our hands, through sure testimonies, through formal declarations and discoveries of deposits having been made by the Dubarry.

" To these first observations, the said Morin has replied that he had his mistress' confidence apparently rather than in reality; that they should not assume he enjoyed the entire confidence of the Dubarry merely because his position as valet gave him more facilities for receiving his mistress's orders and for communicating her orders to those attached to her service; that, moreover, he was too great a lover of truth to refuse to make any declarations which could not be relied on, or to conceal anything which might give us information with regard to the Dubarry.

" We then immediately called upon the said Morin to declare to us what he had been doing before he was with Madame du Barry.

" Said in reply, that he was the son of a vine-dresser at Auteuil, near Paris, after having been in the service of several other ladies in Paris, and had, by mere chance, entered into the employment of the former Comte Dubarry on the 5th of June, 1769; that since that time he had always remained attached to the house of the Dubarry, at first in the capacity of a lackey for four years, and in the capacity of a valet for the rest of the period in the private service of the wife of the former Comte Dubarry.

" We called upon the said Morin, to declare to us what had become of the statues in bronze and a bust in marble, representing Louis XV.

" Said in reply, that he knew nothing about the statue of bronze, that he only knew the *concierge* of the pavilion had been told by the Dubarry to bury it in some place of which he was not aware, probably to prevent it from being mutilated; that he had deposited it in a conservatory with other marbles, with the assistance of the before-mentioned Deliant, floor-cleaner and Picard, terrace-maker, to whom had been given orders to that effect.

" We asked the said Morin what had become of the different pictures, which were in the woman Dubarry's house.

" Said in reply that, after having been advised by several persons as to the necessity of not leaving as evidence any pictures which might fatigue the eyes of the Federates, he had himself, with the

Madame Du Barry

assistance of the above-named Deliant and another lackey, hidden between the window and the blind of the dining-room, one picture representing Louis XV., and had no other knowledge with regard to the portrait of Marie-Antoinette, than that he had seen it and left it hanging in Madame Dubarry's dressing-room; that, moreover, he had himself hidden, with the assistance of the said Deliant and Pretry, the Dubarry's hair-dresser, a large picture in a frame and on its sash representing Louis XV. in the dress of a knight, and that this was in a press in the chapel; attention being drawn to the fact that all the deposits were only made by him by the Dubarry's orders; that the frame of the said picture had been brought to the pavilion, that the armorial bearings which had been detached from it had been shut up by him in a cupboard in an antechamber in one wing of the buildings, in which cupboard there is also a picture representing a frigate called 'The Comtesse Dubarry.'

"Declared immediately afterwards, spontaneously and without any interpellation, that he had himself alone, without the assistance of anybody, buried in the conservatory facing the ice-house, an oak chest well bound with iron, containing, as he believed, a gold dressing-case of which the Dubarry had the key, and that this was in a hole made by himself alone; declared, besides, that he had buried in a hole in the same place a wooden box, and as well as he could remember, without being quite certain of it, a second box in the same hole, both containing precious objects, the nature of which he did not know.

"Had buried by the Dubarry's orders, and at the pressing request of the latter, in two holes opened at the left on entering into his (witness's) garden, viz.: in the first hole about five or six bags of money, sent to him by the Dubarry, the whole shut up in a box, attention being drawn to the fact that besides this box, there was a vermilion goblet belonging to the woman Roussel, and which she gave him to hide; and in addition about nine louis in pieces of about six livres, a louis d'or, a guinea and a half-guinea in gold, the entire shut up in a leathern bag belonging to him, Morin, the latter recalling the fact that in the same box, concealed in the first hole, there were a hundred silver counters with armorial bearings on them, belonging to the Dubarry.

"Secondly, that in the other hole of which he had spoken already, there was a little wooden box fastening with a hook, in which were contained different precious objects which he could not designate, not having had the curiosity to look at them, burying them in spite of the opportunity he had of doing so.

" Having called upon the said Morin to declare to us the quantity of silver which the first hole might contain:

" Said in reply, that he was unable to state exactly the quantity, as these bags, which were more or less large, might contain some 1,200 livres, others more.

" On being asked whether there was not a louis d'or in the box in question:

" Said in reply that, as a matter of fact, he had at first put into this box two rouleaux, each composed of about fifty louis d'or; but that, after the Dubarry's orders, he had taken them out and handed them over to her about fifteen days before she was arrested; that for this purpose he had been obliged to unearth the box, and had then replaced it in the same hole.

" We represented to the said Morin that, from knowledge which we obtained, there should have been found a greater quantity of silver than that announced in his declaration.

" In reply, said it was well within his knowledge that in the month of September, 1792, he had hidden and buried in a corner of the district, with the aid of Deliant, floor-cleaner, and Salenave, head-butler, the sum of 10,000 francs in a number of bags, but that the Dubarry, learning that many persons had been robbed of even what had been hidden, and thinking no place of deposit sufficiently safe, had given orders to the said Deliant and Salenave to remove them, that in consequence the person appearing before us, with the persons above-named, had disinterred the ten thousand francs referred to elsewhere; but that the bags they were in being rotten, they found the money scattered about and brought it to the Dubarry, and that, after they had cleaned it with the help of the woman Deliant, they counted it, and found it was ten louis short of the said sum, according to the count of the Dubarry herself, the person appearing before us adding that it was through an error he told us they had counted it themselves. The said Morin had added in answer to further interpellation, that the money in question had been disinterred some time before the departure and the journey of the Dubarry to London.

" Further questioned to tell us what had become of the money delivered up by him, Deliant, and Salenave to the Dubarry;

Madame Du Barry

" Said in reply, that according to the fresh orders given by the said Dubarry to himself, as well as to the said Deliant and Salenave, the three of them had buried the said sum with the exception of the ten louis, which were missing, in a hole made by them in the pound of the chateau, after having put this money into two earthen jars.

" Declared that at the same period the above-mentioned persons had also interred along with him two coffers, one of which contained the Dubarry's dressing-case and the other many precious objects, each in two particular holes made by them in the said pound; and adding that he himself with the above-mentioned persons also interred at the same time in a hole made by them in the orangery, a third chest containing jewels, as he presumed, the said three chests being locked and the Dubarry having the key to them

" That the said Dubarry, fearing lest the objects above described should be stolen, and not thinking the place of deposit safe on many grounds, gave orders to him as well as to the said Deliant to take them away from the place where they were; that in consequence the person here appearing had in the course of last June, disinterred along with the said Deliant, the above-mentioned chests, and the two earthen jars, and had handed them over to the woman Dubarry.

" We interpellated the said Morin as to whether he knew what had become of the three chests to which he referred, and the two jars containing the money.

" Said in reply, that he had buried in the conservatory the chest containing the dressing-case, as he had declared, that, with regard to the two other chests, the Dubarry had got her joiner to open one of them, and that he (Morin) did not know what had become of the other. As for the money, it had remained in the hands of the said Dubarry, but without doubt the objects contained in the last two chests, as well as the money given up to the Dubarry, formed part of the particular deposits made and ordered by her.

" Declared next, and without any interpellation, that in the loft of the kitchen belonging to him near his garden, he had concealed a small silver cross, a chalice, and its paten; in addition, that in the woodwork near the walls in the fields there was a case containing six gold tea-spoons.

" And thereupon the said Morin having offered to go himself into his garden and the places adjoining it to point out the hidden objects as to which he had made a declaration to us, we accompanied the said Morin forthwith into his garden, where we found in a place at the left-hand side of the garden-gate, in a hole which had been covered up, a deal box; and the said Morin then pointed out to us another place not far from the first, in which, after having got him to dig there, we found a second deal box. Two of us immediately took charge of it, reserving to ourselves the right to open it at the chateau which formerly belonged to the Dubarry.

"The said Morin, in order to follow up the purport of his declaration, conducted us into a loft near the house where we found, in accordance to his statement, and concealed behind a quantity of wood, a silver crucifix, a chalice with its paten of vermilion, belonging to the chapel of the former chateau. At the same moment and in the same place we found a quadrille-box and besides it a rouleau of paper so hidden that it could not be opened without breaking the wax; and, afterwards, a little box of shagreen tied with a half-rotten cord concealed behind the woodwork and the rafters abutting on the garden wall and beside the dwelling of the said Morin.

"We took possession of all these articles and immediately we returned to the drawing-room of the former chateau with the said Morin, where in his presence we made an examination of all the objects of which we had taken possession.

"Having opened the first box buried in the first hole, we found in it and counted in the said Morin's presence: (1) a bag of 1,200 livres, (2) another bag of 1,248 livres, (3) a bag of 1,200 livres, (4) a bag of 1,200 livres, (5) a bag of 900 livres; the entire of the money in the five bags in question as we counted in the said Morin's presence, being composed of new six-franc pieces with the effigy of the former Louis XVI.

"Having next opened the second bag, in Morin's presence, we found there and counted in succession: (1) 99 hexagonal silver counters, bearing on one side the Du Barry arms and having on the other side a cipher; (2) 40 double louis d'or; (3) a bag of 1,185 livres of large and small old crown pieces; (4) nine louis less six livres in white silver, a gold louis, a guinea, a half-guinea, the whole enclosed in a little leathern bag, half-rotten, which sums and moneys comprised in the fourth article the said Morin claimed to belong to him; (5) a silver goblet inlaid with vermilion, belonging to the woman Roussel.

"Having opened the quadrille-box, we found in it four little ivory boxes bearing on the lid the figures of a cushion, a shamrock, a pike, and a heart incrusted with gold, the said boxes containing the ivory cards marked and incrusted with gold, with similar figures.

"Proceeding, after the opening of the little box of shagreen, we found there a dozen gold tea-spoons with strings and the armorial bearings of the Dubarry.

"We immediately shut up all the articles above-mentioned with the number and the nature of them, according to their different kinds in one only and the same bag, which we tied up and on which we affixed the seal in the presence of the said Morin. We put this bag in another and larger bag, having shut up there the cross, the chalices, paten and goblet referred to above, attached to it the seal, leaving it in the drawing-room where we are, not being able to put it elsewhere, as we would be obliged to take off the seals placed on the cupboards, furniture, and apartments of the house.

"As for the rouleau of paper found behind the woodwork, we interpellated the said Morin, calling on him to tell us if he had hidden it and if he knew what it contained.

"Said in reply, that he had not hidden the rouleau in question, and was absolutely ignorant of what it contained.

"We kept in our possession the said rouleau,[1] reserving to ourselves the right to make a particular examination of it, and to send to whomsoever it might belong the different papers contained in it.

"And thereupon at the hour of ten o'clock in the evening we closed the present record with which we had been occupied since ten o'clock in the morning, and for the continuation of our operations have adjourned and fixed to-morrow, the 25th Frimaire, at eight o'clock in the morning, when all the above-named remaining here consent to appear to-morrow.

"And immediately we had the said Morin's answers, declarations, and our operations contained in the record read for him; the said Morin declared they were the truth and persisted in them and has signed with us:

"Signed to the minute, VILLETTE, FAIQUET, HURE, HOUDON, BICAULT, D. MORIN, and LEQUOY, Secretary to the Commission. As

[1] Note by Favrolles.—We have not been able to get any knowledge of what became of this rouleau, in spite of the searches we made for it. We presume it may contain Louis XV.'s letters to Madame Dubarry, as they were not found amongst the papers.

a copy collated and conformable to the minute certified by us, under-signed Commissioners of the Executive Council of the district of Versailles, Justice of the Peace, Mayor of Luciennes, and Secretary of the Commission of Luciennes, the 25th Frimaire, the second year of the Republic. HOUDON, Justice of the Peace; BICAULT, Mayor; VILLETTE, FAIQUET, and HURE. Commissioners; LEQUOY, Secretary to the Commission.

NOTE.—" The sitting of the 25th was only employed in hearing a fresh reading of the said report and in consulting as to the remaining interpellations to be put to Morin; after which we adjourned till the following day.

CONTINUATION OF THE SEARCH MADE BY ORDER OF THE REVOLUTIONARY TRIBUNAL IN THE CHATEAU AND PAVILION OF LUCIENNES FOR THE PURPOSE OF TAKING POSSESSION OF THE JEWELS, GOLD, AND SILVER WHICH WERE HIDDEN THERE.

" On the 26th Frimaire, the second year of the French Republic One and Indivisible, before us, Commissioners, Justice of the Peace, Mayor, denominated in the Report contained in the present document, there again appeared the man Morin, ex-valet of the Dubarry.

" We at once pointed out to the said Morin that the discoveries which he had enabled us to make of several deposits by indicating to us the places where they were put and interred in his garden, may give us some inclination to believe in the fidelity of his declaration in this respect; but that, nevertheless, the examination of the various documents in our hands, the comparison of the objects found in his garden with the quantities, nature, and kinds of all the others which must have been concealed in the said garden by him (Morin) made us feel very great suspicions as to the fidelity of his declaration, and gave us all reason to think that he (Morin) had taken away some money and other objects from the chests and boxes entrusted to him by the Dubarry, whether he concealed them in his own garden or had the intention to remove them from our cognizance. We observed to him, for example, that there ought to be found in the garden eleven bags of 1,200 livres, whereas we found only six bags of about 1,200 livres, each conformably to his declaration.

" In reply to all these observations, he said he would swear upon his honour that he had never put out of the way any of the objects contained in the boxes interred by him, that if the notes in our hands designated a greater number of effects than those discovered by us, these effects were in no wise within his knowledge, that he had indicated the only deposits made by him in his garden and assured us that there was no other.

"In order to arrive at the discovery and the cognizance of all the deposits and to convince the said Morin that we had been informed by the Dubarry's declaration that he had himself been charged to conceal many more things, we had read to him the entire declaration of the Dubarry, and amongst other portions of it, the Article IX., which designates several objects, and notably a shell-box mounted in gold, on which was the portrait of Marie-Antoinette done by Sauvage.

"We interpellated the person appearing before us to declare to us if he had knowledge of what had become of the box in question, observing to him that he had alone been charged by name to conceal it with the other effects designated in the Article IX.

"Said in reply that he had no knowledge of the box which we claimed, that in his capacity of valet to the Dubarry he had certainly knowledge of all the articles which she mentioned, but that he was ignorant of the use to which his mistress might have put them. The said Morin added that notwithstanding the objects declared by his mistress, we ought to find two covers and a gold teaspoon marked with three 'fleurs-de-lis' incrusted in gold, and two knives with gold blades, mounted in Sevres porcelain.

"That he had in his room several effects belonging to the Dubarry, which, not being in a conspicuous position, might have escaped discovery by us, and forthwith he offered to conduct us there to give us all the necessary indications.

"Whereupon we made our way to the buildings called the 'communes,' and going up to the attics, after we had taken official notice of the affixing of the seals to the room of the said Morin, we took off these same seals, and we then entered this room, where the said Morin indicated to us and enabled us to find in a little veneered cupboard at the left, beside the chimney, eight curbs with large silver bridle-studs with pearls marked in relief with the initials of the Dubarry, a smaller curb of the same nature, another with a silver-mounted bridle-stud, with another *idem;* a pair of bridle-studs with strings and ciphers; a gold-laced snaffle; four ciphers in gilt copper suitable to be put on carriages; and five velvet strips of material suitable for the lining of a carriage.

Madame Du Barry

"In another cupboard, and hidden amongst the linen, a little silver nutmeg-grater, fixed in a case also of silver, which is contained in a cover of shagreen. In a little box containing old iron, a hand of gilt silver.

"The said Morin having pointed out to us a bed of sacking under the mattress of which he said we would find two velvet housings of a carriage-seat embroidered with gold and silver fringes, and in the same place a surtout of white cloth with gold lace, we only found there a bearskin.

"Furthermore, having pointed out to us an oak press, in which he had hidden two saddle-cloths of crimson velvet for a woman, and a vest adorned with gold lace we found there nothing.

"Furthermore, on a board at the right where he had placed a bag containing 400 livres in silver given to him to be deposited by the person named Laroche, formerly Abbe, in the month of October, 1792, we there likewise found nothing.

"Having left the said Morin's room, carrying with us the sole and only object found by us after the said Morin's indications, we closed up the room, reaffixed the seals to the door, all in the presence of the said Morin, and we next entered another little room beside the first, after having meanwhile taken official cognizance of the seals affixed to the door and taken them off. The said Morin indicated to us a woman's hatbox, in which we discovered, with several packets of seeds containing their names, nature, and species, a big packet entitled *parsnip-seeds*, in which we found seventeen ells of silver lace for liveries, and that after we had measured them.

"An interpellation having been made to the said Morin as to whether he had cognizance of other objects concealed in his abode, he said not.

"Coming out then from the said second room, we closed it up, reaffixed the seals to it, and immediately we returned with the said Morin to the drawing-room of the chateau, carrying with us the only objects discovered by us on the indication of the said Morin.

"Having put to the person appearing before us an interpellation to tell us if in a red house belonging to the Dubarry there were not deposits hidden:

"Said he had no knowledge of any.

100 livres for getting a passport from the municipality of Luciennes:

"We asked the said Morin if he knew that the Dubarry had given

Madame Du Barry

" Said in reply that he had never heard anything said as to a passport having been solicited by his mistress, that he only remembered
having given by her orders the sum of 100 livres for the purpose of
assistance to one Louis Ledoux, ex-Mayor of Luciennes.

" Having interpellated the said Morin to declare to us all the information he could give us as to the discovery of objects belonging to
the Dubarry and not found:

" Said in reply that he had no other declarations to make except
those embodied in the said report, has persisted in assuring us of the
truth of them, and has signed after having heard them read.

" Signed to the minute: D. MORIN, VILLETTE, HURE, FAIQUET,
HOUDON, BICAULT, LEQUOY, Secretary of the Commission."

On the 28th Frimaire (18th of December, 1793), in consequence
of the declarations of Morin, whose fate it was to be condemned to
death and executed on the 23d of December, 1793, the Commissioners
of the Executive Council of the directory of the district of the Committee of General Safety of Versailles addressed this letter to the
Citizen Public Prosecutor of the Criminal Tribune of Versailles:

" We address to you herewith copy of declarations, depositions
which have been made by Morin in the two examinations we made
him undergo on the 24th and 25th inst. The presence of this man
has been all the more useful to us, inasmuch as we discovered from
his indications, many precious objects hidden in his garden.

" The woman Roussel, chambermaid of the Dubarry, appearing to
us to have been informed of various facts by Morin, and her conduct
leading us to suspect that she might herself have concealed the effects belonging to the Dubarry, we invite you to have the said woman
Roussel transferred in the case only where the different declarations made by her to the tribunal may lead you to think that the
presence of this woman might aid the discoveries which we are
charged to make."

Already on the 21st Frimaire (11th of December, 1793), three days
after the death of the DuBarry,[1] the Commissioners were occupied
with the means for attaining the discovery of the stolen articles.
They had commenced by arresting the floor-cleaner Deliant and his

---

[1] It is a curious illustration of the Commissioners' want of method
that in this letter they spell " Du Barry " both " Dubarry " and " Du
Barry." In their *proces-verbal* they invariably spell it " Dubarry."—
TRANSLATOR.

Madame Du Barry

wife, against whom the Du Barry had given evidence in her declaration between two wickets as the depository of two boxes containing jewels, diamonds and other precious effects. The Commissioners could extract little information from Deliant, who was already dying, and whom they had conveyed to the Infirmary of Versailles, where he died eight days afterwards. But the wife, after having confessed that five or six days before her arrest the Du Barry had put into her apron five or six packets covered with paper, which she had concealed in the dungpit of the melon-bed, forwarded, next morning to Greive, whilst the Commissioners were occupied in searching through Morin's garden, 183 single gold louis entrusted to her keeping by the Du Barry some time before her last journey to England.

On the 16th Frimaire she was examined by the Commissioners. She declared that the Du Barry, at the time of her last journey to England, had sent her three chests containing many precious articles; that the day after the Du Barry's arrest, she had deposited them in the house of the Widow Aubert, her mother, but that, in consequence of the searches made in Luciennes and its out-buildings, fearing lest they might find at her mother's the chests deposited, she had emptied and concealed them in the dungpit near the melon-bed, with the exception of four rouleaux of single louis, a gold goblet with its cover, a purse filled with silver counters, and some flagons; that her mother had next day flung into the artificial pond of the Grand Jet de Marley these objects, with the exception, however, of four rouleaux of louis, which she had kept for herself without telling her husband about it.

Being present this day at the deposit made by Agathe Gournay of a watch enriched with diamonds found in an ornamental pool in the garden of Marly, the woman Deliant, on the pretext of some ordinary troubles, cut her throat with a razor.

The Commissioners sought to fix the account of the money found at Madame du Barry's house in order to remit it to the National Treasury. After a close investigation of the facts set out in the reports, they arrived at a sum of 51,801 livres. There was also a sum of 3,143 livres in assignats found in the chest of drawers of the Du Barry's bed-room, but this sum had been put by the Citizens Lacroix and Musset, representatives of the people, at the disposal of the Citizen Greive, to assist in defraying temporary expenses, and out of this sum there was now left only 29 livres. And this was not the only money spent by Greive; he had besides consumed with his associates 3,000 livres furnished by Vouland and Jagot, and he, moreover, owed 3,151 livres to eighteen bailiff's men whom he had installed at Luciennes. The Commissioners, anxious to introduce a little economy into the house, regretted to see "that the Citizen Greive, too much occupied, without doubt, in the execution of the great measures of general safety with which he announced that he was entrusted, even by his public position, had no time to enter into details," and they reduced the number of men in possession from eighteen to six, and stopped the account of the baker, the butcher, and other tradespeople whose bills they forwarded to the administration of the district of Versailles—the entire amount of these accounts reaching 2,749 livres.

The verification and the collection of the silver plate, jewels, and diamonds gave terrible labour to the Commissioners, who said in their reports: "Perhaps the pleasure of having made the discoveries and the precipitation with which an inventory was taken have caused the necessary formalities in compilation, exactness of description, and examination of the various articles to be neglected, but in general the Commissioners have observed a lack of order, and they cannot prove this fact more clearly than by mentioning the great number of effects not included in the inventories." They complained gently, later on, of having found in different places in the house many shagreen cases which contained, without doubt, some precious objects, and which, however, "do not form part of those inventoried and verified." And they ended with this bitter remark: "All these cases have been found empty."

The general Commission, aided by two other commissions, made an inventory of stuffs at the moment unsaleable in France, sent to Saint-Cyr, which had become a military hospital, the linen, the bedding, the sugar and the brandy, making choice of fifty-five objects now preserved in the Museums or the Royal Palaces :[1]

[1] The State also kept the Favourite's books, as is indicated by this estimate dated Messidor, Year II. of the library of Madame du Barry. (Papers of the Library of the City of Versailles.)

List of books in the Library estimated by the Sieur Blaizot, librarian at Versailles, dated the 3d Prairial, Year II., 14,500 Books.

The said library was naturally preserved in Versailles in the National Library. Afterwards, during the ministry of M. Chaptal, it was transferred to Paris, and since then to Malmaison and Saint Cloud.

Madame Du Barry

1.—Two Pictures by Vien.

2.—A Case with Capital and Base of Italian Granite.

3.—A Venus Callipyge (small proportion).

4.—An Apollo Belvedere.

5.—Theseus carrying away Hermione.

6.—A Vestal nursing the Sacred Fire, followed by two Children.

7.—A group representing Louis XV. carried by four Warriors.

8.—A small bust of Louis XV.

9.—A Fireplace in gilt-bronze, Stag, Wild-boar, and Attribute of the Chase.

10.—A Sea-piece by Vernet (height, 8 feet; length, 5 feet).

11.—Another picture of the same dimensions representing a Ruin.

12.—Four Designs for the Upper Portions of Doors.

13.—Nymph in Marble flying and a Cupid threatening her.

14.—A Woman Bathing, by Falconet.

15.—The Bust of Louis XV. in marble, by Pajou.

16.—A clock representing Love borne by the Graces in bronze gilt, with Ormolu.

17.—Two Sevres Porcelain Vases, on an azure ground.

18.—Two Porcelain Vases in the Etruscan Style.

19.—A Barometer and Thermometer with Cartouches of Porcelain

20.—Two Vases in White Marble and Porphyry.
Figures.

21.—Two Fireplaces in Ormolu of the richest kind.

22.—Figures of White Marble, proportion of 2 feet.

23.—Two Candelabra with three branches representing Two Women grouped.

24.—Two others in the form of a Bottle.

25.—A Gilded Fireplace in the form of a Vase.

26.—A Sevres Porcelain Table, Paintings after Vanloo.

27.—A Porphyry Vase.

28.—A Fireplace in the form of Scent-boxes and Fire-cones.

29.—Three Chandeliers with three Branches in the form of Scent-boxes.

30.—The Bust of the Du Barry by Pajou, on its Case.

31.—A Piano-Forte Party.

32.—Two Large Porphyry Vases.

33.—A Harp in its robe of Black Taffeta.

34.—A Picture representing the Flight of Love.

35.—*The Female Trafficker in Loves,* by Vien.

36.—*The Broken Pitcher,* by Greuze.

37.—*Jupiter in Antiope.*

38.—A Pastoral, by Boucher.

39.—A Landscape by *Visnose.*

40.—An oval Frame 3 feet high richly carved and gilt.

41.—Another 2 feet high.

42.—A Chest of Drawers of old Lacquer.

43.—Another plaque in Sevres Porcelain with very pretty Subjects and Figures.

44.—A Picture representing the " Visitation of Elizabeth."

45.—Another representing the Virgin and the Infant Jesus.

46.—Another not finished, representing the Du Barry as a Bacchante.

47.—A Pastel, a Child playing a Tambourine, from Drouais.

48.—A Child holding an Apple, painted by Drouais.

49.—Picture of a Woman as a White Levite.

50.—Another of Louis XV. in Review Dress.

51.—Another of Louis XV. as a Child.

52.—A coloured Engraving representing a Landscape.

53.—Print representing Madame Lebrun.

54.—A Picture painted on canvas by Robert, representing a Sketch of the Mass (height 14 inches, length 16 inches).

After the particular labours of the different Commissions, the General Commission made a general abstract of all the minutes of inventories, removals, verifications, and sales of furniture which took place successively under its direction.

Madame Du Barry

This general abstract is ended with the memorandum of the only objects sold and estimated, which reaches the sum of .... 707,251*l*. 15*s*.

The jewels, diamonds, crystals, etc., the price of which is not obtained, are valued in the same inventory .... 400,000*l*.

The gold materials, 89 marks, 6 ounces, may be estimated at least at .... 60,000*l*.

Those of silver, 1,449 marks, at 45 livres per mark.. 65,000*l*.

Those of vermilion, 84 marks at 50 livres...... 4,200*l*.

Laces and Fringes, 34 marks...................... 2,700*l*.

Silver Lace and Brule Lace, 121 marks............ 3,600*l*.

Copper, iron, lead, tin........................... 4,000*l*.

General total of the valuation of the movable effects confiscated in Madame du Barry's House .... 1,246,956*l*. 15*s*.

The creditors thereupon presented a series of bills reaching the sum of 956,124*l*. 13*s*. 4*d*. and were referred by the municipality of Luciennes to a commission charged with using the utmost rigidity in the verification of these claims. And such was the rigidity of the Commission, says M. le Roi,[1] that scarcely any of the creditors were paid.

SALE OF NATIONAL PROPERTY.

"In the third year of the French Republic One and Indivisible, the fourth of the month of Thermidor, we, administrators composing the Directory of the District of Versailles, have repaired accompanied by the Citizen Procureur Syndic to the ordinary hall for meeting . . . conformably to the decrees of the National Convention of 10th, 12th, 15th and 27th Prairial of the Third Year, for the first publication and reception of outbiddings in order to effect a sale of the goods hereinafter described, indicated by the placard of the 16th Messidor last. . . . .

. . . .

A Belvedere Pavilion on the summit of the Mountain, being at the end of a wide green carpet, composed of an antechamber, and a

[1] "Madame du Barry," Versailles, 1858. A work prepared from the official Documents in the Archives of Seine-et-Oise.

grand salon on the ground floor adorned and garnished with white marble and gildings with galleries and ceiling, two cabinets adjacent to the said salon, of which one is divided into two, and another salon. . . .

. . . .

To this advertising notice is attached a placard thus expressed:

"*Canton of Marly.*

Municipality of Luciennes.

Goods of the Dubarry Condemned.[1]

Luciennes was knocked down on the 9th Thermidor, Year III. (7th of August, 1795), to Jean-Baptiste-Edward Delapalme, residing at Vaux de Cernay, for the sum of 6,000,000 (in assignats).

[1] "Dossiers" concerning the Du Barry and her family, preserved in the Library of the City of Versailles.

THE END.

INDEX.

A.

395

Index

Index

Index

Index

Index

Index

Index

Index

Index

Index

Index

Index

Index

Index

Index

ABERDEEN: THE UNIVERSITY PRESS

Printed in Great Britain
by Amazon